MW01138435

Swift Boats at War in Vietnam

Swift Boats at War in Vietnam

Edited by Guy Gugliotta, John Yeoman, and Neva Sullaway

STACKPOLE BOOKS
Guilford, Connecticut

Published by Stackpole Books
An imprint of Globe Pequot
Trade division of The Rowman & Littlefield Publishing Group, Inc.
4501 Forbes Boulevard, Suite 200, Lanham, Maryland 20706

Distributed by NATIONAL BOOK NETWORK
800-462-6420

British Library Cataloguing in Publication Information available

Library of Congress Cataloging-in-Publication Data

Names: Gugliotta, Guy, editor. | Yeoman, John (John William), editor. | Sullaway, Neva, 1952- editor.
Title: Swift boats at war in Vietnam / edited by Guy Gugliotta, John Yeoman, and Neva Sullaway.
Description: Guilford, Connecticut : Stackpole Books, [2017] | Includes bibliographical references and index.
Identifiers: LCCN 2016045557 (print) | LCCN 2016049197 (ebook) | ISBN 9780811719599 (hardback) | ISBN 9780811765657 (e-book)
Subjects: LCSH: Vietnam War, 1961-1975—Riverine operations, American. | United States. Mobile Riverine Force—History. | United States. Navy—History—Vietnam War, 1961-1975. | Sailors—United States—Biography. | Vietnam War, 1961-1975—Personal narratives.
Classification: LCC DS558.7 .S95 2017 (print) | LCC DS558.7 (ebook) | DDC 959.704/345—dc23
LC record available at https://lccn.loc.gov/2016045557

∞™ The paper used in this publication meets the minimum requirements of American National Standard for Information Sciences—Permanence of Paper for Printed Library Materials, ANSI/NISO Z39.48-1992.

Printed in the United States of America

To Swift Boat Sailors,
Shipmates who fought nobly in an unpopular war,
To those who returned
and to those who did not.

Contents

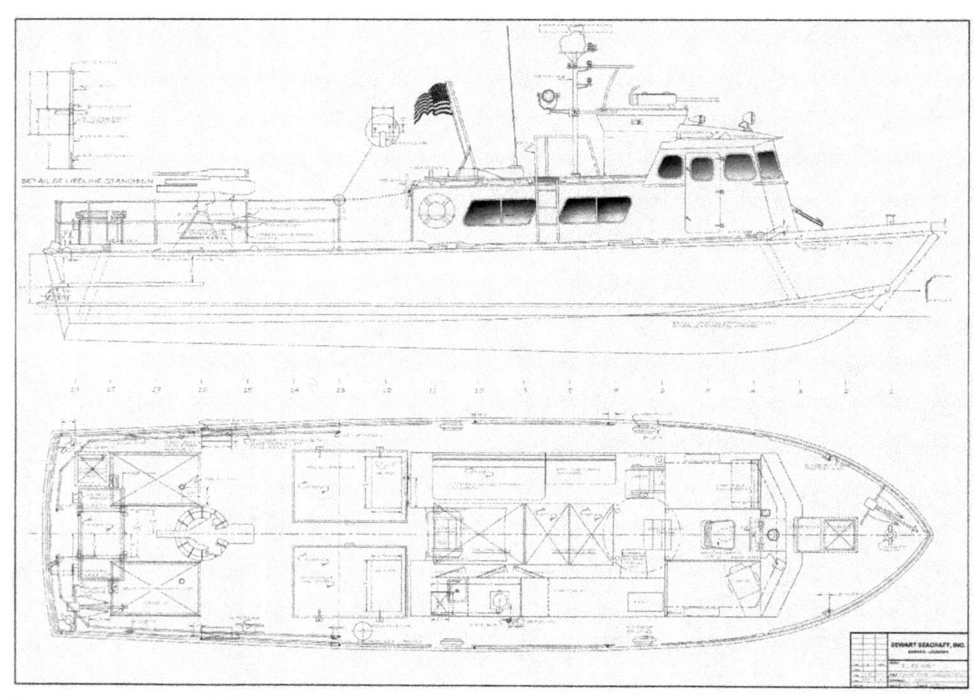

Rendering of a Swift Boat–Mark I.

COURTESY OF JOHN W. YEOMAN

MARK I SWIFT BOAT SPECIFICATIONS

Length:	50 feet 1½ inches
Beam:	13 feet 6½ inches
Full load draft:	5 feet 10 inches
Construction:	Hull/superstructure ¼-inch aluminum alloy construction
Weight:	34,913 lbs. empty. 47,047 lbs. with full war load of fuel and ammunition.
Displacement:	42,500 lbs.
Engines:	Two General Motors 12V71"N" Detroit marine diesels; port model #7122-3000, starboard model #7122-7000, each equipped with two 4-71 blowers and rated at 480 horsepower with Twin Disc 1.5:1 reduction gears and driving two counter-rotating 28 inch bronze screws.
Fuel:	800 gallons, diesel or JP-5 in an emergency, in three fuel tanks.
Construction:	The PCF (Patrol Craft Fast) is divided into seven compartments: forepeak, crew quarters, pilothouse, main cabin, stowage compartment, engine room, and lazarette.

FOREPEAK

The forepeak is used as a storage area. Access to this compartment is through the forepeak hatch in the main deck just forward of the pilothouse.

CREW QUARTERS

The crew quarters has berthing for three personnel, storage areas for personal gear, and a toilet. Access to the crew quarters is either down a ladder from the main cabin or through an escape hatch located on the forward main deck.

PILOTHOUSE

The pilothouse is equipped with the necessary controls and indicators to operate the propulsion engines, diesel generator, two .50-caliber machine guns (located in the gun tub mounted in the aft center overhead), and electrical systems and to navigate the PCF.

MAIN CABIN

The main cabin contains berthing for two; a galley area with griddle, refrigerator, and sink; radio/radar area; a small arms locker; storage cabinets; and two CO_2 fire extinguishers. Access to the main cabin is through the main deck hatch on the aft end of the main cabin, or by ladder down from the pilothouse, or up from the crew quarters.

STOWAGE COMPARTMENT

Below deck in the main cabin, the stowage compartment contains ammunition storage, the forward fuel tank, and the two engine control units. The remaining space is utilized for storage. Access to the compartment is through the bilge hatch located in the main cabin, under the ladder to the pilothouse. Three access hatches are provided in the main cabin, one for the forward fuel tank and two for the ammunition boxes.

ENGINE ROOM

The engine room houses the two propulsion engines, diesel generator, two 24v battery sets, storage access for service manuals and tools, exhaust systems for the engines and generator, a 5-gallon lube oil can, piping necessary for the bilge system, engine and generator seawater cooling systems, fuel system, 24v DC source of power switch, and AC source of power switch. Access to the engine room is through two hinged hatches on the main deck just aft of the main cabin.

LAZARETTE

The lazarette houses the two aft fuel tanks, fresh-water tank, steering gear, rudder tillers, and two 5-gallon lube oil cans. Access to the lazarette is through an access hatch located on the aft port corner of the aft deck. Two soft-patch hatches, on the aft deck, provide access to the fuel tanks.

Electrical: Two engine-driven alternators charge four 24v batteries that provide the main source of electrical power for main engine starting, general purpose lighting, search lights, navigational lights, radar, and URC-58 radio. There are two 24v battery banks. 6.0kW Onan diesel-driven AC generator provides 120v 50 amp electrical power for radios, signal lights, refrigerator, griddle, and cooking outlet.

Electronics: Decca D202 surface search radar, maximum range of 24 miles.

Raytheon DE-736A fathometer, maximum depth range of 240 feet.

AN/URC-58 Single Side Band radio, 2 to 15 MHz, can operate on upper sideband, lower sideband, AM, or CW. Output is 100 watts. This was the PCF's primary communications equipment and was used for long-range boat-to-base communications. This radio normally operated on 120v DC power but could be operated on 24v DC if necessary.

AN/VRC-46 FM radio, 30.00 to 79.95 MHz (short range—boat-to-boat or boat-to-shore for coordination with other units).

	AN/PRC-10/25 FM, 30.00 to 79.95 MHz portable field radio (used by off-boat inspection parties and to coordinate with other units ashore).
Miscellaneous Equipment:	Two main engine-driven bilge pumps. Danforth/White magnetic compass on pilothouse console. 6-inch portable search light, visible at 4-mile range Spotlight, used to illuminate targets at 250- to 300-yard range, mounted on pilothouse roof and controlled from inside the pilothouse by the helmsman.
Armament:	Twin .50-caliber Browning machine guns, with heavy barrels, manually operated. Capable of firing at 450–550 rpm (rounds per minute) and equipped with ammunition bins for approximately 1,000 rounds per gun. Located on the boat centerline, in a guntub mounted on top of the pilothouse. The maximum range of these guns is in excess of 7,000 yards. 81mm Mark 2/Mod 0, trigger-fired or drop-fired mortar with a .50-caliber Browning machine gun, with heavy barrel, fixed atop it and equipped with ammunition cans for 100 or 300 rounds. Mounted on a tripod centered on the boat's fantail. Range of the 81mm mortar is approximately 4,000 yards when elevated and about 1,000 yards when operated in a direct fire mode. Trigger-fired capacity is 10 rounds per minute. Drop-fired capacity is about 18 rounds per minute. 81mm ammunition rounds carried on board in the stern-mounted ready service locker and two main cabin floor lockers. The variety of 81mm mortar rounds included high explosive rounds, white phosphorus rounds, flechette rounds, illumination rounds, and proximity rounds.

	Various crew-member weapons including: M-60 machine guns, M-79 grenade launchers, M-16 rifles, 12-gauge Ithaca riot gun, .45-caliber pistols, various types of hand grenades, Very pistols (flare gun).
Speed:	32 knots, designed maximum
Turning radius:	75 yards at 20 knots
Stopping distance:	2¼ boat lengths (114 feet) in 9 seconds, from maximum speed
Operating Range:	Varies depending upon engine rpm, fuel load, ammunition, personnel, and sea and wind conditions. At 800 rpm, about 8 knots with normal load, flat seas and calm winds, a range of about 840 nautical miles or 100 hours' endurance. At 2,000 rpm, about 23 knots, about 250 nautical miles or 10 hours' endurance.
Potable Water:	60 gallons

Introduction

by Guy Gugliotta and John Yeoman

Lt. (jg) John W. Yeoman was the skipper of PCF 37 and PCF 692. After leaving the Navy, he earned an MBA from the University of Chicago. He then worked as an investment banker in New York, as skipper of mega-yachts and tugboats in San Francisco, and then moved to Maui and into a position as a financial advisor with a major wirehouse brokerage for the past ten years.

See page 288 for Guy Gugliotta's biography.

The first two Swift Boats arrived in Vietnam in the fall of 1965 as the initial installment of what in later years came to be called "The Brown Water Navy." Besides Swifts, this fleet of heavily armed small craft—several hundred of them at the height of the Vietnam War—included everything from tiny, high-powered "skimmers" for ferrying Navy SEALs on secret raids to fiberglass river patrol boats comfortable in a few inches of muddy water to the ponderous Tango Boats, shallow-draft armored landing craft capable of carrying entire infantry units into hostile territory.

Swifts were the most versatile of the lot. They were big enough to navigate the open ocean in search of ships and junks suspected of smuggling contraband arms and war matériel to Viet Cong Communist insurgents, but small enough to disrupt Viet Cong supply lines in the rivers and canals of the Mekong Delta. The boats were fifty feet long and fitted with a brace of .50-caliber heavy machine guns in a forward turret atop the pilothouse, with a third .50-caliber on the fantail riding atop an

PCF 9 patrols with Vietnamese troops on board in the lower Ca Mau peninsula in 1969. The shoreline vegetation has been denuded by Agent Orange.
OFFICIAL U.S. NAVY PHOTO

81mm heavy mortar. Swifts also carried a changing menu of standard small arms—M-60 machine guns, M-16s, .38-caliber pistols, shotguns, bazookas, grenade launchers, and grenades.

Crews quickly found out that "versatile" did not mean Swift Boats were particularly well suited for either the ocean or the rivers. The boats carried too much weight forward, and at sea pitched horribly in any kind of moderate chop. When the winter monsoon began, it never seemed to end, and crews spent a good deal of patrol time hanging onto stanchions, wearing wet clothes, burning themselves with hot food, trying to avoid concussions, and failing to sleep. Getting in and out of harbor could be a terrifying run through an obstacle course, one that required boats to dodge unmarked shoals, surf down twenty-foot wave faces, and avoid broaching when immense crosscurrent seas suddenly grabbed the port quarter.

The rivers and canals, although relatively calm, presented their own challenges. Swift Boats taunted the enemy by their very presence, and the enemy responded with everything from a couple of badly placed Claymore mines to deadly ambushes initiated from hidden mud bunkers. The boats were made of quarter-inch aluminum, which was like tissue paper to enemy bullets, but just strong enough to allow an enemy rocket to penetrate the main cabin before detonating in a cloud of shrapnel. For this reason, crews patrolling the river ate and slept on deck and tried never to go below for more than a few moments. Then there was the noise: The Swifts' twin 12V-71, turbocharged General Motors Detroit marine diesels made it impossible to sneak up on anything. And even at idle speed, a row of hinged metal exhaust pipe covers rattled like castanets. Swift Boat folklore held that although the engines were loud, the jungle smothered the Doppler effect. The bad guys could hear a boat coming, but could not tell whether it was two miles away or just around the river bend. This thesis was never proven, but it provided some comfort—like crossing your fingers.

In all, the Navy sent 116 Swift Boats to fight in Vietnam between 1965 and 1970.[1] About 600 U.S. Navy officers—mostly lieutenants junior grade, but also a few lieutenants and ensigns, served aboard the boats. The enlisted—about 3,000—were mostly second-class and third-class petty officers, along with significant numbers of first-class petty officers and seaman strikers. Fifty Swift Boat sailors died in Vietnam—all but a handful in firefights—and about 400 others were wounded.

After the Navy turned over the last fourteen in-country U.S. Swift Boats to the South Vietnamese on December 1, 1970, the few remaining stateside boats survived as trainers and later as museum pieces, all but disappearing from the American consciousness for decades. But in 2004 Swift Boats surfaced briefly and notoriously when pro-Republican Swift veterans upended the presidential campaign, denouncing the candidacy of Democratic Senator John Kerry, a former boat skipper, who in the 1970s had played a prominent role in the antiwar organization Vietnam Veterans Against the War. That election added the newly minted verb "to swiftboat" to the U.S. campaign lexicon, used to describe almost any particularly virulent form of political smear.

The story of Swift Boats is much more than this. For those who served aboard them, the boats offered unmatched lessons in heroism, teamwork, camaraderie, and the ability to function under life-or-death pressure. Some young men grew up on Swift Boats. Others grew old before their time. Some saw things that amazed and awed them. Others saw things they wished they had never seen. All saw things they never forgot.

Swift Boats showed the Navy at its best—giving kids barely out of high school or college opportunities for leadership and initiative they could never have found elsewhere. Swift Boats also showed the Navy at its worst. They were a flawed solution to a festering crisis, evidence that the Navy, which had been worrying for years about Vietnam, had done nothing to prepare for it. The stories in these pages offer a lesson in how the United States makes war and what war does to the people who fight it. The lesson comes from an earlier time—from a war that Americans long tried to forget and that far too many have long forgotten.

While the first American ground troops—3,500 combat marines—arrived in Vietnam in 1965, the "Vietnam War" per se had begun two decades earlier, at the end of World War II, when Ho Chi Minh's Viet Minh insurgents seized Hanoi from the Japanese, proclaimed independence from France, and within months embarked on a war of liberation against their colonial masters, ultimately defeating them in the decisive battle of Dien Bien Phu in 1954.

The Geneva Accords, negotiated even as the French surrendered at Dien Bien Phu, ended what the victors described as "The French War." The accords divided the country in two at the seventeenth parallel, with elections to come in 1956 to choose a permanent government for a united Vietnam. Ho's Viet Minh Communists, supplied principally by China and allied with the Eastern bloc, controlled North Vietnam from Hanoi, while Prime Minister Ngo Dinh Diem led a U.S.–supported anticommunist government in Saigon in the south. Neither the United States nor South Vietnam endorsed the accords. In 1955, Diem consolidated his power, arresting thousands of suspected Communists and repressing political opposition of all kinds.

The southern Communists were in disarray, but immediately began to regroup for a second insurgency aimed at toppling the Diem government. Their cause prospered. Diem was unpopular, weak, and corrupt, giving the insurgents—with material assistance and support from North Vietnam—ample time to grow stronger. These were the beginnings of what the Vietnamese came to describe as "The American War."

In January 1955, the United States began sending direct military aid to the Diem government through its Military Assistance Advisory

Group. In February, the first U.S. military advisors arrived to begin training the South Vietnamese army. From 1955 to 1960 the United States had between 750 and 1,500 advisors in Vietnam. The Navy, part of the advisory group since its inception, by 1960 had an in-country staff of sixty.[2] Their efforts had met with some success: The South Vietnamese Navy, virtually nonexistent in 1955, had 117 ships and boats and 4,500 personnel by the end of 1961.

But insurgent pressure mounted even more rapidly. In 1960 North Vietnam prevailed on the southern resistance fighters to unite in the National Front for the Liberation of South Vietnam—the Viet Cong—and within a few years the guerrillas had won control of much of the vast Mekong Delta, a 66,000-square-mile landscape of flatland and swamp that formed the bottom half of South Vietnam.

In December 1961, the Navy moved from a strictly advisory role to active military operations, sending U.S. minesweepers to the South China Sea to join Vietnamese warships near the seventeenth parallel Demilitarized Zone (DMZ). This combined force attempted to block the North Vietnamese from smuggling arms and supplies to the Viet Cong. Early in 1962 the Navy began using destroyer escorts on Vietnam's west coast for similar operations in the Gulf of Thailand between Phu Quoc Island and the Ca Mau Peninsula, the final stretch of tropical forest and marshland at Vietnam's southern tip. The U.S. ships themselves did not stop suspect shipping. Instead, they found targets and vectored their Vietnamese counterparts to intercept them.

By the end of 1963, however, it was clear that this plan was not working. Diem's tumultuous reign ended with his assassination late in the year, but the corruption and ill will he had engendered with his repressive policies had radicalized the noncommunist opposition. The North Vietnamese and Viet Cong, better organized and more committed than the South Vietnamese, were gaining followers and increasing the stakes dramatically as they shifted to what they called their "stage three" insurgency. In addition to hit-and-run guerrilla raids and ambushes, they were now ready for pitched battles involving large numbers of troops.

But they too had a weakness. Until 1964, the Viet Cong had waged war—and quite effectively—with a hodgepodge of explosives, both

PCF 695 patrols near Ben Tre in 1970. Twin mounts of M-60 machine guns, port and starboard, were added on the aft deck by industrious crew that "borrowed" the weapons from where they were not needed.
COURTESY OF JOHN W. YEOMAN

imported and homemade, and small arms captured from the French or Americans or donated by the Soviets and Chinese from superannuated stockpiles. Replenishing ammo and finding spare parts for weapons was a constant and increasingly vexing problem. To reach for ultimate victory, the North needed a standardized family of effective small arms and a consistent supply of modern rockets, mines, and other support weapons.[3]

The supplies themselves were no problem; the Eastern bloc was more than willing to upgrade the Viet Cong arsenal. The hard part was the logistics of getting them to the Viet Cong fighters in South Vietnam. The quickest and most economical way to do this was to send them by sea. Cargo vessels disguised as fishing trawlers traveled south in international waters and at the appropriate moment turned west to rendezvous at hidden moorings on the South Vietnamese coast and unload their wares.[4]

In January 1964 a team of eight U.S. naval officers met in Saigon and concluded that the North was moving enough war matériel to support its expanded operations and that the South was making only a token effort to stop it. The subsequent Bucklew Report, named after Navy captain Phillip H. Bucklew, who headed the Saigon team, recommended adding U.S. assets to beef up the South Vietnamese Navy. (The U.S. Navy presence in Vietnam by that time had risen to 742 officers and enlisted.) The report languished. The number of South Vietnamese Navy ships on anti-smuggling patrol rose to twenty-eight, but there were few successful interdictions along South Vietnam's 1,200-mile coastline. These efforts required either more ships or better performance from the ones that were already there—or both.[5]

The most divisive foreign war in U.S. history began on August 2, 1964, when North Vietnamese patrol boats attacked the destroyer USS *Maddox* in the Tonkin Gulf, off the coast of North Vietnam. Three of the boats were damaged, and four North Vietnamese sailors were killed. The *Maddox* suffered neither damage nor casualties. Two days later, U.S. military authorities reported that North Vietnamese boats had again attacked the *Maddox* and a second destroyer, the USS *Turner Joy*.

Questions immediately arose within the Navy and in Washington about the authenticity of what came to be known as the "Tonkin Gulf Incident." But many years passed before the general public came to understand that the initial attack probably owed as much to the *Maddox*'s deliberate provocations as it did to North Vietnamese aggression. The second attack, it turned out, was almost certainly an illusion. Technicians aboard the two ships apparently mistook "ghosts" in the destroyers' radar returns for the blips of enemy patrol boats.

At the time of the Tonkin Gulf incident the Cold War was at an apogee, and U.S. analysts and policymakers were convinced that the collapse of the government in South Vietnam would trigger a cascade of "falling dominoes" and spread Communism across Southeast Asia. On August 7, 1964, President Lyndon Johnson asked Congress to authorize military action in Vietnam. On August 10, the "Tonkin Gulf Resolution" passed unanimously in the House of Representatives and in the Senate by a vote of 88-2. In March 1965, the first contingent of U.S. troops arrived in Vietnam. By the end of the year, there were 200,000 U.S. soldiers on the ground.[6]

Despite the pivotal roles played by the *Maddox* and *Turner Joy* in the opening act, the U.S. Navy was ill prepared to fight in Vietnam, and the Navy knew it. This realization led directly to both the invention of Swift Boats and to their deployment, first on coastal patrol and eventually into the rivers on South Vietnam's northern coast and in the waterways of the Mekong Delta.

The February 15, 1964, Bucklew Report was just a year old when the Navy found out just how badly South Vietnamese waterborne interdiction was faring. On the morning of February 16, 1965, a U.S. Army pilot flying a MEDEVAC helicopter over the central coast of South Vietnam reported an unidentified, camouflaged trawler unloading cargo in Vung Ro Bay. When South Vietnamese troops drove the Viet Cong from Vung Ro three days later they found 100 tons of small arms, ammo, grenades, mortar rounds, and explosives that had come from the trawler.[7]

Less than a week after the discovery of the trawler, Gen. William Westmoreland, the commander of U.S. forces in Vietnam, asked the Navy to attend a conference in Saigon to plan a joint U.S.-Vietnamese Navy offshore patrol. The conference convened March 3 and the plan was approved March 16. Twenty-eight U.S. Navy ships were on interdiction station by March 24. The patrols had two groups of targets. The largest enemy shipments originated in China or North Vietnam and came south in trawlers, which were up to 200 feet long. The smaller shipments were mixed in among the 50,000 junks, sampans, and other small craft sailing up and down the Vietnamese coast carrying everything from livestock to needles and thread. The conference report concluded somewhat ambiguously that the "best tactic," given the circumstances, would be "to assist and inspire the Vietnamese navy to increase the quality and quantity of its searches."[8]

The report recommended that the best way to "assist and inspire" was for Navy ships and aircraft to establish "a defensive sea area" to extend forty miles from the Vietnamese coast. There was nothing ambiguous about what should happen next: the Republic of Vietnam should authorize U.S. naval forces to "stop, board, search, and, if necessary, capture and/or destroy any hostile suspicious craft or vessel found within South Vietnam's territorial and contiguous zone waters."[9] The U.S. Joint Chiefs of Staff immediately approved the proposal and called it "Operation

Market Time." On May 11, with nearly thirty U.S. ships on station, the government of South Vietnam ratified what was by then a fait accompli.

In practical terms, Market Time flipped the Navy's priorities and turned the South Vietnamese government into a loyal bystander. Instead of finding interdiction targets and getting the Vietnamese Navy to chase them, the Americans would find the targets, hunt them down and deal with them, and then turn over the contraband to the Vietnamese. To do that, the Navy needed some sort of watercraft that could work close inshore among junks and sampans, both to follow leads provided by deepwater ships and aircraft and to patrol independently, finding and following the enemy wherever he might go. The ships available—destroyers and small troop carriers—were either too big or too slow to pursue these targets in inshore waters. Market Time needed something else.

The Navy had nothing in its arsenal or on the drawing board that fit the job. The service that did have the necessary boats and ships was the U.S. Coast Guard, and their first eight cutters reached Da Nang in July 1965. This must have rankled the Navy: an Army chopper had proved that the Vietnamese Navy—tutored by U.S. Navy advisors—could not do the work, and now the Coast Guard was fighting the Navy's war.

The Navy moved as fast as it could to develop and build the necessary craft. On February 1, 1965, even before the Vung Ro incident, Naval Advisory Group chief Capt. William H. Hardcastle Jr., the senior naval officer in Vietnam, published a staff study entitled "Naval Craft Requirements in a Counter Insurgency Environment." The mission is "difficult, demanding, and unique," the report said. "A prevalent belief has been that COIN (counterinsurgency) craft can readily be obtained from existing commercial and naval sources when needed.

"Unfortunately," the report continued, no action had been taken "to develop COIN craft specifically suited to perform the many missions needed to combat insurgent activities." In fact, the Navy had not had this type of vessel since the Civil War. The need had now arisen, and since the Navy itself had nothing to offer, it had to find someone who did—and quickly.

Hardcastle wanted something more maneuverable and thus smaller than the eight Coast Guard cutters doing inshore patrol. He called for a

PCF 694 at 30 knots returns to Seafloat in 1970. Skipper John Meehan stands outside the pilothouse on the port side.
COURTESY OF JOHN W. YEOMAN

shallow-draft, metal-hulled boat that was "reliable and sturdy," with screw and rudder guards to provide protection in case of grounding. The boat needed a patrol range of at least four hundred miles and should be able to reach sustained speeds of at least twenty knots. It should have a short-range radar to find targets, a searchlight to illuminate them, and long-range communications gear to talk with the Army and Air Force, if necessary. The boat needed "some berthing space" but no galley. There should be enough weaponry for "limited offense," and the boat should have "quiet operation."

The job of finding such a boat fell to a Navy commander named Cab Davis in the Bureau of Ships (BuShips). He needed a fifty-foot patrol craft that was fast, but soundly built and strong enough to support the installation of heavy weapons. A civilian on the staff recalled that a shipyard in Louisiana provided quick fifty-footers to the companies that serviced oil rigs in the Gulf of Mexico, reasoning that such boats might fit the Navy's specifications.

A few days later the commander, accompanied by a lawyer, a contract specialist, and the rear admiral who was his boss, went to Berwick, Louisiana, to talk to Sewart Seacraft. The delegates bought the design for a "swift boat" similar to Sewart's Gulf runabouts. The Navy asked for about fifty modifications to the drawings. Sewart added a .50-caliber gun tub atop the pilothouse, along with ammo lockers, bunks, and a galley consisting of a hot plate, a sink, and a small refrigerator.

Sewart sent the drawings to BuShips within a week. BuShips bid the job immediately and let the contract to Sewart in mid-July 1965, a little more than a month after the process began. The Navy further modified the civilian design by including a combination .50-caliber machine gun/81mm mortar mount on the fantail and a mortar ammunition box on the stern, as well as dozens of other small adjustments. Even with the requested modifications, Sewart delivered four boats within forty days. The first pair, PCFs (Patrol Craft Fast) 1 and 2, traveled by rail to Coronado, California, and were put to use as training boats for the new Swift crews and maintenance personnel who began arriving at Coronado Amphibious Base in mid-September.[10]

PCFs 3 and 4 went directly by ship from New Orleans to Subic Bay in the Philippines. An advance detachment of brand-new Swift Boat sailors met the boats there and began readying them for deployment. It was during this initial shakedown that the crews discovered that BuShips and Sewart had perhaps been a little hasty. The radarscope was in the main cabin, useless for the skipper and helmsman—the people who actually needed to see it. The scope was moved to the pilothouse. Both boats had a ship's bell, as good as a brass band for announcing the Swift's presence. The bells disappeared. The hull needed to be reinforced to support the aft gun mount. And the toilet, it turned out, was the most useless appliance of all: Located in the forward berthing space, it pitched up and down in the open ocean like a rodeo bull. In the river, it was not worth anyone's life to be caught with his pants down during a rocket attack. Unfortunately, there was no easy solution, so for the next five years Swift Boat crews made their own arrangements, which usually, but not always, involved a bucket of water.

The vast majority of the Swifts sent to Vietnam—108—were Mark I models built to the original 1965 specs and delivered between 1965 and 1967. In 1968, Sewart began building Mark IIs. These had more freeboard in the bow so the boats could ride higher in heavy seas. Sewart also moved the pilothouse aft several feet to keep waves from blowing out windshields, and substituted storm-resistant portholes for the sliding tourist windows in the Mark I main cabin. These were all significant and welcome changes, but the Navy sent only three Mark IIs to Vietnam. Still unresolved were the aluminum hulls' limited ability to endure water mines and other concussions, but the designers could not do much about strengthening the boats without causing them to lose speed and maneuverability. And finally, there was the core dilemma—fifty feet was not enough boat for the ocean, but it was too much boat for the rivers.

These shortcomings persisted in the much more livable Mark IIIs, built in 1969. Five were sent to Vietnam. By that time crews had adopted the philosophy that Swift Boats could "outrun anything they couldn't outfight," which was fine as far as it went, but it didn't go very far. Swifts were never able to cope gracefully with the monsoon, and the thin aluminum never fared well in the river. By 1969, the hulls on most of the older boats were so fatigued and beat up from bullet holes, rocket impacts, groundings, and other abuses that crews paled when confronted with any kind of prolonged transit in the open sea. A functioning bilge pump was a must. In the beginning, a crewman could stomp a Swift Boat deck and be rewarded with a throaty washtub "bong." By 1970, most of the hulls sounded like garbage cans at 4 a.m.

Despite all these weaknesses, Swift crews loved their boats. Most of the crewmen, both officers and enlisted, were in their early to mid-twenties, and there were few things that young men with big egos liked better than having two mean and ugly turbocharged 450-horsepower beasts under the fantail hatch covers. The twelve-cylinder diesels could deliver more than thirty knots—ten knots more than Captain Hardcastle's specs demanded—and stay there for several hours. Given the opportunity—calm seas or a quiet river and a fuel dump at the end of the journey—the boats always traveled "full bore," and too bad if everybody in the neighborhood could hear them coming for ten minutes. Nothing could be done about that. Hardcastle's wish for "quiet operation" remained forever an unfulfilled dream.

Beyond speed, Swift Boats fed many spiritual needs, both for officers and enlisted. Officers enjoyed an early career opportunity for "command-at-sea," even though a Swift Boat was not a "ship." Ships pick up and carry "boats." Boats cannot pick up anything. And being a Swift "Officer-in-Charge" was not the same thing as being "the Captain." As a practical matter, however, OinCs ran their own show and told their superiors either what they wanted to hear or what the OinCs decided they needed to know. Superiors were told nothing beyond that, and the crews backed up the OinCs because they also didn't want superiors interfering in their work.

For junior petty officers, Swift Boat duty meant taking charge of your own engines, guns, deck gear, charts, or electronics without having a Chief second-guess every move. Instead of sleeping on a strip of stretch canvas in a three-tier destroyer berthing space with another guy snoring a foot above your head, you could spread out in a Swift Boat's main cabin, or, weather permitting, sleep on deck under the stars. Crews kept the boats immaculate, partly because that was "the Navy Way," but also because the boat was the most "home" the Navy had ever offered them. Even when in port with shore berthing available, many crewmen preferred to spend their nights on board.

One personal characteristic shared by both officers and enlisted was that they were a bit out of control. Saluting was sporadic, and uniforms got progressively more ad hoc as the war advanced, until most sailors were wearing cut-off utility trousers or jungle greens, boots, and little else. Nobody bothered with rank insignia, and underwear encouraged rashes, so nobody wore any. At some point Adm. Elmo Zumwalt, Commander Naval Forces Vietnam and the Swifties' favorite officer, allowed sailors to grow beards. When hirsute crewmen, many of them fresh from the jungle, unwashed and identifiable only by their dog tags, started arriving in Saigon prior to R&R, military cops—usually Army—were not amused and strongly urged them to get cleaned up if they wanted to make the flight to Hawaii, Bangkok, or Hong Kong.

Swift Boat crews routinely drank beer aboard the boats—after all, it was a "boat," not a "ship," hence the Navy's ban on shipboard alcoholic beverages did not apply. However, whiskey and dope, increasingly available as the war continued, were deemed to be dangerous indulgences that could get people killed. You could get drunk and watch a movie when the patrol was over, and Swift crewmen did that more frequently

PCF 75 leads a four boat sweep around "Football Island" near Sa Dec on the Mekong River, September 17, 1970.
COURTESY OF WILLIAM ROGERS

than most, but crews would not tolerate anything that detracted from underway performance.

This was a lesson rigorously taught by the Navy generally and reinforced by reality. Ships had limited space, and they were dangerous, offering endless opportunities to fall through open hatches, get whacked on the head by metal outcrops, or splatter pots of scalding coffee all over a shipmate when the deck suddenly took a sharp dive. On Swift Boats, the stakes rose. Besides the usual obstacles, there were weapons and ammunition everywhere, along with careful procedures to follow in handling the ammo and loading the guns. With just six crewmembers, everybody had to know each other's jobs. There were discussions about whom to call during an attack if you were the last one left to summon help. Everybody knew how to rig a towline, administer morphine, rescue an exhausted swimmer, or get on the radio to vector a MEDEVAC chopper to a Landing Zone (LZ) to pick up the wounded. Swift Boats were in a deadly serious business, to be undertaken with meticulous attention to detail. Every sailor needed his wits about him.

Weapons trafficking was common and tolerated. A boat could never have enough guns, and over the years boats or their crewmen, or both, amassed significant stashes of contraband. They took AK-47s, old Chinese SKS rifles, and B-40 and B-50 rocket launchers from the enemy. Friendlies provided M-14s, Winchesters, Swedish "Ks," .45-caliber "grease guns," Claymore mines, C-4 high explosive, and the occasional Israeli Uzi or even a vintage Chicago-style tommy gun. These artifacts changed hands frequently, either in trade for money or beer or as gifts left behind or given to a shipmate by a crewman finishing up his tour.

Whenever superior officers happened upon evidence of these or other transgressions they either pretended not to notice (a tactic acknowledged and appreciated by OinCs, who made sure the boss never got burned for looking the other way) or they became enraged, a reaction greeted with utter indifference from the crews. Swift Boat sailors tended to have limited respect for authority. It was one of the reasons that many of them came to Vietnam. And since there was no punishment in Vietnam to fit crimes generally regarded as "chickenshit," they could be ignored. What do you want to do, confine me to quarters? Send me home? Break my heart.

Despite all this, it was impossible to characterize anything resembling an "average" Swift Boat officer or sailor. In theory, serving aboard Swift Boats was supposed to be voluntary, and there were certainly significant numbers of highly motivated "Swifties" eager to fulfill their patriotic duty by fighting Vietnamese Communists. But ideology was seldom, if ever, the only reason to volunteer. Indeed, most Swift Boat sailors probably had little idea what Communism entailed. It was simply "bad," because adults had told them that all their lives.

In reality, the defining principle for young men in the United States in the 1960s was the military draft. Every able-bodied American male after his eighteenth birthday was eligible for the armed forces, and managing one's "military obligation" dominated the lives of the entire generation. In this light, the Navy looked like a pretty good deal. Who wanted to spend his time in uniform pounding hills with the Army or the Marine Corps? Or fight a war—and perhaps die—halfway around the world in a place he had never heard of? Or run away to Canada or go to prison? In the blue-water Navy you were in the ocean away from danger, or you were visiting—but not remaining in—exotic places.

To get volunteers for Swift Boats, the Navy appealed to patriotism, and this worked to a certain extent throughout the war. But the previous 150 years had taught the Navy that volunteering worked best if it had sweeteners. For officers, ego and careerism were the main inducements. In the spring of 1965 a call went out for shipboard junior officers who had qualified as Officers-of-the-Deck underway. For a senior ensign or a young lieutenant junior grade, being an OOD-underway was the best, and practically the only, thing you could do to call favorable attention to yourself. But then what? Drive tin cans for two more years until you made lieutenant and got into destroyer school, or cool your heels on a carrier caddying for airmen who knew nothing about ships? Now the Navy was offering to make you the boss, put you on the fast track for promotion and maybe even get you some medals. The Vietnam War was the central event of the 1960s, said the Navy. You did not want to miss it.

The appeal worked. The early Swift Boat officers included significant numbers of Naval Academy graduates, regular NROTC officers, and other highly regarded career Navy types with considerable shipboard experience and swagger. Nobody knew anything about Swift Boats, but how hard could it be?

The enlisted were a somewhat different story. One significant advantage that the Navy had over other services was that it taught an enormous number of trades that translated directly to civilian life: electrician, machinist, electronics technician, plumber, welder, steam mechanic, diesel mechanic, clerk, cook, and more. Swift Boats didn't offer much that was ostensibly useful in this regard, especially for a high school graduate who had joined the Navy because he did not want to go to Vietnam. For the enlisted, the Navy played on patriotism and added responsibility, but it also reminded them there was combat pay. And when this did not fill all the needed billets, the Navy simply issued orders to "volunteers" who had not volunteered for anything. The Navy did what it needed to do.

From 1965 to 1968, the Swifts worked almost exclusively on Market Time patrols in the open ocean, within twelve miles of the coast. The boats took some casualties in firefights and other encounters with the enemy and also performed a number of gunfire support missions for nearby ground troops and rescues, on land and in the water, of both U.S. servicemen and Vietnamese. Crews interacted frequently with local Vietnamese on many levels, and it became increasingly common to see enlisted crewmen re-up for second or even third tours. Still, the work of tracking and inspecting junks and sampans was mostly routine, even tedious.

Almost everything changed in 1968. The enemy's Tet Offensive, even though it did not succeed, dimmed prospects for American victory. War casualties mounted and U.S. domestic protests intensified. For Swift Boats, Market Time began to appear increasingly irrelevant. Vietnamese boats started taking over some of the routine coastal patrols. Seaborne smuggling all but stopped, and the North Vietnamese opened the Ho Chi Minh Trail, carrying supplies overland to the Mekong Delta, where distribution fell to sampans and other river craft using a 3,000-square-mile labyrinth of rivers, canals, and streams.

As this logistical shift became more apparent, U.S. Swifts began poking their noses into the rivers, and in October 1968 two boats conducted unauthorized raids into Viet Cong strongholds: first in the Cua Lon estuary in the Ca Mau Peninsula, and then on the Giang Thanh River on the Cambodian border. Both OinCs faced disciplinary action for disobeying standing orders, but Admiral Zumwalt intervened and awarded them medals instead, effectively endorsing their actions. The High Command then formalized a fundamental change in the Swifts' wartime mission, with the commencement of "SEALORDS" operations in which the Swifts were tasked with interdicting smuggling across the Cambodian border, "pacifying" waterways, and helping wrest control of enemy-held areas.

The number of firefights increased dramatically. So did casualties. Crews no longer got involved in civic action, instead focusing on raids and ambushes in enemy territory and on ferrying SEALs, Cambodian and Montagnard mercenaries, and other exotic troops on special ops. Being a Swift Boat skipper no longer qualified as a plum assignment. Boat officers no longer needed to be OODs-underway, and the career Navy guys began to disappear; it was not good for a Navy career to be associated with a losing cause. During 1970, the last year of Swift Boats,

SEAL team gun crew at Seafloat in 1970 with the repaired and restored weapons used by the SEAL teams stationed at Seafloat.
COURTESY OF JOHN W. YEOMAN

virtually all the OinCs were reservists from Officer Candidate School winding up brief military careers with a stint in the jungle. They had the same enthusiasm and skill as the early OinCs, but they also understood that they were just showing the flag as placeholders. Or cannon fodder. It depended on the day.

Vietnam undoubtedly radicalized many Swift Boat crewmen, both officers and enlisted. Some were disgusted with the protests at home and the ill treatment they received from family and erstwhile friends. Others were equally appalled by the futility of the war and the pain and divisiveness it caused in Vietnam and in the States. These feelings endured for many years and took many forms, polarizing Swift veterans to a certain degree, although the disagreements rarely erupted in public displays like the Kerry affair.

The last U.S. Swift Boats in Vietnam were turned over to the Vietnamese Navy on December 1, 1970, at Cat Lo, on the Mekong Delta's northeastern edge. The few crewmen with time still remaining on their in-country tours either rotated home or became advisors to the Vietnamese Navy. President Richard M. Nixon, ending the apparent aimlessness of the Johnson years, had promulgated a strategy of "Vietnamization," in which the Americans were to train their South Vietnam allies and give them the weaponry they needed to win the war on their own. This had not worked ten years earlier and, perhaps as no surprise, it failed again. On April 30, 1975, the North Vietnamese and Viet Cong occupied Saigon, and the war was over.

CHAPTER ONE

1965–66

Making It Up as We Go

When Swift Boat volunteers reported for duty at Coronado Amphibious Base near San Diego, they were assigned to six-man crews, given a number, and put into the training queue. When a crew's number reached the top of the list, they went to Vietnam. The Navy intended from the outset that crews would train together, travel to Vietnam together, and serve together. Training was deliberately designed to encourage cohesiveness. As a result, crews developed a remarkable level of mutual trust. In many cases the ties forged at boat school created lifetime friendships.

Training itself, however, was something of a grab bag. Instructors had no experience in Swift Boats—nobody did—and the Navy had no institutional memory that could help. Prolonged Naval blockades and coastal patrol had last been used during the Civil War. Swift crews learned about the engines, the equipment, and the weapons. They practiced the operations the boats were supposed to perform, but since no American sailor had ever actually boarded-and-searched a junk, provided mortar support from a bobbing platform, or stalked enemy trawlers during the monsoon, the entire experience had something of a high school flavor. Trainers had many bright ideas, but until they were tested in situ, all they could do was pass on what they knew, hope for the best, and wait for the reviews. Context also created problems: Crews needed to practice inshore piloting in stormy seas, but the hundreds of pleasure craft in San Diego harbor and its environs had a habit of ruining the ambience by demanding that

Swifts observe International Rules of the Road and complaining loudly and often when the Swifts ignored them.

The one boat school experience that never changed through the years, and that no one ever forgot, was the week of prisoner-of-war training spent in the mountains at Warner Springs, California, or, in later years, on Whidbey Island in Washington's Puget Sound. Called Survival Evasion Resistance and Escape, but known simply as SERE, it was a brutal exercise involving interrogation, beatings, sleeplessness, starvation, and constant physical abuse at a simulated POW camp, all designed to acquaint Swift crews with what might happen should they suddenly find themselves washed up on a hostile shore. No Swift Boat sailor ever had the bad luck to test the training under real circumstances.

On October 1, 1965, the Navy officially established Boat Squadron One at Cam Ranh Bay[1], a spectacularly beautiful South China Sea harbor on South Vietnam's central coast. As boats arrived in Vietnam they were assigned to one of five divisions, one for each Market Time sector along South Vietnam's 1,200-mile coastline. The patrol sectors began in the north at Cua Viet, just south of the DMZ on the South China Sea and then swept southward, curled around the Ca Mau Peninsula (South Vietnam's southern "boot"), and turned north again into the Gulf of Thailand and up South Vietnam's west coast to Ha Tien on the Cambodian border.[2]

The divisions were numbered in the order they were established. First was Division 101 at An Thoi on Phu Quoc Island in the Gulf of Thailand, with responsibility for South Vietnam's west coast. Next came Da Nang, Division 102, the northernmost base in the South China Sea. Division 103 was at Cat Lo, near the South China Sea tourist city of Vung Tau on the northern edge of the Mekong Delta. Divisions 104 (Cam Ranh) and 105 (Qui Nhon) were on the South China Sea central coast between Da Nang and Cat Lo. By June 1966, there were seventy Swift Boats spread among the five divisions. In 1967, after other kinds of patrol boats had arrived in-country, the divisions lost their middle zeroes and simply became Coastal Divisions 11, 12, 13, 14, and 15. Boat Squadron One became Coastal Squadron One. The reason this name change was necessary was never made entirely clear.[3]

The boats spent the vast majority of their time in coastal waters, boarding and searching junks and sampans suspected of smuggling arms and supplies to the Viet Cong. Boats generally operated with two crews who swapped out every twenty-four hours to minimize downtime, keeping the boats constantly on patrol.

Swifts coordinated closely with the Coast Guard cutters that had preceded them to Vietnam. Destroyer-sized "high-endurance cutters" could pursue trawlers and other deepwater ships; these and the Navy's shallow-draft landing ship tanks (LSTs) also frequently served as mother ships for deployed Swift Boats. The Coast Guard also had eighty-two-foot cutters, more seaworthy but less maneuverable than Swifts; they were also much slower, with a top speed of eighteen knots. Speed and the Swifts' 81mm mortars, deadly accurate to a range of 4,000 yards, heightened their value as a quick-reaction artillery alternative for beleaguered ground troops. Swifts soon acquired a reputation for prowess in gunfire support, casualty evacuation, and seaborne rescue.

Once crews arrived in-country they quickly began learning about the enemy. During a patrol in the Gulf of Thailand on Valentine's Day 1966, PCF 4 approached a bamboo pole flying a Viet Cong flag about 250 yards offshore near the town of Rach Gia. After exploding several grenades near the base of the flagpole without incident, a crewman moved to cut the flag loose. Suddenly a remotely triggered mine detonated in a tremendous explosion, sinking the boat and killing four crewmen and wounding two others. Viet Cong fire hindered recovery, but the boat was eventually lifted from the water and shipped to Subic Bay, where it was deemed beyond repair, forcing the Navy to scrap it. These were the Swifts' first casualties in Vietnam, and PCF 4 was the first lost boat.[4]

In March, PCFs in tandem with Coast Guard cutters conducted their first river patrols in a twelve-day operation to interrupt enemy supply routes in the Rung Sat Special Zone, a mangrove swamp southeast of Saigon laced with an intricate web of canals.[5] At high tide, any part of the Rung Sat could be navigated by sampan, and it had long served as a haven for robbers, river pirates, and, now, the Viet Cong. The Long Tau River—a principal Rung Sat waterway—was the critical shipping link between the sea and Saigon. Keeping it open and keeping it safe were priorities for U.S. forces.

During the twelve days of Operation Jackstay, six Swift boats engaged the enemy nine times. Two months later, also in the Rung Sat, PCF 41 came under heavy-weapons fire from the banks of the Dinh Ba River. Shrapnel killed the helmsman, wounded the radioman, and destroyed most of the pilothouse equipment. Seconds later a mine exploded next to the boat, causing hull damage. The crew got away from the kill zone, but could not control the stricken boat, and it ran aground. With dusk approaching, the crew jettisoned the aft .50-caliber machine gun, the radio equipment, and some ammo, and escaped in the life raft. A U.S. Army reaction force later reached the boat and attempted to tow it to safety, but the bottom was too badly damaged, and it sank in twenty-five feet of water.[6]

Besides learning about the Viet Cong, the crews also learned what their boats could and could not do. Seas higher than six feet were almost impossible to negotiate. Squadron reported this back to BuShips, and the Navy began thinking about a different and more seaworthy design. But change did not come fast enough. In October 1966, PCF 56 lost a crewman over the side as it tried to negotiate heavy surf at the mouth of the Hue River in South Vietnam's northern reaches. The crewman's body was found two days later on the beach.[7]

A month after that PCF 22 lost a man overboard in the approach to Hue, but was able to rescue him. PCF 77, waiting outside the surf line and ready to offer assistance, was suddenly rear-ended by a sea estimated to be between twenty-five and thirty feet high. The wave lifted PCF 77's stern and drove the bow deep into the trough, causing the boat to "pitch-pole"—flip end over end. Three crewmen died and the boat sank keel-up in ninety seconds. The bow section eventually washed up about one and a half miles north of the Hue River. The rest was never found.[8]

Despite these tragedies and other setbacks, the Swifts and their Coast Guard allies had considerable success tracking, attacking, and destroying enemy trawlers and other shipping vessels, recovering more than one hundred tons of weapons and other war matériel. Swift Boats had learned their business.

Oops

John Louk

Lt. (j.g.) John Louk retired from the Navy in 1980 with the rank of lieutenant commander. He obtained his undergraduate and graduate degrees and completed a second career as an engineering manager at Wabash Valley Power Association in Indianapolis.

It was a perfectly calm night, a rare occasion in the South China Sea. Flat seas, no wind, no moon. I was Officer-in-Charge of PCF 16, on routine patrol at a cruising speed of ten knots off the coast of Vietnam at the DMZ.

Around midnight we detected an unusual radar contact. It was seaward of us, not more than a mile or two away. If there had been any weather at all, we might have dismissed it as an electronic anomaly, but there was no doubt. The water was like a pond, and we saw the blip on repeated radar sweeps. Usually the only thing you found at night in the coastal waters of the South China Sea was a "fish stake," a long wooden pole attached to fishing traps and gear to help Vietnamese fishermen locate and retrieve their catch. We never found fish stakes anywhere near the DMZ because fishing was illegal there. And this radar contact pinged stronger than a wooden pole. This was something else. We turned the boat and went to have a look.

Vietnam was the latest stop in a journey I had chosen long before. I just flat-out loved the Navy. I grew up watching *Victory at Sea*, became a Sea Explorer as a teen, and enlisted when I graduated from high school.

I spent nearly six years as an Electronics Technician, made First Class, installed radar at GITMO during the Cuban Missile Crisis, and wore a Good Conduct ribbon. Then I decided to become an officer.

I won a trip to Officer Candidate School (OCS) through something called the "integration program," in which no college degree was required. When one interviewer (a commander or a captain, I can't remember) asked me why I wanted to be an officer, I told him I was looking for a chance to "do" the Navy "my way." I did not lack confidence.

So at twenty-four I became an unrestricted line officer, an ex-enlisted "mustang." I ended up on the USS *Lexington*, an aircraft carrier out of Pensacola. I punched every ticket they had: division officer, combat information center radar navigator, Officer-of-the-Deck underway. And that was it. I was napkin number 179 in the wardroom—representing my seniority among the *Lexington*'s line officers. I'm sure I had a good chance to become napkin 178 if I had wanted to wait around, but I didn't. It was the spring of 1965 when I read about a call for underway-OOD-qualified junior officers to volunteer for a new small craft to be deployed to Vietnam. I signed up. Be the captain of my own ship—the goal of every officer! Fight in a war! They didn't call it the armed forces for nothing.

And so I became one of the original Swift Boat officers—a "plank owner." Training at Coronado was sort of a mess, but it got the job done. We were inventing Swift Boats as we went along. We learned about the weapons, learned about the gear, and drove around the ocean near San Diego, practicing board-and-search and small-craft navigation. Our job-to-be was the interdiction of enemy boat traffic in the coastal waters of South Vietnam. Boat Squadron One—the Swift Boat command—was invented and went to Cam Ranh Bay to set up shop.

My crew and I were sent to Subic Bay, Philippines, to await the new boats, coming to us on a freighter from Louisiana. After they arrived we had to set them up for deployment. This required us to reinforce the fantail gun mount of the .50-caliber machine gun/81mm mortar so the recoil wouldn't rip it from the deck; transfer the radar from the main cabin to the pilothouse so the helmsman and OinC (me) could actually use it while underway; and get rid of the ship's bell, as good as a neon sign if you wanted to let the bad guys know you were coming.

When we finished with all this, we put the boats aboard a big LSD—a floating dry dock—for the trip to Vietnam. We arrived in Da Nang on January 23, 1966, and there we established Coastal Division 102. We lived aboard a floating barracks and made shakedown cruises to get us ready to patrol the coastline from the DMZ south to Chu Lai. We learned that a small base north of Hue was supposed to be part of a Vietnamese national forest, and dire consequences were promised to any who harmed a tree or otherwise messed up the area. Uh . . . there was a war on, but like I say, these were early days, and we were making it up as we went along.

We got some pointers from the Coast Guard, who had preceded us, but then we were on our own—conducting twenty-four-hour patrols boarding and searching waterborne traffic to check for contraband. Our Vietnamese-language skills were limited, and at first we didn't have any South Vietnamese sailors aboard to help us with translation. But we looked formidable, and we were pretty good at spotting nervousness. Still, what were you going to do with a large motor-driven coastal junk jam-packed above and below decks with everything from cases of beer to cooking utensils? You did what you could.

That is maybe why we weren't overly excited at first by our midnight radar contact. We were still fairly new at a job that had zero institutional memory, so if there was something sticking out of the water that we had never seen before, it was no big deal. There were a lot of things in Vietnam we hadn't seen before.

As we approached the contact, we saw that it was moving, slowly drifting to port. We compensated by coming left to keep it dead ahead. We slowed to steerageway as we closed, finally losing the contact altogether in the close-in sea return on the radarscope. Then we turned on the pilothouse searchlight and pointed it forward. I immediately saw and recognized a submarine periscope (*Victory at Sea*!), traveling about five knots with a wake, and heading almost due north (015 degrees magnetic).

As we crossed the wake, our fathometer registered a sharp rise in depth, then quickly returned to normal soundings. We reversed course and did it again with the same fathometer reaction. I was convinced we had accidently discovered a submarine. I leafed through my mental encyclopedia of Naval Lore. You needed two or more sensor contacts to make a classification of "certain sub." We nailed it plus one: the radar contact, the fathometer, and Mark One Eyeball.

I knew I had to tell someone ASAP what we had found, but I didn't know what to do next except hang around and keep alert. I also had no idea whose sub it was, but I understood that an 81mm mortar, a bunch of machine guns and automatic rifles, and a single .38-caliber revolver were not going to do any damage to anything underwater. Maybe the spare Danforth anchor on the stern?

The periscope disappeared. Time to send the alert. We grabbed the encryption tables and quickly found the appropriate words (positive, submarine, visual, radar, etc.). We put together an encoded flash precedence voice message and transmitted it to the Coastal Surveillance Center at Da Nang.

Very soon we found ourselves in the middle of a monstrous predawn airshow. P5M Marlin surveillance seaplanes on maritime patrol began to converge on our position. The marines scrambled some A4 Skyhawk attack jets and the Air Force sent an F-105 "Thud" with spare ordnance hanging from the pylons.

But almost as quickly as the operation started, everything changed. Da Nang called everybody up: Break it off, forget the contact, don't try to find it again, and "resume normal operations"—in other words, mind your own business. That wasn't hard for us, since I had no intention of wandering north of the DMZ in search of whatever it was we had found. But I was curious. I later asked my Division Commander what the order was all about, but he didn't know. Neither did anyone else I asked, or, if they did, they weren't saying.

Then years later, when I was attached to a Beach Jumper unit deployed to White Beach Okinawa, I first overheard, then sought out a Navy SEAL who told me about a clandestine operation aboard a submarine off Vietnam. He wouldn't tell me the exact nature of the operation or its ultimate outcome, but he confirmed that some #$&$@^& patrol boat had screwed it up.

Oops.

S.E.R.E.

Rod McAlpin

Lt. (j.g.) Rod McAlpin left the Navy in 1969 for a career in manufacturing, eventually owning his own business. He retired to Litchfield, Connecticut.

THE FORMAL NAME FOR IT WAS "SURVIVAL, EVASION, RESISTANCE AND Escape," but to anyone who ever served in Vietnam it was simply S.E.R.E. It lasted a week and was extremely unpleasant, and when we were undergoing Swift Boat training to go overseas, we anticipated it with extreme dread. We weren't stupid.

Here's the script: Your boat gets shot up and sinks in enemy territory. You and your crew make it to the beach, but you have nowhere to go, nothing to eat, and no weapons of any kind, except maybe a knife. You must learn how to forage and survive . . . in the jungle, in the desert, in the woods, in the mountains above the tree line—you get the idea. Soon the bad guys come looking for you, so you run, you hide, whatever it takes to evade them. But in the end, they find you and take you prisoner. And then, in phase three, the prison camp, they interrogate you, starve you, and beat the crap out of you for several days. You have three tough choices: quit, escape, or simply endure the abuse. They do the endure part whether you escape or not. When it's over, you're filthy and pissed off, but you've learned a lot of stuff about hunger, humility, mind games, and torture that could come in handy if, God forbid, Charlie ever captured you.

So one Sunday during Swift training at Naval Base Coronado in the summer of 1967, our instructors advised us that we would be going to

Coronado Beach the next day for some boat exercises. A bus would pick us up at the base at 0630, so don't bother to eat breakfast. The school would provide a brown-bag breakfast and lunch. We actually believed this.

We did go to the beach. But not for boat training. This was S.E.R.E., phase one: Survival. No beautiful girls sunbathing in bikinis. Just a remote and vacant stretch of seaweed-covered beach in the middle of nowhere, with waves lapping at the shoreline and occasionally offering a dead crab or fish which, little did we know, would soon become part of our desperation menu. The instructor told our group leader, a lieutenant commander, that this landscape would be the base for him and his troops—three dozen of us. Then he dropped a couple of small bags of rice at his feet, probably to ensure that we wouldn't starve too soon, and walked off into the sand dunes.

By this time we had figured out what was going on, but we were hungry, so we spent the rest of the day stabbing small fish and an occasional crab in the surf with spear-sticks. We boiled this menagerie in a pot with the rice to make a meager, tasteless sandy stew, but we weren't choosy. Anything to quiet the hunger pangs. This was the opening meal in what would be a week's worth of scrounging for rattlesnakes, rabbits, and such for S.E.R.E stew or driftwood barbecue.

All this was just the intro for the next phase—internment at a prison camp high up in the mountains of Warner Springs, California, where temperatures ranged from ninety degrees during the day to subfreezing at night. I don't remember how we got there, but we were taken to a sixty-by-eighty-foot compound that had been erected in a forest just below the snow-covered mountaintops—far from the beach. The camp, enclosed with steel mesh fencing topped with spooled barbed wire, had sentry boxes and gun turrets along the entire perimeter. A handful of wooden buildings dotted the dusty courtyard. We arrived dirty, hungry, and very tired. Lack of food will do that to you. It saps your energy and plays havoc with your mind, thereby making it much more likely that you'll crack under interrogation.

Our first night at the prison camp, we were herded into the woods to a checkpoint designated by the instructors. This was the start of nighttime Escape and Evasion. The objective was to negotiate roughly two miles of darkened woods to reach a lighted outpost. The enemy had set traps along the way. Escapees who reached the outpost without being captured would get a meal. Or so they said. But what did we have to lose? Maybe they told the truth. And we were really hungry.

An overcast night made it impossible to see anything. The enemy had all the advantage. I struggled through the underbrush, trying my best to be quiet and still make decent progress toward the outpost. I heard gunshots throughout the night as one escapee after another fell into enemy hands. Then, at what I thought was about halfway, I reached a clearing of sorts, which seemed to offer an unimpeded crossing. I checked all the entry and exit points carefully, then started streaking across the open span, hoping to make cover on the far side.

I never saw what was coming, never even sensed it beforehand. I ran headlong into a huge coil of barbed wire that had been spread across the belly of the clearing. I don't know which was worse: the pain from myriad impaling points stabbing into my legs and lower torso, or the extreme disappointment of missing the carrot at the end of a successful journey. From that day forward the front of my right thigh carried a vivid reminder of my barbed wire encounter: a six-inch scar that looks like a thermometer, the mercury bulb being the initial entry gash. I was captured shortly thereafter and returned to the prison compound.

At the compound we were further starved, tortured, and morale-busted for the next three days or so. We all visited the dreaded "black boxes": coffin-like solo boxes, two-man boxes, and a large five-foot-square enclosure designed to handle multiple prisoners. We endured solo interrogation, in which a guard forced you to your knees, sat on your chest, and literally bent you over backwards. His MO was to weaken your resolve to the point where you would eventually disclose more than just your name, rank, serial number, and date of birth.

The guards tortured and beat our CO so badly in several of these interrogation sessions that he suffered a broken leg and had to be removed from the exercise. These sessions, as planned, weeded out the weaker souls who either could not or would not continue. They were pulled out of S.E.R.E. training and consequently lost their opportunity to go overseas. (And we were the lucky ones?)

The guards told us from the beginning that our main objective as prisoners was to both Resist and Escape in any way we could during the camp phase. When I ended up with four others stuffed into a black box probably designed for three, we decided to kick out the locked door and make a break for it. The door succumbed quickly, but when we bolted for the nearest camp exit, guards in the watchtowers opened up with .50-caliber machine guns. The noise alone was a shock, but I think I remember rounds of live ammo kicking up the dirt in our path. Real or imagined, it brought us to an immediate and complete standstill.

Our captors then rounded us up, made us strip naked, and forced us to climb into a trough filled with cold water. They held us under water until we nearly drowned. Then, still naked and bitterly cold from the subfreezing nighttime temperatures, they told us to lie on the ground and roll in the dirt until totally covered in mud. Only then could we put our uniforms back on.

The end finally came in the middle of the night after several days of this when one of the hated "enemy" guards assembled us and delivered the welcome words: "Exercise Secured." The hot oatmeal and fresh fruit that followed may have been the most well-deserved and relished meal of our lives.

Our captors immediately dropped their foreign accents and began to relate both the positives and negatives of our S.E.R.E. experience. I had an incredibly hard time dealing with this chitchat. These guys had become the hated symbols of our week in captivity. They had spent their time mocking us, degrading us, physically abusing us, and causing us real pain, and now we were all supposed to be friends? It was almost impossible to move on emotionally after all this, and my instinct to break every bone in their bodies was almost too overwhelming to ignore.

Of course, it was just an exercise. Imagine if it lasted longer than a week. Imagine if it was the real thing.

Shakedown Cruise

Jim Franklin

Lt. Jim Franklin was separated from active duty in 1967 and worked first in banking and then as a teacher, eventually retiring to Seattle with his wife.

IT WAS THE FIRST REAL PATROL FOR PCF 61, A BRAND-NEW BOAT FOR a brand-new Swift Boat division at Qui Nhon, far up the exposed northeast coast of South Vietnam. I was the Officer-in-Charge, and my crew and I had been together since training at Coronado. We already had five months in-country, and we were good, but we'd been working out of An Thoi and the relatively placid waters of the Gulf of Thailand. Qui Nhon was a different story.

We got underway the afternoon of May 23, 1966. The weather was lousy—high winds, rain, and big, heavy swells that kept getting bigger. Our patrol area was forty klicks to the south, around the mouth of a large bay leading to the town of Song Cau. Soon we were bucking through seas between three and four feet high. It was a rugged ride, but nothing we hadn't handled before.

Our job was to keep watch on the water traffic in our area and to board and search any boat that piqued our interest. We were looking for VC contraband—weapons and medicine—and we were also ready to provide fire support with mortar or machine guns to U.S. or Vietnamese ground forces in the area if they needed it.

This patrol, however, was all about the weather. Very few junks were at sea, and we couldn't board anything anyway. By 2100, we were about eight klicks north of the entrance to Song Cau Bay with seas between five and six feet high, about the limit of what we could handle in open water. Operating close inshore was pretty much out of the question. We decided to head into the bay and find a smoother ride.

The trip to the bay's entrance took about an hour, but we didn't finish it. Instead we picked up a large radar contact about four klicks due east from us, straight out to sea. We went for a look, making slow progress and taking a pounding from the head seas. Eventually we spotted our contact. It was a fifty-foot motorized junk, except the motor wasn't running. Instead, the junk was falling into the weather and wallowing in the troughs as waves crashed over the side. About ten or eleven men were on deck, alternatingly waving at us and trying to bail. They weren't having much success, and the junk was taking on water at a rapid rate.

Towing wasn't going to work, so we decided to offload the crew. Working from the aft helm, Connell, our boatswain, brought the boat around to the windward side of the junk, blocking the weather for a moment, and then delicately brought us alongside the junk where we tied up loosely so we could begin the evacuation.

But that's not what the deckhands had in mind. Rather than immediately abandoning ship, they began yelling down to people in the holds below. We knew that junks this big had a large storage capacity. What we didn't know was that the cargo on this junk was people. Mobs of them.

It was a trickle at first, and then a flood. I stood with Grey, our leading petty officer, and Gerich, the engineman, on the fantail. Soon we were helping men, women, and children, young and old, onto our deck. I called for more help, and soon our entire crew was distributing the new arrivals everywhere—below decks, crouched on the bow, and even clinging to stanchions on the roof of the main cabin. Sometime in the middle of all this, the passengers began passing up pigs, dogs (the eating variety), and crates of chickens. Suitcases and bales of belongings were also in the mix. Grey gave me a look, and without a word he and Gerich began passing the animals and luggage for me to toss overboard. Luckily, the people were so focused on saving themselves that no one said anything about their belongings. Or anything else. We fired several shots in the air at one point in hopes of imposing some kind of crowd control, but it made no impression. Fear of drowning overcame any fear of weapons.

We had been in radio contact with Qui Nhon ever since we first spotted the junk, and once we saw the extent of our task, we called for help. The destroyer escort USS *Vance*, patrolling offshore, began steaming toward us, but it would be several hours before she arrived. It was going to be our job to stay afloat until that happened. It was going to be complicated.

Despite the nonstop pandemonium, our actual evacuation probably lasted no more than fifteen minutes. But even as the last evacuees crowded in next to us on the fantail, the junk began to go. We cast off our lines, and within moments the junk foundered and sank. For an instant all of us—crew and refugees—went silent.

The *Vance* was two hours out. I took the after helm and tried to find a slow enough speed and a careful course that would somewhat neutralize the high seas and improve the ride for our passengers. Our freeboard had all but disappeared—I was afraid to look—and it affected our maneuverability. I was having a hard time driving, and the refugees noticed. It took them a while to recover from the trauma of one near drowning, but as time passed they began to call out to one another with increasing frequency and higher volume. We did not know what they were saying, but they had undoubtedly realized that they might simply have exchanged one watery coffin for another. We kept the hatches and doors battened down, and Miller and Ballard, our radarman and gunner's mate, were supervising the below-decks survivors. They reported a packed house, with a lot of seasickness and perturbation. The folks on deck were more worried about holding on.

Several times out of An Thoi we had ferried Special Forces units to and from their op areas, and I remember thinking that twenty-five of those guys, heavily armed, was enough for any Swift Boat. Now we had many times that number. I mentioned to Grey how fortunate we were that the Vietnamese were small people.

After more than an hour of barely making headway, the *Vance* radioed that they had us on radar. An hour after that they came up on our windward side, like we had done for the junk, and the waves subsided in their lee. The *Vance* dropped several ladders to us and offloading began. The passengers didn't need any coaxing. Once they saw the size of the *Vance* relative to PCF 61, brand-new or not, they were up and out in no time.

The final count was 157 men, women, and children. One of our crew counted more than twenty people emerging from the forward cabin alone—an extraordinary number, and every other space on the boat was filled just as compactly. The CO of the *Vance* told us we showed about six inches of freeboard as we approached them, and that we looked more like a floating mass of humanity than a patrol boat.

We stayed aboard the *Vance* for an hour and then went back on patrol, eventually scooting into Song Cau Bay, our original destination, where we cleaned up the mess. We felt pretty good about our boat and about ourselves. The squadron commander wrote us a letter of commendation.

Our passengers, we found out later, came from a small village outside Song Cau and had decided to leave en masse because of increased conflict with the VC. They were on their way to Nha Trang, about 100 klicks south, and had just picked a bad day to travel. Eventually, however, they made it—minus animals and luggage.

In 2004, my wife and I visited the Song Cau area and tried to find out if anyone remembered our adventure, but no one did. I hope those people found the peace they were searching for.

Man Overboard

Gary Liedorff

Gunner's Mate Third Class Gary Liedorff left the Navy in 1967 for a career in the commercial air-conditioning business in the San Francisco Bay Area, retiring near Sacramento, California, in 2004.

I REPORTED TO ACTIVE DUTY AT TREASURE ISLAND IN SEPTEMBER 1965. I was a local San Francisco Bay Area kid and engaged to be married. I was eighteen. The whole idea in joining the Navy was to not go to Vietnam, and at first things looked bright. I was close to home and close to my fiancée. After waiting around for a week or so, I got orders to join Swift Boats.

So what was a Swift Boat? None of my buddies had the vaguest idea. I talked to a couple of the admin folks. Not a clue. The only thing I knew was that I had to report to Coronado Amphibious Base, near San Diego—which, still, was not so bad. Nice place, and when I arrived I was happy to learn that Swifts were small craft. I had spent a lot of time on our family's sixteen-foot pleasure boat—launching it, driving it around, maneuvering. It was great fun and I was pretty good at it. Maybe that's why the Navy had picked me for this. They told me I was going to be one of the very first Swift Boat crewmen.

A few days later, however, I learned that Swift Boats were going to Vietnam. Suddenly my grand plan for escaping the war wasn't working out. I decided to make the best of it. If this was how I was going to fill my draft obligation, then so be it. Besides, Swift Boats were pretty impressive—three times as big as my dad's boat, real fast and with lots of guns. I was looking forward to finding out how they performed. Pretty glamorous.

We trained for several months—boat handling, weapons, POW training, boarding procedures. Then I climbed aboard a plane at Travis Air Force Base and said goodbye to my fiancée, my father, my mother, and my sister. My mother did not handle it well. She was distraught, consumed with anxiety. I tried to reassure her, but what did I know? Swift Boats may have been really cool, but I was scared as hell.

The glamor wore off fast. We arrived in Cat Lo February 19, 1966, and three days later I spent my nineteenth birthday filling sandbags. There were only four boats based in Cat Lo when we arrived, and a lot of the base still needed to be built. That was our assignment. Sandbags, trenches, bunkers. No latrine, no mess hall. Just sweat and C-rations for the first six weeks.

Our boat finally arrived in early April. We loaded it up with guns, ammo, gear, and food. Then it was time to find out what patrolling was going to be like. Our job was to cruise the rivers of the Mekong Delta and search everything on the water that could carry contraband. The first couple of weeks I was terrified. We got in our first firefight before dawn one morning. Muzzle flashes in the jungle about 250 yards off our port bow and tracers coming toward us. We returned fire and in a matter of seconds it was over.

We relaxed after that, and found patrols to be even less glamorous. Most were boring and uneventful. We had the occasional exchanges of gunfire but not often. After a few months of this, the High Command took us out of the river and sent us on coastal patrol. This was called Operation Market Time, in which we spent our days going up and down the coast boarding and searching watercraft—same as the Mekong except the boats were bigger.

And finally the glamor disappeared altogether. We were on patrol in the middle of the night, something like ten miles off the Vietnam coast in the South China Sea. We were looking for enemy trawlers, pitching and rolling dramatically in fifteen-foot seas. All it took was a slight chop for a Swift Boat to behave like a bucking bronco. Given this shortcoming we often wondered why the Navy had put the toilet way up in the bow. You could forget about using it even in moderate seas.

It was 0320, pitch black, and I had to go. Our method was to brave the ocean spray and make our way hand-over-hand along the rail to the fantail. Then you would drop your pants, grab hold of the rail, and hang your butt over the sea. I had almost completed this maneuver when a rogue wave swept over us and washed me overboard. I don't know if I yelled, but within moments the boat was out of earshot. Between engine noise and the weather I doubt if my screams would have mattered.

Not good. I don't remember what my first thought was, but rational analysis kicked in shortly. I knew I wasn't going to be able to tread water for long, but they had taught us a neat trick in boat school: You take off your pants, tie knots in the legs, pull up the zipper, and then raise the pants and slam the open end into the water. Air gets trapped inside and you lie between the inflated legs (thank God I wasn't wearing shorts), which hold the air because they're wet. It worked!

So I was okay on buoyancy. Then I started remembering all the snakes we saw swimming in the bay near Vung Tau with their heads above water just looking for something to bite. I didn't know if they were in the ocean also. Then I started to think about how to get ashore—a long way—and what I might find there—probably Charlie. Again, not good.

At that point I started praying and hoping for the best. Oddly enough, I didn't really get scared. The water was warm, my ride was stable, and my mind was racing from "what if" to "what if," without lingering on any topic long enough to imagine the worst thing that could happen. I knew that my departure would be discovered fairly quickly, and this proved to be the case. I had the 0400 watch, and one of my crewmates came down to wake me up about 0350. When I was nowhere to be found, it was surmised that I had been washed over the side about a half hour earlier. Out in the ocean I did the math. I was maybe eight miles back at that point. In seas as rough as we had that night, top speed was no more than eight or ten knots, so the return trip was going to take a while, say another half hour—if they found me at all. Don't think about that.

Fortunately, just when I needed help, the ocean became my friend. The boat did a 180 and was coming back down the coast on a reverse track when Mother Nature lifted me on top of a big swell and perched me there just in time for the boat's radar to ping me. They were fifteen minutes away and they had me—at least intermittently—on their screen. Of course I didn't know this right away, but I figured out what was happening when the searchlight came on maybe 200 yards away, tacked back and forth a couple of times, and then found me.

Only then did I fully understand my predicament, and suddenly I was overjoyed. Whitley, our Leading Petty Officer and a ropy six-footer, leaned over the side of the boat and grabbed my arm on the first try. And then I was back aboard, none the worse. I was late for my watch, but nobody gave me a hard time about it.

The last part of my tour, like the first, was pretty slow. I got badly spooked when I reached my final week, convinced Charlie was going to grease me on my last day, but it didn't happen. I got home February 18, 1967, and spent big parts of the first few days hugging my mom while she calmed down. I didn't tell her right away about getting swept overboard—in fact, I didn't tell her about it for years afterward. She needed to relax, and it was wonderful to watch it happen. She didn't need another: "Oh, by the way . . ."

Getting There Is Hard . . . Getting Out Is Better

Dick Olsen

Lt. (j.g.) Dick Olsen left the Navy in 1967 and retired in San Francisco after a forty-year career as an investment advisor.

I JOINED THE SWIFT BOATS IN THE FALL OF 1965. THEY WERE BRAND-new in Vietnam and I was a brand-new Officer-in-Charge of a brand-new crew training at the Amphibious Base in Coronado, California. Every week, as training progressed, the staff gathered us all in a big room so we could find out where we were going.

Early on I didn't pay attention. Crews had numbers, and ours was sixty-eight. When I started, they were still in the forties. But things moved along, and we moved up, until one day we learned we were destined for Cat Lo, the only Swift Boat base that included inland patrols in the rivers of the Mekong Delta. Boats there were getting ambushed and having firefights. We were nervous.

We flew commercial from San Diego to San Francisco, rented a car, and spent the day sightseeing. We drove across the Golden Gate Bridge and looked at places we might never see again. Then we took a bus to Travis Air Force Base for our flight. We left in the evening, believing we were en route to Clark Air Force Base in the Philippines, and then to the Subic Bay Naval Base. Instead, we flew first to Hawaii, then to Midway, and then perhaps to a couple of other islands. I don't remember. It got

Skipper Dick Olsen and crew upon arrival in Vietnam in April 1966.
COURTESY OF RICHARD OLSEN

dark soon after we took off, and it stayed dark. It seemed like the flight—and the night—would never end. Then we landed in Okinawa, and the pilot told us we had reached the end of the line.

"We have to go to Subic Bay," I said. "In the Philippines." We were 1,000 miles short.

"That may be," the pilot said, "but this plane stops here."

We checked around. There were no flights that day to Subic, and the Air Force wouldn't put us up. We took a bus to Naha Naval Air Station and hung out there for three or four very long days. It turned out we needed official authorization to get off Okinawa, and we spent our time trading messages back and forth with the Swift Boat command in Coronado until we had it.

Eventually we did reach Subic, where we spent another five days training and shaking down some boats that had just arrived from the States. Only when we finished with that did we get our orders to Cat Lo. I gathered up the crew and went to see the OinC of the Swift detachment. "How do we get to Vietnam?" I asked. He laughed: "That's up to you."

We went to Cubi Point Naval Air Station. They had flights, but not enough seats, so I told my Chief Petty Officer to take the rest of the crew and get going. We would all meet in Saigon, I said, at the Naval attaché's office—wherever that was.

Late in the day I caught a World Airways cargo flight that landed at Tan Son Nhut airport about 0200 the next day, April 12, 1966. The base, the ground crew told us, was under mortar attack, and they advised us that we should get out of there as soon as possible. I didn't see any explosions, so I grabbed my gear, left the plane, found a cab, and went to Saigon, where I found my way to a building that housed some sort of Navy command. The front door was unlocked, so I went in and fell asleep on a couch. Shortly after sunup a lieutenant woke me up. "What are you doing here?" he demanded. I was only a lieutenant junior grade. I told him my story. Eventually I rounded up my crew and called the folks in Cat Lo to let them know we had finally arrived. They sent a boat upriver to pick us up.

Our new home was a small village near the tourist city of Vung Tau on the northeastern edge of the Delta. Mostly we did Market Time

Dick Olsen and his crew six months after their arrival. Lt. (j.g.) Olsen is on the left.
COURTESY OF RICHARD OLSON

Aft mount with .50-caliber machine gun mounted piggyback atop an 81mm mortar.
COURTESY OF RICHARD OLSEN

patrols, searching junks and sampans along the coast and seizing contraband to keep it from getting into the rivers and into the hands of the Viet Cong. These patrols typically lasted twenty-four hours. We left the base before noon, relieved the boat on station, and stayed until we were relieved at noon the next day. Then we returned to the base, took showers, relaxed, ate, slept, ate again, and left again the following day. Patrols were generally uneventful except during the monsoon season, when heavy seas tossed us about, and immense waves snuck up on us in the night.

The river was somewhat different. Besides searching junks, we had to watch for pieces of wood or other floating objects tethered to something that might be an underwater explosive. If a boat approached the float, the VC triggerman on the beach pushed the plunger. We tried to avoid anything on the surface that didn't move with the current.

During the day there was a lot of traffic on the rivers, but as the afternoon gave way to nightfall, the locals went home. There were no boats on the river after dark except ours. The riverbanks were heavily overgrown, perfect for ambushes. We liked dark nights and hated the full moon. We saw flares, heard B-52 bombing runs that sounded like thunder, and saw C-47s spraying torch-like stripes of tracer from their miniguns. Time passed, and we began anticipating the day we would go home. One morning my commanding officer summoned me to his office and handed me my orders. I had extended my time in the Navy so I could go to Vietnam, and now my time was up.

"What about transportation?" I asked.

"That's up to you," he said.

Stupid question. I said good-bye to my crew, who still had about a month left, and then hitched a ride to a nearby Army helicopter base and began asking around to see if anyone was going near Tan Son Nhut. One pilot said he was going to Long Binh—about 38 klicks (24 miles) away. Close enough, except the pilot wasn't sure he could get off the ground with me on board. I figured what the hell, and I tossed him my gear. We struggled into the air and made it to Long Binh. It was late in the day and there were no rides to Tan Son Nhut, so I found a vacant building and slept on the floor with a bunch of Army soldiers, all of whom were in the same fix—orders to Tan Son Nhut, no way to get there.

Early in the morning we heard there was a bus leaving Long Binh. We jumped aboard and managed to get seats. The unpleasant news was that the windows were covered with heavy mesh screens to protect us from bad guys throwing grenades. The good news was that the bus traveled very fast to avoid the incoming, and we got to Tan Son Nhut in no time at all.

My plane didn't leave until later, so I wandered around. As the day progressed, I spotted a lot of soldiers and airmen walking toward a big amphitheater-type place, so I joined them. It was Bob Hope doing a show—just like in the newsreels and on TV. It was great seeing him in person. I laughed at the jokes by Bob and Phyllis Diller, applauded songs by Vic Damone and Anita Bryant, and ogled Joey Heatherton and Carole Baker.

And then I was on the plane. No more Military Airlift Command—this was a charter jet with stewardesses. I had a glass of real milk and a bowl of real ice cream. When we took off, a feeling of exhilaration and relief hit me so powerfully that I felt the tension drain right out of my body. Early the next morning I looked out the window and saw the Golden Gate Bridge.

During our training in San Diego a buddy of mine asked me why I volunteered to go to Vietnam. I told him I wanted to see if I had what it took to look danger in the eye and not blink. I did.

Chapter Two

1967

Doing Damage

On July 11, 1967, a U.S. patrol aircraft spotted a steel-hulled North Vietnamese trawler in the open ocean about eighty-five miles southeast of Da Nang in the South China Sea. Market Time surveillance tracked it until July 15, when PCF 79, along with other U.S. Navy and Coast Guard units, intercepted it about three miles off Cape Batangan.

The trawler opened fire with automatic weapons and a heavy machine gun, but in a classic "crossing the T" maneuver worthy of Horatio Hornblower, PCF 79 cut across the trawler's stern, giving the after gunner an unimpeded look at the target. Firing the 81mm mortar like a shotgun, Boatswain's Mate First Class Bobby Carver put an incendiary round almost point-blank into the trawler's pilothouse, blasting it apart and lighting the trawler afire. The ship was forced to run aground 200 feet from the mouth of the Sa Ky River, about halfway between Da Nang and Qui Nhon.

The Navy seized more than 10,000 rounds of ammunition and grenades from the wreck, including nearly 3,000 heavy mortar shells and Claymore antipersonnel mines. Also recovered were 1,200 weapons, including automatic rifles, machine guns, rocket launchers, three and a half tons of plastic explosive, and one and a half tons of dynamite.

The trawler was the eighth that Market Time patrols had stalked and intercepted since the patrols began in March 1965. Three trawlers were destroyed, one was damaged, two—including the July trawler—were captured, and two turned back into international waters.[1]

The Navy had built Swift Boats with interdiction in mind, and trawlers were high-value targets, capable of bringing one hundred tons of supplies to Viet Cong insurgents in South Vietnam. Between 80 and 110 feet in length, they displaced between 275 and 300 gross tons (a Swift Boat weighed about 22 tons). The vast majority of the cargo—weapons and ammunition—came from Communist China, with a sprinkling of light automatic weapons from the Soviet Union and other Eastern bloc countries.

The trawlers' diesel main engines and most of their auxiliary equipment had been manufactured in East Germany between 1963 and 1965. Nevertheless, the trawlers were slow, with a top speed of only ten or twelve knots, and a substantial draft—between six and a half feet and eight feet. Once found, they could not escape. Identifying them, however, could be tricky and dangerous work. None flew flags, although one had the flag of Nationalist China painted on the sides of the pilothouse. Three had false masts and booms to imitate fishing boats, and four carried nets and cordage. And if all this failed to convince, the trawlers could defend themselves with automatic rifles, heavy machine guns, and recoilless rifles. Their armament improved as time passed.

The trawlers usually tried to close the coast at first light. Needing to avoid detection but lacking maneuverability, they had to see to reach a pier or an anchorage. Once in contact with their Viet Cong allies, they could lay up for the day beneath palm trees or camouflage netting, or take cover among other anchored watercraft while they unloaded their cargo. They got underway at nightfall for the trip home.[2]

The Swifts, and their Market Time allies at sea and in the air, gradually strangled North Vietnamese coastal infiltration in 1967. Increasingly, the enemy turned to overland smuggling through Laos and Cambodia along what came to be known as the Ho Chi Minh Trail, bringing the cargo into the Mekong Delta via sampan and river junks. Overland resupply was much more cumbersome and labor intensive than trawlers, but much less risky. With trawlers, the North Vietnamese rolled the dice—load up, get underway, and take a chance on sneaking into the South unmolested. Mess it up and lose one hundred tons of supplies. Overland, it took many more people to move the goods, but they carried smaller loads. Getting caught occasionally was the price of doing business.

Squeezing North Vietnam's logistics had been the goal when Market Time began, and in 1967 it became clear that it was working. The mission had expanded beyond coastal interdiction in 1966 when the Navy had brought in its first tranche of river patrol boats—PBRs—to interdict traffic in the Mekong Delta. These nimble fiberglass boats drew only eighteen inches of water and were driven by a pair of water jet engines—no screws or rudders. They had crews of five, twin .50-caliber machine guns forward, and a third .50-caliber mounted aft. Their mission, called Operation Game Warden, was to do the same thing in the rivers that the Swifts were doing along the coast.[3]

In February 1967 the Navy added the Riverine Assault Force, a fleet of small vessels designed to move troops within the Delta and to support their operations. These new arrivals completed the "Brown Water Navy." By the end of 1967 there were nearly 400 warcraft of all kinds operating along the coast and in the rivers of South Vietnam. The Navy presence had grown from 4,500 men in March 1966 to about 27,000 by the end of 1967.[4]

"The United States Navy has not received due credit for the sizeable contributions its forces have made to the war in South Vietnam," Gen. William Westmoreland, the commander of all U.S. forces in Vietnam, remarked at a September 19 meeting. "Market Time activities have, for all practical purposes, sealed off the coast. Game Warden operations are increasingly denying the enemy the use of inland waterways. Thirdly, the Riverine Operation has no parallel in the history of warfare. The fine efforts of the Navy should not continue to go unnoticed."[5]

Besides stalking trawlers, in 1967 Swifts added responsibilities that were beyond what had by then become their "traditional" activities. They provided gunfire support for beleaguered allies and rescued two downed airmen from the sea—one near Da Nang, the other in the Gulf of Thailand. They continued civic action with local communities, offering medical assistance and other services to South Vietnamese civilians.

One Swift Boat was badly damaged in a firefight and needed extensive repairs. Two Swift sailors died in accidents, and in early December PCF 79 was ambushed during a loudspeaker PSYOPS patrol near Cape Batangan. Only five rounds of enemy fire hit the boat, but one of them killed BM1 Bobby Carver, the aft gunner whose mortar round had stopped the July trawler.[6]

By mid-1967 a great number of Swift Boats had seen almost constant use for at least a year, and hulls in many cases seemed to be wearing out. Maintenance teams discovered that seawater corrosion had caused some hulls to shrink to half their original thickness. It turned out that Sewart had made the hulls with a new alloy that could not handle seawater erosion. Hulls were exfoliating aluminum like paint peeling in the summer sun. The squadron started sending stricken boats to Subic Bay and Sasebo, Japan, to have their hulls replaced.

Any hope that the heavy weather disasters in the turbulent Hue River in 1966 were somehow due to a particularly nasty winter or to Swift crew inexperience were dashed in 1967. In July, the squadron sent a four-boat detachment to a temporary base near the mouth of the Cua Viet River, just south of the DMZ that separated North and South Vietnam. The river mouth was shallow, with sandbars extending several miles out to sea. This effectively turned the channel into a funnel. In good times there was some chop as the river forced its way out the narrow passage into the South China Sea; in bad times—the monsoon—the river mouth became a horror. The Cua Viet, swollen with runoff, sluiced into the funnel at dramatic speed, boring into the storm surge from the sea. The summer chop turned into a constant barrage of twenty-foot seas with cliff-like surf worthy of Hawaii on a big day.

On November 6, with the monsoon in full cry, PCF 76 was conducting a "weather probe," sampling the river mouth to see if it was possible to navigate the channel, reach the ocean, and go on patrol. It was not. The boat overturned in the surf. With help from other boats and from a helicopter that picked up two men with a sling, the crew was rescued, but the boat was pounded to bits and never seen again.

A bit over three weeks later, PCF 14 capsized in the channel while trying to rescue Vietnamese whose sampans had overturned in the surf. PCF 55, on hand to help in the rescue, rolled eighty-five degrees in the surf and lost all but one man overboard. He, his crew, and PCF 14's crew were rescued. PCF 55 made it back to port; PCF 14 did not. On November 30 the squadron closed down the Cua Viet detachment.[7]

Trawler

Bernard W. Wolff

Lt. Bernard W. Wolff returned from Vietnam and received an MBA from the University of Pennsylvania's Wharton School. He remained in the Naval Reserve until 1974. He embarked upon a career exporting American-made specialty chemicals from his business headquartered in his hometown of Roswell, Georgia.

THERE WERE FOUR NORTH VIETNAMESE TRAWLERS IN ALL, EACH ONE carrying one hundred tons of supplies destined for the Viet Cong. We didn't know about all of them right away, but ours showed up at 1630 on February 29, 1968. It was in international waters about 125 miles east of Vung Tau, heading southeast in the South China Sea at ten knots. A P-3 Orion surveillance plane spotted the trawler and began stalking it, marking the trawler's hull number—498—and taking note of the deck cargo on board and the 12.7mm heavy machine gun on the bow. The trawler exhibited no signs of being a fishing boat.

Every Market Time unit along the coast was aware of such trawlers, and when it became obvious that this one was headed our way my crew and I were aboard the *Winona*, a "high-endurance" Coast Guard cutter on station in the Gulf of Thailand off Vietnam's southwestern tip. We were one of the Swift Boat relief crews on Market Time patrol. Two boats, each with two crews, used *Winona* as a mother ship. Two of the crews would go on patrol while the relief crews stayed aboard the cutter. We were using PCFs 72 and 92. After twenty-four hours the boats would come back to the cutter and the crews would swap out. My crew and I were off-duty February 29, along with Lt. (j.g.) Bob Finley and his crew.

We liked it on the *Winona*. The Coasties treated us well. Our home base at An Thoi, a remote island off Vietnam's west coast, was pretty much the end of the supply chain for U.S. forces. Food there was lousy, and creature comforts were limited to a floating barracks. On the cutter the food was terrific, living quarters were comfortable, and the ride was a lot easier than it was on a Swift Boat. The cutter's crew enjoyed having us aboard, too. Whenever we came in to refuel and reprovision we'd tell them stories about what had happened on patrol. It broke up the monotony.

Winona was 254 feet long, a blue-water ship for the open ocean. It was more than a match for the trawler, which was less than half its length. *Winona*'s challenge was that its crew had never confronted a serious armed belligerent during what until then had been a relatively short time in-country. The cutter may have been two-thirds the size of a destroyer, but it had fewer than half as many men. The Coast Guard was not set up for sea battles.

As soon as the P-3 reported in, we changed course, rounded the tip of Vietnam, and headed north into the South China Sea at top speed—about seventeen knots. By sundown, we had the trawler on radar and reduced speed to shadow it, staying unseen just over the horizon. We exchanged communications with the P-3 and other Navy units that continued to track the trawler as it proceeded south. Three smaller Coast Guard cutters and Swift Boats from Cat Lo—not ours—were gathering outside the mouth of the Bo De estuary, the principal South China Sea entrance to the Viet Cong strongholds in the lower Ca Mau Peninsula and the only navigable way in for an overloaded trawler riding low in the water. If the trawler made a run for the Bo De, the blocking force had it covered. Anything else was up to us.

Winona's skipper needed all his gunner's mates to serve the five-inch, .38-caliber cannon that was *Winona*'s main armament. He also had a crew for an 81mm mortar mounted forward of the bridge and above the five-inch. For his six .50-caliber heavy machine guns—three each port and starboard—he was short of trained people and would have to man them with boatswain's mates, or deck crew. The fifties had no protective armor. The skipper needed a gunner's mate experienced with fifties to deal with malfunctions. He asked Finley to lend him his senior gunner, GMG3 William J. Lockerman, to man a fifty and serve as an all-purpose troubleshooter. As a Swift Boat gunner, Lockerman knew everything about .50-caliber machine guns.

At 2100 the trawler turned west and began to close the coast of Vietnam, its speed increasing to thirteen knots. At midnight it cut its speed in half, turned right thirty degrees, and shortly afterwards crossed into South Vietnam's twelve-mile contiguous zone. It was now officially an invader. *Winona* sounded General Quarters. The captain sent Finley and me to the wardroom, getting us out of harm's way. We were joined by the steward's mate, a potential hospital attendant if the wardroom was pressed into service to treat casualties—if it came to that. Both our crews, minus Lockerman, were below decks in the crew's quarters. Lockerman stood next to the starboard fifties.

We listened as *Winona* closed the trawler and fired a warning shot across its bow with the five-inch. We waited. Then we heard the trawler answer with the 12.7mm heavy machine gun it had on the forecastle. The five-inch opened fire in earnest, and kept shooting. The starboard fifties fired a few rounds, then suddenly and strangely fell silent, except for one gun. Bob and the steward's mate sat calmly at the wardroom table, but I nervously paced the deck, frustrated because I wasn't involved. Loud "whacks" echoed from *Winona*'s hull as enemy rounds smacked into it. The 12.7 wasn't enough gun to do serious damage to a ship the size of *Winona*, but it could wreak havoc among any crew out in the open.

The lone .50 caliber continued firing steady bursts from the starboard side of the ship. Return fire from the trawler intensified, and the whacks converged on the .50-caliber mount. The five-inch kept shooting for perhaps two minutes—an eternity in combat. Suddenly, we heard the sound of a huge explosion. *Winona* shook from the shock wave. Moments later the captain came up on the ship's PA system and jubilantly announced that the trawler had been engaged and destroyed "without any casualties—at least on THIS ship!"

Bob and I, shut up in the wardroom, heard everything but saw nothing. Subsequent conversations with crewmembers and with Lockerman filled in the blanks. When General Quarters sounded, the trawler was between 1,200 and 1,500 yards ahead of *Winona*, about seven miles off the coast. The moon was half-full, Lockerman said, but even so, the trawler was hard to see.

As the cutter closed the gap, *Winona*'s captain told his signalman to send the trawler an international flashing light order to "stop." The signalman sent the message three times, and each time the trawler ignored it. At that point the trawler was 800 yards off Winona's starboard beam—point-blank range. The captain ordered a five-inch round to be fired across the trawler's bow. The trawler immediately turned east. The captain then ordered the mortar crew to fire a star shell over the trawler to illuminate it. This was the catalyst, Lockerman said later, and "all hell broke loose."

The trawler began shooting its deck gun as soon as the star shell burst overhead. It was *Winona*'s first combat experience, and, at least at first, it did not go well. When the enemy opened fire the mortar crew took cover. In the process, the wrench they used to set the star shell's fuses was lost overboard. Without it, the star shells could not be properly set to illuminate—they were useless. After the first shell burned out, the entire scene went dark. Amidships, the boatswain's mates manning the starboard fifties, like the mortar team, left their guns and took cover inside the ship. Lockerman stayed put. He was at that point the only gunner on board with a clear look at the muzzle flashes coming from the trawler. He kept shooting.

Meanwhile, the five-inch was firing blindly. Without star shells, the fire control director had no visual target. The gun kept firing, but without clear purpose. In the confusion the gun crew apparently lost sight of the enemy's muzzle flashes and tracers. For the next two to three crucial minutes *Winona*'s only response to the trawler was Lockerman's fifty. But finally *Winona*'s fire control director spotted the enemy muzzle flashes and locked on to the target. It took only one well-placed round to obliterate the explosives-laden trawler in a massive ball of fire.

At sunrise we could see a mass of bullet impacts in the bulkhead behind Lockerman's firing position, but somehow he had emerged untouched. Over the PA system the *Winona*'s captain thanked the crew for a job well done, and added his thanks to "our Swift Boat guests" for their contribution. Later we found out that two other NVA trawlers had been engaged and destroyed farther north. One was hit and blown up, while a third was blown up by its crew after it ran aground. The fourth trawler never risked entering territorial waters and survived unmolested.

Lockerman, a quiet, competent man who later joined my own crew, never discussed the trawler battle during the remainder of the time I knew him. And as far as I know, the Coast Guard never said anything about him either, and did not offer him the recognition he deserved. He was Navy and *Winona* was Coast Guard, and his contribution appeared to fall between the cracks of the two services. Lockerman battled the trawler to a standstill for vital minutes to give *Winona*'s crew time to react. For me, Lockerman was the real hero.

To Build a Better Boat

Herb Pollock

Herb Pollock earned a master's degree in business administration from the University of Michigan and went to work for Whirlpool in 1972 as a business systems analyst. In 1988 he retired to Holland, Michigan, where he bought an historic residence and restored it.

By the time the Vietnam War began, I had already worked for ten years as a naval architect and marine engineer. I had done a little bit of everything, civilian and military, and had become something of a specialist designing amphibious assault boats for the Navy. But I dreamed of building beautiful custom racers for wealthy yachtsmen. So in 1963, with one job ending and nothing else immediately on the horizon, I moved back to my hometown on the shores of Lake Michigan to try my hand as an independent naval architect. My wife taught school to keep us in grocery money.

I was living a quiet, pleasure boat–focused life when Congress passed the Gulf of Tonkin Resolution in 1964, beginning the Vietnam buildup. It didn't affect me right away. I was older and draft-exempt, classified "4-F" for near-sighted astigmatism. I filled the time designing and building a midget ocean racer for myself and racing it successfully, trying to enhance my reputation—and, I hoped, win a commission to build a fancy boat for someone else.

This interlude ended after two years when a venture capital firm, formed in response to a Navy invitation to bid on an armed river patrol boat for Vietnam, asked me to design and build a prototype. The money was too good to turn down, so I abandoned my plans to become a gentleman yachtsman and commuted to Buffalo, where I designed a thirty-footer to meet the Navy's specs.

The firm didn't win the contract and subsequently folded, but the experience gave me a chance to renew Navy Department contacts in Washington. I learned that the Navy had a desperate need for fast, armed small craft to use in Vietnam and didn't have any. As a stopgap for river patrols in the Mekong Delta they were using old, slow, steel-hulled utility boats the French colonials had left behind. What "armament" they had consisted mostly of hand-held weapons. For coastal patrol the Navy was relying on eighty-two-foot Coast Guard cutters, a humiliating acknowledgement that they had no inshore craft of their own.

The Buffalo job ended in the spring of 1966, and I was at loose ends again and thinking about a summer of yacht racing. Then a Washington acquaintance called me to tell me about an opening in the Naval Ship Engineering Center Small Boat Design Department. He felt I should apply because I was perfect for it. I had experience in shallow-water design and I understood how Navy contracts worked.

I wasn't enthused about moving to Washington, but I liked the idea that my specialty was in demand and the idea of getting a regular paycheck. But the decider was probably the death of a close sailing friend, a Naval Academy graduate killed when the Viet Cong overran the shore station he commanded. I figured I ought to do something in his memory.

My wife and I moved to Washington in June 1966. The Navy's Small Boat Department consisted of eight people. A well-known yacht designer from the Massachusetts Institute of Technology ran it. There were two naval architects from Webb Institute, a small school in New York; a draftsman; a contract specifications writer; a couple of all-around technical guys; and, now, me.

By then the Navy had already selected the design for the first generation of boats, or Mark I: Patrol Craft Fast, otherwise known as Swift Boats. Sewart Seacraft, the designers, had originally sold the boats as transports to carry crews to and from offshore oil rigs in the Gulf of Mexico. The boats themselves were being bought and delivered as we went to work. The Small Boat Department had not participated in the design selection but had helped reconfigure it for military use, and the redesign would allow it to accommodate a Navy crew, weapons, and ammunition.

My first assignment was to familiarize myself with the Swift—review the hull structure and make sure the propeller diameter and pitch were correct for the engines being used. Everything checked out for a planing boat of that size and speed, but that was no surprise. Sewart had been building the same design for years. They knew what worked.

One thing, however, struck me as odd: The boat seemed small for patrol and interdiction missions along an exposed, open ocean coastline. By comparison, World War II Patrol Torpedo boats, designed to operate at high speed on the open sea, were seventy-eight feet long. And the Coast Guard was using eighty-two footers for coastal work in Vietnam. The Swift Boat was fifty feet long. On the other hand, the Sewart boats had the advantage of being easily adapted for wartime and could be built rapidly in relatively large numbers—forming a quick fix for the fleet's small-craft shortage.

Once the Swifts were on station conducting coastal Market Time patrols, we began to get reports of how they performed—especially when they performed badly. Several times underwater mines exploded beneath the boats, but strengthening the hull bottom to resist the blasts would have added too much weight. We also thought about boosting performance with turbocharged engines, but tests showed that running at low rpm for a long time—typical for a Swift trying to save fuel while on station—caused turbo engines to clog badly. We took note of other reported shortcomings. In most cases we could sympathize, but we couldn't really do anything to fix them.

Swift boat seaworthiness was a different story. The civilian Sewart boats in the Gulf of Mexico could go slow or suspend ferry service altogether during dirty weather and wait for kinder times. Armed Swifts didn't have those luxuries while patrolling the South China Sea or the Gulf of Thailand during the monsoon. Heavy seas smashed windshields and cabin windows. One boat pitch-poled—flipped end over end—and others capsized in the surf trying to return to base. There was so much of this that the Navy told the Small Boat Department to design an improved Mark II Swift Boat.

I got the job. The task was to make the boat a better sailor, but without sacrificing speed. We decided to retain the existing hull form, but we raised the bow freeboard height, so the boats could stay on top of heavy swells instead of burying their noses in walls of water. We moved the pilothouse cabin aft several feet to keep waves from smacking the windshield too strongly. We got rid of the large, passenger-friendly side windows in the main cabin, and replaced them with small round portlights—better able to resist wave slap. We also made some improvements to the crew habitation area. Sewart Seacraft again won the contract.

Aside from design changes, we also had to deal with a completely unanticipated hull problem. Sometime during construction of the Mark I Swifts, Alcoa, the aluminum company, had persuaded the Navy and Sewart to use a new, "stronger" alloy for the hull. It may have been stronger, but after a few months on the job we learned that the hulls were "exfoliating," shedding layers of aluminum like interior plywood that has been left outdoors. This can happen when spent brass from expended .50-caliber machine gun rounds festers in hidden corners of the boat, breeding galvanic corrosion with the aluminum. But the Swifts' problem was much simpler: the new alloy was no good in seawater. The Navy replaced the bad Mark I hulls and made sure the problem didn't carry over to the Mark IIs.

Our job was winding down, but this only became apparent bit by bit. First the government decided to demolish the main Navy Building on Constitution Avenue and sent the Small Boat Department out to Little Creek, Virginia. Fair enough, except the department staff was all different. Next, the holdovers from Swift Boat days—including me—were shunted off to Prince George's County in the Maryland suburbs. Then in late 1968 and early 1969 we learned that the Swifts had abandoned coastal patrol and were doing river patrols and raids in the Mekong Delta, jobs for which they were ill designed and ill suited. River patrol brought new and different complaints: the boats made too much noise; they presented too large a target profile; they had no armor. But we learned that it was too late to do anything about these new difficulties. The Navy was checking out of Vietnam, and our main task now was shepherding the boats through Vietnamization—preparing them to be turned over to the Vietnamese Navy. In other words, we pushed paper. Naval architecture was over.

My wife was working in a Washington think tank doing projects related to the land-based Vietnam War, but I was marking time. I started taking graduate courses at American University, and I came to realize that I had no desire to settle into a civil service career. My work in Washington was done. We moved back to Michigan and I entered the MBA program at the University of Michigan, being careful not to talk too much with my classmates about what I had been doing in D.C.—they didn't want to hear about it on college campuses in 1970.

My MBA led me to a career as systems analyst, and ultimately, an early retirement that sent me back to the world of sailing and boats. I have often thought about how my time with Swifts took me out of my go-it-alone shell and put me in touch with the rest of the world. It gave me tasks that had tangible and immediate life-and-death results. I did my best to make a better boat. I hope I made them better for those who sailed them.

Smell Like a Rose

Rod McAlpin

Lt. (j.g.) Rod McAlpin's stories, S.E.R.E. and Even the Best of Intentions, appear on pages 29 and 85.

IT'S THE FALL OF 1967 AND I'M OFFICER-IN-CHARGE OF PCF 73, DOING coastal Market Time patrols out of An Thoi, Phu Quoc Island, to intercept enemy junks and boats trying to infiltrate supplies and personnel into South Vietnam. One day our division commander tells me he has extended PCF 73 the privilege of hosting two rear admirals to give them a first-hand look at Swift Boat patrol capabilities. I should show them our underway routine, and, while doing so, give them a full demonstration of our firepower.

I no longer remember the names of these two gentlemen, but they were evidently desk admirals, filling advisory billets in the Navy's Saigon hierarchy. And even though they presented themselves as tourists interested in witnessing the Navy's newest wartime watercraft in action, I suspected they might also be on an inspection tour, looking to find fault with the Navy's newest young warriors. I noticed right away that they had not dressed down for their experience, arriving on board in pressed khakis with combination covers (brimmed hats) bearing lots of gold "scrambled eggs."

As I politely introduced the admirals to my crewmembers, I could almost see the officers' eyes gleam. These two 50-year-old wunderkinds probably thought they had seen it all, but they haven't seen this. In a

PCF 73 returns to base.
COURTESY OF JOHN BECKER

Swift Boat, even a ride in moderate chop is akin to riding an out-of-control roller coaster. The engine noise alone makes conversation almost impossible, and the guns make your head feel as if it's going to explode. And if you thought you were somewhat "stiff" to begin with, just wait until it's over. A desk will never look so good!

Our guests first queried me about my unusual crew, which included a Hawaiian (QM1 Ulloa, Senior Petty Officer), a Mexican American (BM3 Castillo), and a Filipino American (EN1 Paje). They were impressed with this diversity. Then they asked me how we interacted with friendly locals. To this topic I suggested we begin our outing with a quick visit to our "adopted" family, who lived on a barrier island along the route we would take to the free-fire zone. Each crew was assigned an adopted South Vietnamese family for the duration of our in-country year, and ours resided on the island of Hon Nhum Ba in the Gulf of Thailand near the Cambodian border. We visited often, bringing clothes and food that our families had sent us from home.

We never got a handle on the family's surname, but first names were easy to remember. Zang was a fisherman. His wife was Madam Marie, and they had two boys, Michel and Be, and two girls, Yum and Wa. We were always treated with great deference and some awe. The arrival of an extremely noisy, fast, and heavily armed Swift Boat was an extraordinary event at Hon Nhum Ba, and usually brought most of the village down to the beach.

On this trip we brought some pillows and some American cookies and canned food. We used a single mooring line to tie up at a tiny, somewhat dilapidated pier, then leapt gingerly to the rickety, bleached-board surface. Our high-level guests were hardly enthralled by the facilities but managed to land upright with their dignity intact. We said hello with much bowing and curtsying in return, and used our broken Vietnamese to introduce the new arrivals. The family got it, of course. They could see the stars and the scrambled eggs.

PCF 694 engages in mortar fire support for troops ashore in the Seafloat operating area in 1970. Engineman John Miller (left) stands by to trigger fire on command. In the elevated mode, the 81mm mortar could accurately hit targets 4,000 meters away. In the horizontal mode, accuracy was good to about 1,000 yards.
COURTESY OF JOHN W. YEOMAN

A Swift Boat with its bow pushed into the jungle to disembark troops. Hanging on the left and right bow hand rails are half-inch-thick sheets of Kevlar to protect the bow gunner.
COURTESY OF JOHN W. YEOMAN

Fortunately for the admirals, our midmorning visit meant we did not have to stay for lunch. In the past, Madame Marie had graciously treated us to interesting meals of curried chicken and pinto beans, cabbage and hot peppers, squash, stewed monkey (or at least that's what we were told), rice, and "whickey" (Vietnamese for whiskey). I was always quite relieved that we never were asked to visit the kitchen prior to mealtime.

Nevertheless, our stopover on this morning also turned out to be timely because Zang and his fishing junk had been stranded for the better part of two days in a nearby canal while he waited to procure a much-needed junk motor and family food supplies. After a quick visit, we reboarded the boat for the twenty-minute trip to the canal, where we rescued Zang and towed his junk and supplies home.

The admirals didn't say much during all this, which I judged to be a good thing. Trying to fit in with the Vietnamese was one of the most important jobs we had, and one of the most difficult, given the cultural canyon that separated us. We were good at it, and the admirals seemed to understand that. But, of course, you never know with admirals, unless they're reaming you out.

After saying goodbye to Zang and the family, we got back aboard the boat and made our way to an empty spot in the ocean where we could put on our show. We fired the twin .50-caliber machine guns from the turret above the pilothouse, our M-16 automatic rifles, and our M-79 grenade launchers. We'd never used the grenade launchers in a firefight, but the concussion from a well-placed round would kill all the fish within reasonable range of the underwater explosion, leaving them to float to the surface to be easily netted by Zang and his sons. We didn't tell the admirals about this.

A Swift Boat returns to base after a patrol. When operating in rivers and canals, Swift Boats carried cargo nets over the bow to help troops embark and disembark. Back aft, flak jackets are hung over the life lines to protect the aft gunners.
COURTESY OF JOHN W. YEOMAN

The centerpiece of our armament was the 81mm mortar that was mounted on the fantail. It was dual-purposed. Most often we used it to lob shells at inland targets called in to us by spotters accompanying friendly ground forces on the beach. But it could also be fired at point-blank range at a target like an enormous shotgun. The admirals, tricked out in flak jackets and helmets, were ready for the main event.

They were obviously impressed with the first couple of rounds, but when we pulled the trigger the third time, nothing happened. We'd had a misfire, leaving a live round in the mortar tube. This happens when the propellant for the mortar shell does not properly ignite, or only partially ignites and fails to send the round on its targeted path. The round should not explode until it hits something on the fly, but a misfire, under any circumstances, is not an occurrence to take casually. For us, the misfire set into motion a series of prescribed moves we had practiced intensively during boat training. For our admirals, however, there was nothing routine about the event. When I ordered everyone to go to the forecastle, I never saw two old salts move so quickly.

Then Gunner's Mate Hart stepped to center stage. As the admirals watched from the bow, he slowly brought the mortar tube to a level position. Then he cautiously bounced the barrel down several times against the stops, slightly below the horizontal—elegantly "walking" the misfire toward the end of the tube until it started to spill out. He froze the tube in place, walked around to the mortar mouth, grabbed the defective round and gingerly carried it to the side of the boat where he dumped it overboard. Sighs of relief were easily audible from the forecastle.

Some days are like that. Even when something goes wrong, everything goes right. My crew had done it all by the book with easy competence, setting up Hart, who performed with Oscar-worthy aplomb. The two admirals could tell Saigon how squared away we were and tell their grandkids an adventure story. In Vietnam that was as good as it got—a modest thrill, no harm done, kudos for the good guys.

Rogue Wave

Stirlin Harris

Boatswain's Mate Second Class Stirlin Harris graduated from the University of North Carolina after a semester of summer school in 1968 and worked as an independent filmmaker based in upstate New York. In 2015 he published his memoir, Who the F#&K Do You Think You Are?, *which is what Elizabeth Taylor said to him when he called her out for being late during the filming of* The Blue Bird, *the first and only Soviet-American coproduction of a feature film.*

My nerves were shot. For three months we'd been at Cua Viet, just south of the Demilitarized Zone. It was the sort of place where you never made a move without mentally tracing your path to the nearest bunker. During the evening movie, shown on the beach where you had to sit in the sand unless you were lucky enough to have a folding chair, it felt like the battle scene on the screen cued the real-life artillery barrage that seemed to begin simultaneously. We scrambled for cover as shells whistled in and exploded around us. I prayed for a cease-fire, or at least a brief truce, so the North Vietnamese might take a few days off. I had no such luck, but I did learn that there was something at Cua Viet just as bad—or even worse—than the NVA's nightly H&I.

I was at the helm in the pilothouse of our Swift Boat, bringing us in after a twenty-four-hour patrol. It was November 1967, and we were out in the ocean, trying to come home. Not so easy. To get to our base, we had to pass through the mouth of the Cua Viet River, swollen

Boatswain's Mate Second Class Stirlin Harris.
COURTESY OF STIRLIN HARRIS

with monsoon floodwaters. When the river smacked into the ocean, the impact created waves that grew progressively larger as the water shallowed at the river mouth. If you were watching from the riverbank, you would have seen our boat completely disappear into this maelstrom, mast and all, leaving you to wonder if we'd gone down. Then suddenly we'd pop up again, bobbing miraculously atop angry seas that climbed up to twenty feet in the air. Get trapped on the downside of one of these monsters and bad things could happen.

One reason I respected our skipper so much was that he expected each of us to know our jobs, and he let us do them without getting in our way. I was the boat's boatswain's mate, and I often took the helm in maneuvering situations. Coming alongside an underway destroyer in a rolling sea, for instance, was a tricky maneuver that could take out your lifeline stanchion—or worse—if you screwed it up. As I discovered on this day, however, coming into the Cua Viet during the monsoon was much worse. It was like riding a rollercoaster, except you couldn't afford to just hold on. If you did nothing, the waves would certainly kill you. And as I was soon to find out, doing something didn't necessarily mean salvation.

At first, I gave it the textbook treatment: Stay on the back of the wave and keep your bow pointing toward the sky. This was one of the cardinal rules learned at amphibious school about how to drive landing craft—one of the things boatswains do. The last thing you wanted was to get in front of a wave and surf up onto the sand with troops inside, only to be left high and dry by the receding wave and exposed to enemy fire.

We weren't headed for a hostile beach in our Swift Boat, but the same principle applied—or so I thought. Our problem was that this was much more complicated than negotiating a shore break to land troops on a sandy beach. Here there was no beach, and most of the time all you could see was water—two immense bodies of water smashing together and rising to towering heights as they looked for space to get where they

PCF 80 on ocean patrol. During the early years, boats patrolling in the ocean were painted U.S. Navy haze gray.
COURTESY OF STIRLIN HARRIS

PCF 99 on ocean patrol.
COURTESY OF STIRLIN HARRIS

were going. And you were in the middle of it with no choice. You got on the back of the wave because if you tried to surf the front, one of two bad and possibly fatal things could happen: you'd roll over if you couldn't hold your stern square to the sea; or, even worse, you'd get pitch-poled, burying your nose in the trough and then getting flipped over, bow-to-stern, by the following wave. This had happened to a Swift the previous year. Three crewmen died and the boat itself pretty much disappeared.

I picked a swell—a gigantic swell—climbed up the back, let it get ahead, and then punched the throttles, maintaining just enough speed to stay behind the crest as we headed into the channel. We were committed now. There was no turning back. We'd be instantly sideswiped, rolled over, and pulverized by the surf. So okay, here we go.

Except there was something else. The river mouth was narrow, and there was a lot of floodwater trying to get out, and a lot of tidewater trying to get in. There wasn't enough room for all of it to move at the same time, so waves of extra water were crashing into the riverbank and headlands and rebounding at odd angles back into the channel, where we bobbed like a cork. Suddenly one of these rogues slammed into our starboard quarter, picking us up as though we had been a surfer madly paddling to get to the crest of the wave.

And there it was. All of a sudden I was staring at the trough below us as we began what seemed like an endless downhill sled run, the wave curling behind and high above us, getting ready to slam down and bury us. Then, even worse, the boat started to yaw to the left, the bow falling off to port. If I couldn't stop it, we were doomed to founder like a semi that swerves to miss hitting something on the highway.

Amphibious school hadn't trained me for anything like this. Instinct took over. I slammed the port throttle full ahead, spun the helm hard to starboard, and then grabbed the starboard throttle and slammed it into full reverse—hoping to corkscrew the boat and break the death grip the wave had on us. The Detroit diesels and gearboxes absorbed the abuse, delivering 450 horsepower apiece to our two screws—one moving us forward, the other in reverse. It seemed like we hung forever in the balance, forty-five degrees to the wave, the boat shuddering as our diesels screamed, the four turbochargers sucking desperately for more and more air. And then, all of a sudden, the wave passed beneath us.

A Swift Boat attempts to depart Cua Viet river for sea during rough weather. The combination of incoming storm swells meeting monsoon floodwaters and a falling tide at the river mouth created treacherous conditions for 50-foot Swift Boats transiting the channel.
COURTESY OF STIRLIN HARRIS

Swift Boats nested at Cua Viet.
COURTESY OF STIRLIN HARRIS

No time to rejoice. I shoved the starboard throttle ahead and climbed onto the back of the wave that had almost done us in. "Watch for the next one on the starboard quarter," I called to the skipper, who stood beside me. "I'll put us in reverse." On-the-job training: what I had done had seemed like a good idea, and it had worked.

"Here it comes!" my skipper warned. I backed the boat down, both throttles this time. The wave crashed over our fantail, making us shudder and blanketing us in a wall of green water. Spray kicked up high and came sleeting against Bill Dodd, our twin fifties gunner otherwise known as "The Dude," who was perched in the gun tub above the pilothouse and getting the ride of his life. "Thank God we have diesels," I thought to myself. A spark plug–fired engine would have sputtered and died beneath such a deluge.

Using my newly learned back-and-fill technique, we soon made it past the river mouth and into calmer water. The Dude poked his head down into the pilothouse: "Boats," he yelled. "I could have leaned out and touched the wave."

A scary thought. The Dude was about fifteen feet above decks during normal times, and we had practically rolled him into the water. "We're going to lose boats," I said to the skipper. We both hoped we were wrong.

We weren't. Two days later we found ourselves once again trying to navigate the surf to get back from our patrol. My system worked. We made incremental runs on the backs of waves, and when the skipper cued me, I'd back down into the quartering sea, then immediately shoot forward again. Many years later I used as a screen saver on my computer a photo that showed our boat in the surf. All you can see is the top of the mast, probably twenty feet above the keel. It reminded me that no matter how bad things get, it's nothing compared to what we had endured.

We had just tied up and taken another deep breath when we heard shouts. A Swift Boat, one of those that was leaving the Cua Viet to relieve us, had overturned in the channel. We got underway immediately,

Swift Boat crew quarters at Cua Viet base.
COURTESY OF STIRLIN HARRIS

heading back out into the surf to see what we could do. Soon we spotted our target. It was eerie and unnerving—a Swift Boat, as helpless as a large bathtub toy, diving and surging as it floated upside down in the surf.

It was PCF 76. We saw four of the crew clinging to a life raft near the boat. We started to inch toward them. The skipper, Dan Daly, and his boatswain's mate, Bill Fielder, clung to the overturned hull. A helicopter hovered overhead and plucked Fielder, then Daly off the boat and hauled them to safety. I eased off the throttles as we came up on the life raft so the other crewmen could swim to us. The skipper took control of the boat from the aft helm and held us steady while my guys reached down and hauled the survivors to safety, timing the grabs as we bounced up and down in the waves.

Fielder later told us about the sinking. The boat was trying to feel its way out of the Cua Viet to get to sea and having a tough job of it. Daly was driving, and Fielder was in the boat's main cabin, holding on for dear life. Daly concluded that it was impossible to negotiate the surf and started to turn back, hoping to flip the boat around to change direction. It didn't work. The boat got whacked by a rogue wave, much as we had, but couldn't hold steady. Before they could make any kind of a move, Fielder said, they broached, rolling over immediately.

Beneath the deck in the main cabin, two storage compartments held about 2,000 rounds of belted .50-caliber machine gun ammunition. When the boat flipped, the lids to the two compartments fell off and the ammo crashed down on top of Bill, pinning him to the roof of the now inverted cabin. Dazed by the blows to the head, Bill needed some moments to gather his wits. But Bill was an E-6 boatswain, a senior man in the most demanding rate the Navy had. He kept his cool. Water was rushing into the open cabin portal, and although there was some air trapped inside the hull, he knew he had to get out fast. He kicked and crawled frantically, freeing his body from the heavy ammo belts, which had pulled him underwater. Careful not to lose perspective and forget which direction was up, he focused on the light still coming through the cabin entrance, and then he stripped off most of his clothes and swam for it. When he reached the surface, he was able to grab the boat's exhaust pipe and haul himself halfway up the stern of the vessel, where Daly was able to give him a hand up.

Much later the skipper told me that we also rescued some Vietnamese fishermen whose fragile sampans had broken apart in the channel's treacherous surf. While some parts of that day remained etched in my mind forever, I don't recall having pulled anyone else out of the water, but the skipper's logbook confirmed it. The next morning the village chief from across the river came over to thank the Swift Boats for rescuing the fishermen. We didn't get them all, he told us. Not everyone was as lucky as we were.

VC Tax Station

Larry Irwin

Lt. (j.g.) Larry Irwin separated from active duty in 1969. He retired to Menlo Park, California, after a forty-plus-year career working in Silicon Valley.

THERE IS A WELL-KNOWN STORY THAT HAS BEEN CIRCULATED ABOUT Lt. (j.g.) Mike Bernique's escapade on the Giang Thanh River that runs eastward from the Gulf of Thailand at Ha Tien, along the Cambodian border. The tale describes how the swashbuckling young naval officer disobeyed orders, went up the river, and attacked and captured a VC Tax Station. Lt. (j.g.) Bernique was sent to Saigon to be disciplined, but was saved when Admiral Zumwalt heard the story and decided that this was the kind of aggressiveness the brass wanted to see. Rather than face discipline, Bernique was awarded the Silver Star.

This story triggered in me a memory about that Tax Station. I was the Officer-in-Charge of PCF 10 and served from October 1966 to September 1967, leaving Vietnam about a year before the Bernique incident. Because I had an interest in photography, I had managed to talk my way into the ancillary duty of "Official Division Photographer." This meant that I had custody of all of the photographs that had accumulated in the division's files. One of these was entitled "VC Tax Station." The outpost was described to me as being just inland of the coastal town of Ha Tien, but was strictly out of bounds because we were forbidden at that time to go into the rivers.

PCF 10 is moored at the Ha Tien pier. The Special Forces camp sits on the hill in the background.
COURTESY OF LARRY IRWIN

At the mouth of the Giang Thanh was a U.S. Special Forces camp on the bluff to the west overlooking Ha Tien. One of the services that we in the PCF division provided was to ferry Special Forces teams to and from their excursions into the Ca Mau Peninsula. This was more than appreciated by these two- or three-man teams, who were typically in the field for three or four days. Without the lift from us they would have had to walk back to base. This simple act was loved even more so by the Special Forces teams because we were able to provide them with fresh salami and cheese sandwiches that were washed down with a cold beer (which we stored aboard illegally). Then they were able to grab some much-deserved shut-eye on the ride home. One team rewarded us with a tour of the Special Forces Camp at Ha Tien, during which they walked us through their jungle live-fire trail where they were training a troop of about 200 Cambodian mercenaries.

On one of the trips back from Ca Mau to Ha Tien I remembered the picture of the VC Tax Station. I started a conversation with one of the Special Forces sergeants about the outpost. He hemmed and hawed a bit, which of course got my interest up, so I kept after him. I finally said, "From the picture, it would seem that you could take a couple of guys down the river with rifles and a Browning Automatic Rifle and shut the Tax Station down." I noted that it was only about an hour's walk from the Special Forces compound. The sergeant finally agreed that the job could be done, so then I asked, "Why not?" More wavering ensued. I was able to discern from what he said and what he didn't say that the mayor of Ha Tien was getting a large slice of the tax collection. That really got my interest going, so I pressed on: "Why do we (U.S. types) care that the mayor is getting a kickback?" No answer.

Walking the trail.
COURTESY OF LARRY IRWIN

I then said that I would take the issue up with my boss and the Special Forces captain who was in charge of the compound. That produced an immediate "better not do that" response from the sergeant. He then very warily implied—but never said directly—that maybe it was not just the mayor who was getting a kickback. I learned later that the Special Forces captain at Ha Tien compound was your classic mercenary soldier, a native of Poland, and not a U.S. citizen. I immediately stopped the conversation at that point, realizing that I was getting into very treacherous territory.

I never mentioned this incident to the staff at the division as I had no real evidence. It was a guess on my part, and I didn't want the sergeant to get in trouble. When I thought back on this after burying it in my memory for forty-five years, I wondered what would have happened if I had reported the incident to the division commander and if it would have resulted in the Tax Station being taken out by the Special Forces. As it turned out, the VC Tax Station was still in place when Bernique decided to disobey orders and go after it.

It has been documented in a number of the Vietnam histories that Admiral Zumwalt, the Commander Naval Forces Vietnam at the time, had gotten at least some of his inspiration for Operation Sea Lords from Bernique's attack. Sea Lords put the thin-skinned and very vulnerable Swift Boats in the rivers and cost many Swifties their lives. If the Tax Station had been destroyed earlier, maybe Zumwalt would have had second thoughts about putting Swift Boats in the rivers and all those lives would not have been lost.

Perhaps some memories are best left untouched.

Chapter Three

1968

Changing the Rules

By 1968, Market Time had become routine, predictable, frequently tedious, and largely unproductive. The North Vietnamese all but halted ocean supply shipments early in the year when it became apparent that their trawlers could not sneak by Navy and Coast Guard patrol craft.[1] The enemy also suffered a major setback when the January-February Tet Offensive failed to win a hoped-for grand battlefield victory. Still, the scope and audacity of Tet fueled growing public skepticism in the United States about the supposed progress of the war and gave new impetus to the antiwar movement.

For Swift Boats, post-Tet was a time of transition. Attention shifted away from Market Time and coastal waters and began instead to focus on the rivers of the Mekong Delta. Part of this change may have derived from a High Command desire to show "real" progress in the wake of Tet, but at least two more factors were in play.

The first was the September arrival of Rear Admiral Elmo Zumwalt as Commander Naval Forces Vietnam. Zumwalt's willingness to listen to fresh ideas, no matter where they came from, immediately won the hearts of Swift Boat sailors. His ex post facto endorsements of individual Swift Boat river raids—in violation of standing orders prohibiting extended river incursions—made Swifts' escape from Market Time all but inevitable.

The second factor was boredom. Swifts Boats with two crews, using Coast Guard cutters, Navy LSTs, and Navy destroyer escorts as mother ships, rotated on 24-hour shifts with mind-numbing regularity. Market Time units in 1968 boarded or inspected 600,000 vessels of all kinds. The return on this investment was low. The number of hostiles encountered on the open sea was negligible.[2]

At the same time, the war itself acquired new intensity, and Swift Boats found themselves embroiled in deadly, confusing encounters of uncertain provenance and tragic outcome. On April 1, a Cambodian ship offloading cargo to sampans in the Gulf of Thailand shot down a P-3 Orion surveillance aircraft that may have strayed into Cambodian airspace. The plane crashed five miles south of the PCF base at An Thoi. Swifts scrambled in hopes of rescuing survivors, but all twelve crewmen were killed.

Then, in the early hours of June 16 on the other side of Vietnam, three rockets fired by aircraft near the DMZ destroyed PCF 19 and killed five of its seven crewmen. The U.S. Coast Guard cutter *Point Dume*, rushing to provide assistance, saw at least one rocket hit the boat. *Point Dume* picked up two badly wounded PCF 19 survivors, but got trapped in the kill zone along with a second Swift Boat, PCF 12, and for the next hour the two rescuers dodged periodic rocket and automatic weapons attacks from what they described as both helicopters and fixed-wing aircraft. Neither suffered damage.

Not as lucky was the Australian guided missile destroyer HMAS *Hobart*, on station in the same area along with the U.S. guided missile cruiser USS *Boston*. Both ships were attacked from the air around 0300, and three rockets hit *Hobart*, killing two sailors and wounding seven others.

Subsequent investigation showed that shore observers some time before PCF 19's sinking had reported sighting enemy aircraft near the DMZ. U.S. warplanes counterattacked and shot down what they described as several enemy "helicopters." Investigators subsequently concluded that these targets, identified by radar, included PCFs 19 and 12. *Hobart*, quite likely, was also hit by friendly fire. (The official investigation does not deal directly with *Hobart*.) But a separate personal account written much later by Jim Steffes, the engineman aboard PCF 12, described repeated communications with Da Nang in which his OinC was unhesitatingly assured that there were no "friendlies" in the area, even as PCF 12 was dodging intermittent attacks from the air.[3]

The Swifts' transition to the rivers was incremental. The groundwork was laid in March 1968 when eight Vietnamese crews began training at An Thoi as a prelude to getting their own boats. They matriculated in July and went aboard the first four Swifts turned over by the Navy in a program that evolved into "Vietnamization." Zumwalt accelerated this process and by the end of the year there were twelve Vietnamese boats, most of them doing Market Time patrols. As they took over the coastline U.S. Swifts began hunting in the rivers.

In July, probably in part because of the South Vietnamese coastal debut, the squadron gave U.S. Swifts permission to probe up to 1,500 yards into hostile rivers and coastal harbors. This ostensibly modest adjustment had immediate consequences, particularly in the Gulf of Thailand and the Ca Mau Peninsula, a huge expanse of tidal flats, rice paddies, and swamp that had sheltered thousands of Vietnamese insurgents for decades.

In the early morning of July 22, 1968, two Swift Boats poked their noses into the mouth of the Bo De River, the eastern mouth of a tidal estuary that cut across the Ca Mau Peninsula near the very tip of South Vietnam. PCF 28 had spotted enemy movement on the riverbank near where the Bo De emptied into the South China Sea. Joined by PCF 95, the two boats traveled nearly a mile into the river, each one shooting ten rounds of 81mm mortar and then firing .50-caliber machine guns at both riverbanks before they turned and headed back out to sea.[4]

It was a classic "harassment and interdiction" mission designed to demonstrate Swifts' new directive to raid long-time enemy sanctuaries. The enemy, however, was ready, and opened up on the return trip with heavy automatic weapons and recoilless rifles. PCF 28's OinC was wounded, and both boats received minor damage. The operation lasted only a half hour—from 0245 to about 0315—but the Swifts had learned an important lesson: Getting into enemy territory was not a problem. Getting out was a different story. And if 1,500 yards was as far as you could go, the enemy could trap you on his turf by waiting you out on the trip in and dry gulching you on the way out. This tactic came to be known in Swift parlance as a "static ambush."

On the other hand, what happened when you did not bother to turn around, but instead just kept going? On October 4, Lt. (j.g.) Mike Brown took PCF 38 into the Cua Lon River from the Gulf of Thailand, feeling his way through the muddy tidal flat known as "Square Bay" and into the western side of the same estuary that PCF 28 had infiltrated three months earlier.

Intending at first to take only a modest look-see, PCF 38 instead encountered a never-ending sequence of targets—junks, sampans, moorings, houses, guard posts flying Viet Cong flags, and an entire village abandoned by the inhabitants. PCF 38 laid waste to everything it saw, running the entire river and scooting out the mouth of the Bo De into the South China Sea in the late afternoon. Brown faced disciplinary action for disobeying orders, but after reading the after-action report Zumwalt recommended everyone for medals.

That was lesson two: If you tried something that had never been done before, you stood a good chance of getting away with it. Once.

On October 14, ten days after what the Swifts came to refer to as "Brown's Run," PCF 3 stopped to take a break from a tedious Market Time patrol at Ha Tien, a pleasant Gulf of Thailand town on the Cambodian border at the mouth of the Giang Thanh River. During the stopover, Lt. (j.g.) Michael Bernique, the OinC, learned that a Viet Cong tax collector was doing business a few miles upriver. Bernique decided to take a look, in the process violating another standing order that Brown had ignored—stay at least 1,000 yards from the shore.

Rounding a river bend, PCF 3 spotted seven armed VC on the riverbank and opened fire, killing four and sending the rest running for cover. The crew nosed into the riverbank to investigate the ambush site, prompting concealed insurgents to start shooting. The PCF crewmen killed two more gunmen and wounded two others.

Bernique was initially summoned to Saigon to explain why he had disregarded orders, but Zumwalt instead awarded Bernique a Silver Star—as he had done for Brown. The Giang Thanh River was now "Bernique's Creek."

Even the Best of Intentions . . .

Rod McAlpin

Lt. (j.g.) Rod McAlpin's stories, S.E.R.E. and Smell Like a Rose, appear on pages 29 and 61.

We were conducting a routine board-and-search patrol off the Ca Mau Peninsula at dusk when a U.S. Army support detachment called us from their base west of the town of Song Ong Doc, near the river of the same name. They were under mortar and recoilless rifle attack by local VC units and needed help. Could we close on the shoreline and use our 81mm mortar to drive them off, or at least keep them at bay?

You never argue with a request like that, and besides, anything out of the ordinary was a welcome change. We were off the southwest corner of Vietnam in PCF 73, so far from our base on Phu Quoc Island that we were operating from the U.S. Coast Guard cutter *Yainstat*, on station in the Gulf of Thailand about ten miles offshore. We had taken two crews to the cutter so we could swap out every twenty-four hours. That way there was always a boat on patrol, and no need to drive back and forth from An Thoi, a three-hour trip on the best of days and a bone-rattling ordeal in heavy seas during the northeast monsoon. It was wearying, tedious, and, when nature was feeling particularly vindictive, occasionally terrifying work. I was the Officer-in-Charge on this trip. It was December 8, 1967.

We closed to within a few hundred yards of the shoreline just north of the Ong Doc River and then anchored and began shelling the enemy positions near the U.S. base, about five klicks east of us, with high-explosive, incendiary and starshell mortar rounds, working from grid coordinates radioed to us by the ground forces' advance spotter. After maybe an hour, our friends told us they had a badly wounded Vietnamese boy who needed serious medical attention as soon as possible. He was nine or ten, they indicated, and had suffered horrific shrapnel wounds from the enemy shelling.

We volunteered to make a run up a canal we called Breezy Cove, just north of Song Ong Doc. We could get close to the support base, pick up the youngster, and take him back to the cutter, where a fully outfitted medical team could treat him. This seemed pretty straightforward to us at first, but it wasn't. It was now fully dark, and the monsoon was blowing the seas into a vicious chop. And we had lots of things to do at the same time: up anchor, check the twin fifties up forward, and set blackout conditions for a canal run. In the canal we wouldn't have to worry about staying upright and dry. In the canal we had to worry about fast reactions and weapons that didn't jam.

I was in the pilothouse using the twin engines to hold the bow steady on the mooring line so we could retrieve the anchor from about twenty feet of water. As the anchor broke ground, we suddenly realized that the unpredictable and unrelenting winds had caused the boat to steadily drift down on the anchor line as it was being pulled in and the line was now fouled in the screws. We quickly shut down our engines so we could take a look underwater.

We now had an entirely different set of problems. The anchor was aweigh and we had no means of making headway to hold our position. We were an ungainly, drifting hulk at the mercy of the wind, the seas, and the firepower of anyone eager to punch our clock. We were moving inexorably toward the beach and we didn't have a lot of time. We needed to unfoul the screws, get underway, and fetch the wounded kid.

Our boatswain's mate quickly stripped to his skivvies and made several dives to assess the extent of the problem and unfoul the anchor. The rest of us hung over the fantail, shining every light we had so he could see what he was doing in the dark water. Another target for Charlie.

Freeing the anchor probably didn't take all that long, but I couldn't tell you. Given the circumstances and our desperation, it seemed like forever. But then we were free. We killed all our lights and returned to general quarters. Then we began feeling our way into the canal.

It was pitch black. Navigating by radar, we inched our way through a watery gulch only thirty feet wide at best. We were lucky it was high tide. Instinct told me we would have run aground if we strayed from the midpoint of the canal. And we were sitting ducks. The banks of the waterway were dense with all sorts of tropical vegetation, making a perfect hiding place.

We were probably lucky again that Charlie didn't figure on a Swift Boat coming upriver, so he hadn't rigged an ambush. And it wasn't any easier for him to see us than it was for us to see him. On the other hand, the rumble of the diesels was something we couldn't conceal. Sporadic gunfire punctuated the entire trip. A number of rounds hit the boat, and our radarman was cut by flying glass.

Finally, we reached a bend in the canal where we were supposed to make our pickup. Our mortar rounds had obviously had an effect, and the shooting had become quite random as we approached a rickety "mooring" composed of poles stabbed into the mud bottom and tied together with old, warped planks haphazardly thrown together to accommodate small fishing boats. We tied up delicately, staying only long enough for the detachment team to place our precious cargo on board. The boy was even worse off than we had been led to believe. Bandages and tourniquets covered what seemed to be an unending number of wounds. Medics had an IV in his arm. I hoped it was morphine.

We retraced our route. Nothing had changed. The water was shallow, navigation was tight, and the travel extremely slow and tenuous. When we got to the canal mouth we pushed the throttles all the way forward and ran full bore to the cutter, which was waiting about four klicks away in the open ocean. The seas grew worse with each klick. The bone-jarring jolts we received from flying into, up, and then over the top of the swells compressed our spines and brutally pounded every joint every time the airborne hull banged back to the surface of the sea.

Our job was tough, maybe impossible. We wanted to get the boy to the cutter as soon as we could, but we didn't want to kill him in the process. We needed to go fast, but nature wouldn't allow it. I wondered as I maneuvered through the whitecaps whether the boy felt any pain. And then we were there. We passed his broken body to waiting hands and said a prayer. The outpost at Song Ong Doc survived, and the District Senior Army Advisor there wrote us a Letter of Commendation. We felt pleased.

On the *Yainstat*, doctor and staff worked through the night. The little boy didn't make it. I suppose we did our best, but it wasn't good enough. We felt rotten.

Shooting High

Stirlin Harris

Boatwain's Mate Second Class Stirlin Harris's story, "Rogue Wave," appears on page 67. Harris graduated from UNC in 1968 and worked as an independent filmmaker in upstate New York.

I SPOTTED THE BLIP ON THE RADAR SCREEN ABOUT 0200. IT WAS A DARK night. No moon. We were patrolling southward in the South China Sea about 3,000 yards off the coast of South Vietnam, just below the Demilitarized Zone. We were in moderate swells, getting swiped broadside and rolling unpleasantly. No big deal. Swift Boats were never an easy ride, and PCF 80 was no exception. We were on routine Market Time patrol, October 1967. We were looking for smugglers coming south with weapons and supplies for the Viet Cong and North Vietnamese. I looked at the blip again. Maybe we had found some.

I had traveled a long, twisted road to become a second-class boatswain's mate in the U.S. Navy. A little less than three years earlier I was a conscientious objector, living with my Canadian girlfriend and her family near Toronto. They were urging me to think about life's basic values in a different way—to believe that wars could be stopped if people simply refused to participate in them. Just as this idea was becoming attractive to me, my parents, ninety miles away in Rochester, New York, forwarded my draft notice. My girlfriend's mother proposed a simple solution—since I was already registered as a landed immigrant in Canada, why not renounce my U.S. citizenship? I decided to do it. I told the officers at the U.S. consular office in Toronto of my intentions. They asked me to think it over for three days and come back if I still felt the same. I did. So three days later I became a stateless person.

With hindsight, of course, this decision seems precipitous at best, but being twenty-one years old, full of myself, and unhappy with the way events were trending in Vietnam, I didn't really appreciate the consequences—or the complications. But I got up to speed pretty fast. First, my girlfriend and I broke up, leaving me marooned in Canada only a few months after becoming an immigrant. I was okay with that, and my pacifism was intact, but I had nothing going for me in Toronto. So I decided to return to the states to finish my senior year at the University of North Carolina, where I was just a handful of credits short of graduation.

Not so fast. When I went to the U.S. Consulate in Toronto to apply for a visa, I was denied. No surprise there, I figured, considering what I had just done. But no sweat. I crossed the Peace Bridge in Buffalo with my New York driver's license.

"What were you doing in Canada?" the immigration officer asked me.

"Visiting friends."

The blip reappeared at two o'clock on the radar screen with every sweep, sparkling orange as I peeked through the rubber shield that kept the gleam from the scope from lighting up the pilothouse and giving away our position. The blip was moving slowly in the same direction we were moving. A boat. I could see a jagged line of surf through our starboard door, tumbling with an eerie, phosphorescent glow. It separated us from the sampan and probably made it hard for its crew to hear us. Swift Boats are noisy, with a loud, distinctive rumble, even when they travel slowly.

"Hey Dude," I called quietly over my shoulder. "Come and see this." Our radio/radarman Bill Dodd, also known as "The Dude," climbed up into the pilothouse, putting his hand on my shoulder to steady himself.

"What you got?" he asked, putting his eyes to the rubber hood. He peered intently at the softly humming radar.

"You're the radarman, you tell me," I answered. We both knew what it was.

"What's going on, guys?" Walt, our engineman, called down from the gun tub above us where he sat behind the twin .50-caliber machine guns. Dude poked his head up into the alcove and told him what we were tracking—most likely a sampan trying to sneak down the coast. Walt, with the best view high atop the pilothouse, peered ahead to his right. Nothing but surf. "Get me the night vision scope," he said.

The Dude handed it up. The scope was mounted on an M-16 and magnified available light about 1,000 times, bringing recognizable shapes into a semblance of focus. Everything you saw was painted in a fluorescent green wash. Walt gave it twenty seconds: "Yep, it's a sampan alright, and those guys are paddling like they've got somewhere to go."

We were wallowing along about as slowly as we could to stalk the sampan without overtaking it. "Dude, take the helm," I said. "I'm going to wake the skipper."

When I showed up in Rochester, my parents were happy to see me. But they weren't thrilled to learn that I was no longer a U.S. citizen and had snuck across the border. Fortunately, my father was an adult, a practical man, and—most important for my purposes at that point—a distinguished attorney in a firm founded by my great-grandfather more than a century earlier. He told me the rest of my life would be chaos if I remained an illegal alien and suggested I get my citizenship back.

"OK, how do I do that?"

My father didn't know immediately, but he knew how to find out. He called our congressman, whom he knew well, and enlisted his assistance. Then Dad and I visited the U.S. immigration office in Buffalo. The man in charge was a retired Army colonel who, for some reason, took a liking to me. He and my father started researching the possibilities. "You really did it, didn't you?" the colonel said. I meekly shook my head in agreement. My job was to shut up and listen, but I knew what was coming.

And I was right. The plan, worked out between my dad, the colonel, and my congressman, was for me to go back to Canada and reapply for a visa to the United States, declaring my wish to become an American citizen. Once back in the United States I would volunteer for military service, beginning a three-year track to citizenship. Graduation at UNC would have to wait.

And, of course, I was done with being a conscientious objector. I was okay with that. I had come to believe that a true CO had to live on a wholly different plane. It was like taking holy vows. You couldn't pick

Boatswain's Mate Stirlin Harris mans the aft gun mount, ready to shoot the 81mm mortar in trigger fire, horizontal mode. The swivel tripod allowed the 81mm mortar to be used in both elevated mode and horizontal mode. In the horizontal mode, the 81mm mortar functioned as a cannon shooting high explosive, white phosphorous or flechette rounds.
COURTESY OF STIRLIN HARRIS

and choose which aspects of pacifism suited you and which didn't, and I wasn't prepared to live like a monk. So I agreed to the plan. I wasn't thinking about killing people, but I had concluded that if I was going to enjoy the freedoms earned by the veterans who preceded me, shouldn't I, too, be willing to serve?

I climbed down into the boat's main cabin where our Officer-in-Charge, Lt. (j.g.) Tom Jones, was asleep. I was the boat's leading petty officer. I had relieved the skipper at midnight, along with Dude and Walt. The skipper led the other watch with "Hooch" and Kellner, our two gunner's mates.

"Skipper." I touched him on the shoulder.

He awoke with a start: "Yeah, Boats, what is it?"

I told him about the radar contact.

"Call General Quarters," he said.

"Aye, aye sir."

We did it quietly. I called up to Dude, "GQ," and then woke the gunners. Kellner relieved Dude at the helm. The skipper stood beside him next to the radar screen. Hooch took over the twin fifties, and Walt joined me on the fantail. Dude was in the main cabin with the radios.

Walt and I took the canvas cover off the rear gun mount, the boat's biggest weapon. It was a trigger-fired 81mm mortar with a .50-caliber machine gun piggybacked on top. The Navy had modified a standard 81mm, making it possible to retract the firing pin. You could drop-fire, sending rounds on a high arc like a conventional mortar. Or you could trigger-fire it on a horizontal plane, transforming it into a muzzle-loading 81mm cannon. Shooting it was my job.

We were at battle stations. The skipper had fixed our position on a chart of our operations area. But there was a complication—a friendly "ville" just inland from the beach. Because of it we wouldn't be using the fifties, which had a killing range of well over a mile. We'd try to take the sampan with small arms.

"Stand by to illuminate, Boats," the skipper ordered.

"Roger that, sir," I answered. I spoke through a sound-powered phone plugged into the gun mount. "Walt, load me a flare." The mortar box held about 100 rounds, including high-explosive, incendiaries, and flares. Each round looked like a miniature rocket, almost three feet long, with fins and bags of powder tied to the tail—the propellant.

"Cocked?" Walt asked. He cradled the flare in his arms.

I reached down to retract the firing pin. "Cocked," I replied. Walt inserted the round, tail first, down the throat of the mortar. It hit the breech with a solid thud.

"Ready to shoot," I said into my mike.

"Seventy degrees elevation and shoot about two o'clock," our skipper replied. I pointed the mortar and fixed the elevation. The flare would explode high in the air, lighting up the sampan right below it.

"Seventy degrees and two o'clock." I keyed the phone.

"Fire!"

The mortar recoiled violently against its hydraulics, shaking the entire boat. About three seconds later we heard a distant "pop" and the sky lit up bright as day. The flare, suspended from a tiny parachute, floated lazily earthward. Below it we could easily see crew of the sampan paddling furiously.

"Dung lai!"—"Stop!" our skipper called over the loudspeaker. "Lai dei!"—"Come here!" The men in the sampan kept paddling.

"Boats?"

"Yes sir?"

"I want you to keep them lit up, fire flares as needed."

"Flares as needed, aye, aye sir."

"Now load HE and sink the bastard."

I enlisted in the Navy and was sent to boot camp at Great Lakes. With four years of college under my belt I aced all the exams and decided I wanted to be a photographer's mate. The last box to check on the form was "U.S. Citizen." I checked "No," and found out my choices had shrunk: Sea Bees (construction battalion) or boatswain's mate. Probably, I surmised, because neither one required security clearances.

I chose boatswain's mate and went to assault boat school to learn how to drive amphibious landing craft. The division lieutenant looked at my background and offered me a desk job. I turned it down, reasoning that I'd rather be on the boats. The division boatswain's mate looked at my background, handed me a swab, and sent me to clean the head. I did what he said and earned his respect. With his guidance I made second class boatswain seventeen months after my enlistment. Then I volunteered for Swift Boats. I had already decided that I wasn't interested in posing as a conscientious objector. Now I decided I wasn't interested in posing as a sailor, either. If you joined the service and learned the skills, you should be prepared to fight the war. And I wanted to know what it was like.

I told Walt to load a high-explosive round. Up forward Hooch and The Dude opened fire with M-16s. Red tracer converged on the sampan, which now turned toward shore. Nobody returned fire. I began to wonder: were these really VC or NVA, or just local fishermen who hadn't lit a lantern as required by local regulations? Often we came up on dark sampans, weapons at the ready, only to find sleepy men fumbling around to find their light and turn it on.

The HE round slid down the tube. I lowered the mortar and pointed it at the sampan. Dude and Hooch hadn't hit anyone with the M-16s, and the sampan had almost reached the shore. Everyone aboard was getting ready to jump out. It was all up to me, and I had to shoot now.

I took aim at the sampan. I didn't like this. It reminded me of the patrol a couple of months earlier when we spotted a herd of cattle grazing on the beach in the DMZ. We were supposed to kill them—food for the enemy. The skipper came back aft to talk it over. I looked through his binoculars.

"Gee sir, I can't tell if they're South Vietnamese or North Vietnamese cattle." I didn't have the stomach for it. It's easy to shoot when someone is shooting at you, but when it's all one-sided you have too much time to think. "I'm sorry skipper, but I just can't shoot 'em. I'll be happy to drive the boat and you can shoot." He didn't like the idea either. Nobody did. And in the end we left them alone.

Now here it was again. But these were people, not animals. They could do us harm. Or they could be harmless. I aimed just a little high and squeezed the trigger. The cannon roared, the boat shuddered and the mortar round went straight across the surf line toward the sampan. It hit just where I aimed, maybe ten feet beyond the beached boat, setting off an explosion and sending up a shower of sand and shrapnel. Was this my reappearance as a conscientious objector? Not at all. I would have done anything to protect my shipmates, but this wasn't that moment. And I didn't want to kill innocent fishermen.

We broke off our action. I said nothing. It was a respectable miss, easy to understand when I was shooting from a rocking platform. At first light, a U.S. Marine patrol found the sampan where we had reported it, and it was full of RPGs (rocket-propelled grenades) and other kinds of ammunition. No bodies.

Bad guys, after all. And I think they escaped.

The Little Girl from Tamassou Island

Bernard W. Wolff

Lt. Bernard W. Wolff's story, Trawler, appears on page 51.

PCF 52 LEFT THE SWIFT BOAT BASE AT AN THOI IN MIDAFTERNOON and headed for the west coast of Vietnam to begin a twenty-four-hour patrol. I was Officer-in-Charge. The whole area was cloaked in thick smoke, reducing visibility to about a mile. It was 1968, early spring, the time of year when farmers burn the straw on their harvested rice fields to provide nutrients for the coming crop and kill the insects that prey on it.

We didn't see many junks, or much of anything else because of the smoke, so after a long, slow run along the shoreline with no sign of enemy activity, we headed north to Tamassou Island for dinner. We had a barbecue grill we had brought from Cam Ranh Bay, and Quartermaster Bart Barthelmeh and Gunner's Mate Jerry Thompson were good at concocting marinades that made mundane food taste interesting.

After dinner, we headed south along the shoreline for the night. Fishing junks had stayed ashore first because of rough seas and smoke, and then because of wind. The next morning was equally uneventful. The sea remained empty and the shoreline was quiet. We tried churning mud with our props as we hugged the mangroves along the shore, trying to attract enemy fire. None occurred. It was shaping up to be yet another boring patrol.

As the time approached for us to be relieved, we returned to Tamassou Island and dropped anchor off the northern side. A small sam-

The first aid station on Tekere Island, An Thoi.
COURTESY OF BERNARD W. WOLFF

pan came out to ferry ashore our landing party, which included me. As was customary, I took along our first-aid kit and some food and gifts for the local folks. Doctors were a rare luxury in the villages, and adults and kids with cuts and sores came forward and gave thanks when we applied stinging ointment. They stood in line whispering "Bák Sĩ" (doctor) in quiet reverence, waiting for their turn.

Some kids brought a shy young girl to me, gesturing toward her crooked right forearm. She had fallen from a tree weeks before and broken it. The bones had pierced the skin, and now she had an angry red scar at the middle of her infected inner forearm. We decided the little girl needed to go to the clinic at An Thoi, and we took her and her mother to PCF 52. We were shocked when the mother returned to shore, leaving her daughter behind, alone and scared. But Bart gave her a peanut butter-and-jelly sandwich, and she perked up. I asked her how old she was. "Mòùi lam, fifteen," she said. She looked no more than twelve.

During the long transit to An Thoi, we let her have a turn at the helm, took pictures of her in the gun tub, and tried to make her feel at

The little girl from Tamassou Island.
COURTESY OF BERNARD W. WOLFF

home. Her bright smile never faded, and she got visibly more excited as we approached the end of our journey.

About 1700 we overheard a series of radio transmissions from a Swift Boat up north, telling us that a Cambodian gunboat was just over the border from Vietnam. Even though Cambodia was neutral, the gunboat would train its three-inch guns on Swifts, and we would train our .50-caliber machine guns and mortar on it, each of us running along next to the border until the gunboat anchored.

This time, however, events took a different turn. The surveillance aircraft that worked with us, a Lockheed P3 Orion with the call sign "Hurdy Gurdy 9," was in the vicinity and wanted to take a look at the gunboat. "Barbados," the Coastal Surveillance Center in An Thoi, granted permission. We listened offhandedly to the chatter, hearing the familiar voice of Hurdy Gurdy 9's radio operator, who sounded just like Smokey Bear.

Suddenly, the tone changed: "We're pulling up! We're pulling up!" the familiar voice said. "Damage assessment unknown!" We learned later that

Hurdy Gurdy 9 had accidently entered Cambodian waters and overflown the gunboat, which had opened fire.

"We're gonna have to ditch," a new voice said in a nervously resigned tone.

"I don't know if we're gonna make it," another Hurdy Gurdy crewman said. I resisted the urge to come up on the radio and encourage them to ditch in the shallow waters of the area.

"We're going to try to make it to An Thoi," Hurdy Gurdy said. An Thoi had a small airfield, maybe enough to land a P3, but it would be tricky. We called Barbados to tell them we would take station at the end of the runway in case the P3 crew had to ditch early. Our passenger was fascinated by the radio, and pointed excitedly at An Thoi as we reached the harbor entrance. Thank God she couldn't understand what Hurdy Gurdy was saying.

"I'm getting out of here," radioed one crewman. "I'm hitting the silk." Bart came into the pilothouse from the main cabin. The FM radio said two crewmen had parachuted. Hurdy Gurdy approached. Rather than

The northside of Tekere Island, An Thoi.
COURTESY OF BERNARD W. WOLFF

The village on the south side of Tamassou Island.
COURTESY OF BERNARD W. WOLFF

coming directly into the airport, it went into a classic landing pattern, one of its engines blazing furiously.

The little girl was beginning to wonder why we were not going ashore. We told her something important was happening and to be patient. And then we heard once more from the radio: "We're ditching! We're ditching!" with that terrible note a person gets in his voice when he is a few seconds from dying, and knows it.

"Hurdy Gurdy 9, this is Barbados, over," the surveillance center radioed in a tearfully shocked and panicked voice.

"Hurdy Gurdy 9, this is Barbados, over."

"Hurdy Gurdy 9, this is Barbados, over."

We headed south at full speed, weaving our way past a series of beautiful and peaceful emerald islands as we charged toward the probable point of impact. Then we rounded a corner and saw the ball of smoke, cut off at the bottom, rising skyward. A villager said later a wing had separated during landing and Hurdy Gurdy 9 crashed practically nose first.

"Hurdy Gurdy 9, this is Barbados, over."

Two landing gear assemblies were bobbing amid a wide field of surface debris.

"Hurdy Gurdy 9, this is Barbados, over."

Feeling numb, I radioed Barbados: "Negative survivors on scene."

"Check again!"

"I'm sorry," I said. "They're all gone."

We cruised through the debris field. The little girl didn't understand why we weren't at An Thoi. I sure as hell wasn't going to tell her. I told the crew to keep her below in the main cabin. We had done this once before.

We stopped at a spot where debris floated to the surface. I was steering from the aft helm. Robinson, the boatswain, stood beside me with a boathook. When the human remains began to rise from the depths, Robinson retrieved them and placed them on the port engine hatch. The longer we stayed, the worse it got.

The rear hatch to the cabin opened, and the smiling face of the little girl appeared.

"Keep her below!!!" My voice was hoarse.

I looked north toward Cambodia in a cold rage, wanting to track down and attack the gunboat. I had never felt such anger before. I would never feel such anger again. I wanted revenge, and I didn't care if I died in the process. The little girl's happy face appeared at the rear window of the pilothouse. The crew politely restrained her.

Eventually more Swifts arrived, and Barbados allowed us to return to the base, drop off our grisly cargo, and pick up body bags. The little girl gleefully watched as we approached the pier, thankfully oblivious to what was on the fantail. I took her to the clinic, introduced her to one of the doctors, told him her story, and said good-bye. She held my hand briefly.

Then I went looking for body bags. I asked some volleyball players. The game stopped. One of the players led me to a small building. I took the bags and returned to PCF 52. We filled a bag, handed it over and went back to the crash scene. Later I learned that the two Hurdy Gurdy crewmen who had bailed out had hit the tail of the plane and died.

Our normal routine resumed, but with one exception. Whenever our Swift Boat arrived at the An Thoi pier, I could see the little girl looking for me from the clinic window. She would rush out, hold my hand and walk with me, telling me about her progress as I went to the briefing office. Afterward she would meet me again and we would go together to the clinic and check her progress. She accompanied me when I went back to the boat and waved good-bye to all of us. Everybody in the crew brought her treats. She loved chocolate.

The bone infection was serious but was responding to treatment, and the doctor had reset the arm so it would be normal after healing. She would need to stay several weeks before she could return to Tamassou Island.

The little girl was still convalescing when we were transferred to Da Nang. We stopped by to say good-bye. When she understood that we were leaving, her eyes filled with sadness. It was the first time we didn't see her smile while she was with us. Except for my photo, I never saw her again. I pray that she's had a happy life.

Brown's Run

Michael Brown

Lt. Cdr. Michael Brown left active duty in 1978 for a career as an engineering contractor and consultant. He retired to Bradenton, Florida.

In 1977, several years after the Vietnam War had ended, two admirals were reviewing my service record to figure out what I should do next. I was a 1965 Naval Academy graduate and a brand-new lieutenant commander. If I kept my nose clean, the admirals told me, I would make captain, but I would never make admiral. Too much of an independent thinker, they said—too inclined to do things my way instead of the Navy Way.

When you have this sort of early mid-career conversation with Navy brass, the message conveyed is that it might be best if you became a civilian. I could put in my time and retire as a four-striper. Nothing wrong with that, I suppose. But that was the trouble. I had never "put in my time," and the admirals knew it. They had me dead to rights.

It didn't begin that way. I had spent my first two and a half years in uniform as a junior gunnery officer aboard two light cruisers. When I got orders in February 1968 to report to Coronado, California, for Swift Boat training, I got in touch with my "detailer," the guy in Washington who was supposed to look out for my specific interests.

"I thought Swift Boat duty was a 'voluntary' assignment," I said.

Engineman First Class Michael Haney (left) and Boatswain's Mate Second Class Daniel Stark (right) at the aft mount on PCF 93. The aft mount was a .50-caliber machine gun mounted atop an 81mm mortar. They were attached to a tripod on a swivel. The 81mm mortar could be used in a drop fire mode for long-range fire support or fired horizontally in trigger fire mode as a cannon during close-quarter canal operations and ambushes.
COURTESY OF MICHAEL BROWN

"True enough," the detailer replied, but reminded me that I had written a letter in 1966 volunteering for Swifts. That was almost two years earlier, I argued. Why should I go now? I lost that argument.

And so I went to Coronado, became Officer-in-Charge of a Swift Boat, and flew to Vietnam, arriving at the U.S. Naval Base at Cam Ranh Bay on April 10, 1968. I was assigned to do ocean patrols out of Coastal Division 14, one of the safest jobs in Vietnam. Except the Navy did not want me at Cam Ranh Bay. Instead, the Division 14 commanding officer told me things were heating up in the Gulf of Thailand and Coastal Division 11 needed boats and crews, so I would be going to An Thoi to search coastal traffic for contraband. The Viet Cong controlled most of the west coast of Vietnam below the Cambodian border, which meant Coastal Division 11 was *not* one of the safest jobs.

Still, my crew and I started our tour tamely enough. We went on training patrols and drilled on search procedures and emergency measures, like rigging the boat for towing and being towed. Patrols were normally twenty-four hours long, followed by forty-eight hours off. After a couple of months we had nothing to show for our time and dedication to duty. We had done everything by the book, looking for suspicious activities and inspecting hundreds of sampans and junks, but had found nothing.

Then one day we were off the coast near the town of Rach Gia, south of the Cambodian border, when a small boat approached us carrying three or four U.S. Army soldiers from a small outpost in the nearby Cai Lon River. Local VC had raised their flag on a pole directly across the river from the outpost, and the Army guys hadn't been able to knock it down or even approach it. Would we follow them in and blow the flag away with our 81mm mortar?

At this time Swifts were not supposed to be in the rivers. But we knew some boats had violated the directive. And who would know? So we drove down the Cai Lon about six klicks until we spotted the flag. We set up a firing exercise. We had four kinds of ammo: high-explosive (HE), incendiary (white phosphorus, or "Willy Peter"), flares, and flechettes, composed of hundreds of tiny darts that came out of the mortar like buckshot from a cannon-sized shotgun. We fired twenty rounds of all types of ammo at that flagpole. Did not knock it down. We radioed the outpost that we were giving up, and then we left. The outpost thanked us for our effort.

I did not give the incident another thought until several days later when the division commander called me into his office and chewed me out for being in the river. I have never been able to get away with doing things I shouldn't do, so this did not really come as a surprise. DivCom explained to me the seriousness of my actions, which, under ordinary circumstances, could have resulted in severe punishment.

But as it turned out, my crew and I had inadvertently destroyed a VC mortar position being set up to fire into the Army outpost later that evening. An outpost patrol had found fresh blood trails and drag marks where bodies or wounded had been taken away from the site around the flagpole. We had accidently saved the outpost from a mortar shelling.

The Army wanted to give us a commendation. The Navy wanted to court-martial us. The Army prevailed. We never got any medals, but we never got any reprimands either. We got away with it.

A bit later, once again near Rach Gia, we were giving Capt. Roy Hoffman, the Swift Boat Task Force Commander, a ride back to An Thoi after a tour of all the coastal patrol areas south of Cam Ranh. Hoffmann, sunning himself in the gun tub atop the pilothouse, at one point yelled down: "Brown, how many VC did you kill today?"

"None," I responded. "We have never run across any enemy troops or found any contraband in the time we have been in-country."

"Why not?" he asked.

The VC do not have to mess with us, I told him. They controlled all the canals and rivers for 100 miles inland, in the Coastal Division 11 Op Area, and never had to use the gulf where we patrolled.

About a week later, Coastal Squadron 1 sent a message to all divisions: "River mouths and estuaries are likely target areas, go get 'em tigers."

That was the day the Swift Boats became a riverine force.

The days of inconsequential patrols had ended. We probed canals and raided VC strongholds. We got into firefights. People died—ours, as well as theirs. Finally, in October 1968, we were sent to the very tip of the Ca Mau Peninsula, land's end for South Vietnam. We had never patrolled along the Ca Mau coast, so a senior boat officer, a short-timer, came along to show us the ropes. My crew and I were most interested in the Cua Lon River, the gateway to a known VC training area. To get there, boats had to navigate a large, shallow, café au lait–colored body of water, affectionately known to us as "Square Bay." At the south end of the bay marking the entrance to the Cua Lon was a small island referred to as "Fish Island."

Getting to the river was hard and could be managed only at high tide. In fact, most of Square Bay was nothing but a mud flat most of the time. Miscalculate the water depth and a boat could spend hours aground waiting nervously for the tide to rise. There was one story about a Swift Boat and its crew that had gotten trapped in a small tidal pool so close to land that a group of VC started wading out to get them. They called for help and, together with two helos from a nearby Army base, man-

Radarman Second Class Marvin Sedlachek rearming after a firefight. The aft ammunition box could store up to 100 rounds of 81mm mortar rounds of various types including high explosive, illumination, white phosphorous, and flechette.
COURTESY OF MICHAEL BROWN

aged to hold off the attackers until nature lifted them off the flat. In our pre-patrol briefing at An Thoi, DivCom told me that I should learn how to navigate the bay, but under no circumstances could I go farther inland than 1,500 yards past Fish Island.

The short-timer lieutenant showed us how to get into the river but had no interest in proceeding any farther, so we obeyed orders, turned around, and headed back out to the gulf, where we deposited him aboard a Coast Guard cutter for transport back to An Thoi and a flight home, his tour in Vietnam complete. That took most of the night, but at first light we noticed we had high tide, so we headed immediately for Square Bay and the Cua Lon.

Just past Fish Island, Gunner's Mate Nagy in the forward gun tub spotted a small boat in the middle of the river with two men in it. The whole area had been designated a free-fire zone, with nothing but bad guys living there. We sped up to overtake the boat and capture its crew,

PCF 93 patrols in the lower Ca Mau Peninsula in 1969. Agent Orange was used to defoliate river and canal banks to deny the enemy the cover they needed to ambush Swift Boats.
OFFICIAL U.S. NAVY PHOTO

but they ran for the riverbank. Nagy laid down a trail of warning shots in front of the boat, but it seemed to gather speed. I gave Nagy permission to take the boat under fire. He shredded it, and the two passengers disappeared into the river. We maneuvered to a spot between the riverbank and the wreckage to catch them when they surfaced, but we never saw them again. They were our first two enemy KIA.

We were going to leave the river, but as we turned the boat, several houses on the south bank came into view. They were only about 200 yards away, so we decided to investigate. As we approached we could see rising smoke from fire pits. Someone was living there—maybe the two men we had seen on the river. Drawing closer, we could see a couple of pigs, as well as chickens and water jugs in front of the houses. I decided to destroy the water jugs, but it seemed like killing the livestock was appropriate as well. After we finished shooting, I pulled out our signal pistol and shot a flare onto the roof of the first house, setting it afire. We fired the next house in line, and the next and the next.

We noticed more houses up the river. And about fifty yards inland a VC flag was flying on a pole. We burned those houses, too. We were right: These were VC or VC sympathizers. We kept seeing more houses farther upriver, and we decided to keep going until we ran out of ammunition. A mile farther along we saw what appeared to be a guard station, like a lifeguard stand on a beach. We leveled it with a mortar round. About 300 yards farther than that the river turned to the right. I decided we should see what was around the bend.

When we rounded the bend, we were all in shock: There was a city, complete with buildings, streets, piers, small- and medium-sized boats, even large junks—everything. I would later learn that we had reached Nam Can, the provincial capital. This was much more than we bargained for. Who knows what we would find there in the way of opposition? I thought. We should turn around and get the hell out of here.

But we couldn't stop ourselves. The strangest thing was there was no one in sight. I had heard rumors that friendlies in this area had evacuated to refugee camps farther north, so I could understand why there would not be many people here, but completely empty? There were also rumors that the VC and North Vietnamese were training between 5,000 and 6,000 troops here. Where were they?

We started blowing things up. We shot the motors from sampans and threw grenades in them to sink them. We mortared the junks. We destroyed hundreds of boats and buildings. There was still no resistance, so we decided to keep going until someone shot at us. It never happened. We stayed until late afternoon. It was time to get out while we still had enough ammunition to defend ourselves from an ambush. Charlie knew that when Swift Boats went into a river they would only go so far and then turn around. That's when ambushes happened.

It was decision time. I asked the crew what they wanted to do—turn around, or keep going? I knew the Cua Lon eventually connected to the Bo De River, which exited to the South China Sea. What I did not know was how far we had to go to find it. I had no charts, just a vague recollection from maps at division headquarters. We checked our fuel status. We would have to get to the South China Sea, then circle back around the tip of the Ca Mau Peninsula and get all the way to the Coast Guard cutter. We talked it over and decided it was worth the risk. We would keep going.

It was a good choice, albeit with some anxious moments. I expected to see the Bo De around the first bend, but it wasn't there. There was a smaller river. Was that it, my crew asked? No, I said, the Bo De was much larger. The Cua Lon made several more turns after that, and each time I expected to see the Bo De—and each time it wasn't there.

And then it appeared. We rounded a big bend to the right, and there was a large river coming from the east. We turned south, picked up a little speed, and stayed in the middle of the new river, which was several hundred yards wide. Finally, we took one last S-curve and the South China Sea was straight ahead.

Not so fast. Just as we put the helm amidships and pointed the boat toward the ocean, Boatswain's Mate Stark came forward from the fantail: "I think someone just shot at us," he said.

Just so.

I had been sitting in the pilothouse doorway with my feet hanging over the side of the boat when I heard the hissing sound a bullet makes as it whizzes by. I turned to Quartermaster Clayton, at the helm, and told him to hit the throttles. At that instant an AK-47 opened fire from our port side. Clayton was shot in the leg and fell out of the helmsman's chair. Other rounds hit the instrument panel in front of the helm and a ricochet splattered into the radar unit. Shrapnel hit me on the left side of my face and on my left arm, but all I was thinking about was taking the helm, adding speed, and steering the boat.

Fortunately, I think we had surprised the enemy, and that one spate of small-arms fire was all there was. Then the Bo De spat us out into the South China Sea and safety—except that two Swift Boats from another division were lying offshore. They were stunned to see us, and challenged us to identify ourselves. We were on their turf, and at first they thought we could be enemy troops who somehow had captured a Swift Boat. Then, when we told them our story, they found it incredible.

There was nothing further we could do. I filed an after-action report by radio to Coastal Division 11, and we left for our home waters. We rounded the tip of the Ca Mau Peninsula and found the Coast Guard cutter. Don't even get off the boat, we were told as we pulled alongside. DivCom wanted to see us in An Thoi—ASAP. Clayton and I went to sick bay to get patched up, the rest of the crew refueled and cleaned up the spent brass, and then we were on our way, dreading what would likely happen.

Our fears seemed to be justified when we met up in mid-transit with our relief boat. We pulled alongside for a moment, and the OinC just looked at me and said: "I would not want to be you right now."

But we lucked out again. Fortunately, Admiral Zumwalt had read my after-action report while we were underway. He called the Squadron Commander to express his appreciation for what we had done. He was recommending us for medals. We had disobeyed a direct order, but once again we got away with it.

Our trip from sea to sea marked the beginning of full-scale river warfare by Swift Boats in Ca Mau, and our story has been told many times. What many forget, or never knew about, is how stupid we were to do this—not just going into the Cua Lon, but staying there all day. PCF 38, the boat we were using that day, had electrical problems. The starter motors did not work, and when we came in off patrols, we could not shut down the engines. Had they failed anytime during the day while we were in the river, we would have been stranded in the middle of nowhere. We were all alone with no backup. We were lucky to get out alive.

A Turning Point

Michael Bernique

Lt. (j.g.) Michael Bernique left the Navy in 1969. He obtained a master's degree in International Relations from the University of Chicago and began a forty-year career in the electronics industry, which included the chairmanship of a NASDAQ–listed company. He retired to La Jolla, California, and passed away in March 2016.

My crew and I arrived in Vietnam in late summer 1968. The squadron sent us to Coastal Division 11 at An Thoi, where we spent our time bobbing like a cork in the Gulf of Thailand on PCF 3, conducting Market Time board-and-search. Toward the middle of October I became increasingly frustrated with what appeared to be a waste of time and effort. All I had to do was look at the charts of the Ca Mau Peninsula and the areas surrounding the coastal towns of Ha Tien and Rach Gia. Why, with all the marvelous rivers and French-built canals that crisscrossed the lower Mekong Delta, would an armed VC smuggler take a chance against us in the open ocean?

On October 14, I put into Ha Tien, a sleepy Cambodian border town and an occasional stopping place for a little R&R and a quick beer. I walked up to the old French military outpost above the town and met the U.S. Army major who was lead advisor for the Regional-Provincial militia forces ("Ruff-Puffs") in the area. He told me that VC were hanging out along the Giang Thanh River that extended inland from Ha Tien. They were collecting taxes from the locals. A couple of Vietnamese officers at

Skipper Michael Bernique
COURTESY OF MIMI BERNIQUE

the outpost advised me against going upriver since there were "beaucoup VC up there!" All this did was confirm my suspicions that I was wasting my time in the gulf. I decided to take a look upriver. The Army major had never been upriver—the Ruff-Puffs wouldn't go—and asked if he could come along. Sure, I said.

I had to feel my way into the Giang Thanh to get through the shallows at the river mouth, but once past the mudflats we had plenty of depth, so we proceeded at speed. Most of the terrain along the northern riverbank was open ground with rice paddies. The southern bank was more heavily wooded.

After about three miles we came around a river bend and spotted four armed men in black pajamas on the northern riverbank. They had stopped two sampans and were, in fact, collecting taxes. I closed the distance at top speed, and they fired on us. Big mistake. They were no match for our machine guns. We had to make a couple of passes, but it was over in a matter of minutes. We took care not to hit the sampans, which immediately left the area. I beached the boat and went ashore with two men to pick up enemy weapons and collect information.

There were four enemy dead. We had never seen mutilated bodies, and now we had to fieldstrip them. It was quite a shock. Our .50-caliber

PCF 82 trails PCF 5 at 30 knots on the Giang Thanh River east of Ha Tien. The river runs from Ha Tien to a canal that runs along the border between Cambodia and Vietnam.
OFFICIAL U.S. NAVY PHOTO

machine guns had literally cut one man in half. Even as we completed this task, the VC opened up on us with automatic weapons from firing positions beyond some open muddy ground dotted with rice paddies. Our three-man landing party was directly in front of the boat, preventing our machine gunners from responding. Even though the enemy fire was fairly heavy, I felt we had no choice but to charge the VC. They continued to fire on us as we sprinted across the muddy ground, but then, fortunately, they broke and ran. We killed two more of them, with no injuries to us.

We took what documents we could find, which amounted to not much, and collected one fully automatic AK-47 assault rifle, four Chinese SKS semiautomatic rifles, and a very old rifle with French army markings. When we returned to our boat, the Army major was laughing and calling me "dinky-dau." Crazy, in local pidgin.

We continued upriver for several uneventful miles, and we then turned around and went back to Ha Tien where we dropped off the major and started back to An Thoi. It was then that I made a crucial decision not to keep quiet about our probe of an inland waterway, a violation of Swift Boat standing orders that did not allow approach within 1,000 yards of the beach. I fervently believed that we belonged in the rivers, and decided to say so. I composed a detailed message and sent it along to An Thoi. Prior to our arrival, in old Navy tradition, we tied a broom to our mast to signify that we had "swept the seas." When we arrived at An Thoi a helicopter was waiting to sweep me off to Saigon to explain my actions to the Navy High Command.

At COMNAVFORV it was obvious there was no consensus about what had happened. According to the first officers who interviewed me, going up the rivers was not what we should be doing. One diminutive captain—a staff officer who shall remain nameless—actually told me that "one hundred dead VC were not worth one dead American." I replied that I would never sacrifice an American, but I would take those odds in a war anytime.

Then I was shown to the office of Admiral Zumwalt himself and invited to recount my story. This proved to be a very different affair. It

PCF 96 patrols the canal along the Cambodian border.
COURTESY OF WILLIAM ROGERS

The local bar at Ha Tien where Mike Bernique learned of tax collectors assessing civilians on the Giang Thanh River.
COURTESY OF MIMI BERNIQUE

quickly became apparent to me that Zumwalt was in favor of my actions. He did me the honor of renaming the Giang Than River "Bernique's Creek" in all naval messages.

During the interview an aide entered the room to inform us that Prince Sihanouk of Cambodia had just accused the United States—and me by name and boat number—of having invaded Cambodia. "Well," I said, "You tell Sihanouk that he's a lying son of a bitch."

What was true was that the Cambodian border is very close to the Giang Thanh River, almost touching it at some points. There are no sign-posts or barriers, of course, and you are left to wonder over which rice paddy the border lies. But in the end, that didn't matter. In accordance with international law and the principle of "Hot Pursuit," I was in the clear. Hot Pursuit means that if you are in close visible contact with the enemy and exchanging fire you may disregard boundaries until the firing ceases. Still, at the conclusion of the interview Admiral Zumwalt pulled me aside and gave me a directive: if this occurs again, he said, "drag the bodies back."

For my actions on October 14, 1968, I received the Silver Star. Subsequent reports have said that I received the award "instead of" being court-martialed. This is not true. I was never threatened with a court-martial.

I stayed in Saigon overnight and returned to An Thoi. A few days later Zumwalt summoned me again. This time there were a number of

Admiral Elmo R. Zumwalt, Jr. awards the Silver Star to Michael Bernique for his actions on the Giang Thanh River. In the background, Michael Brown awaits the award of a Silver Star for his raid on the Song Cu Lon and Bo De Rivers.
OFFICIAL U.S. NAVY PHOTO

officers gathered around a large table in his office. It was clear they were planning heavy naval activity upriver from Ha Tien. Admiral Zumwalt wanted to know how far I thought "Bernique's Creek" was navigable. Would it reach the Vinh Te Canal? I replied that I was sure it would, but if there was going to be a mission up the river I wanted to be the lead boat. Zumwalt laughed. "Of course."

We headed up the river on November 16 with three boats. Our Division Commander rode with me as Officer in Tactical Command. We were to proceed up Bernique's Creek to the Vinh Te, meet up with elements of the riverine forces and several PBRs, and continue all the way to the Bassac River—quite a distance.

We had traveled only about five miles when we came across a sizable group of what looked like VC clustered around a fairly large, partly beached sampan. They were actually Cambodian paramilitaries, we learned later—shadowy irregulars who fought the VC. They shot at us, and we returned fire, but we were traveling at top speed and were past them before anything conclusive happened. I wanted to return and go after them but DivCom overruled me. We kept going upriver with the throttles open.

The rest of the trip was completely uneventful, including our meeting with the riverine forces and our journey down the Vinh Te Canal. We stopped at Rach Gia, and shortly thereafter helos came in carrying three relief officers to take our boats back to An Thoi. The three original OinCs—myself, Terry Costello, and Tuck Brant—then learned that an "international incident was brewing," involving us. We climbed aboard the helos for yet another trip to Saigon.

We went immediately to naval headquarters and were ushered into a large meeting room. You can imagine our condition after two days on the river. We were in combat gear, and Tuck Brant even had some grenades in his pocket. And we were pretty ripe.

The room held three tables covered with green felt. Grim-faced senior officers sat around them. One stood up: "The inquiry is ready to begin," he said. "Get the tape recorders rolling."

We were stunned. We had no idea what this was all about.

Fortunately, Captain Hoffman, the Swift Boat squadron commander, intervened at that point: "Hey, wait a minute. These are my men, and they were following my orders," he said. Hoffman was not shy. "This is decidedly not an inquiry."

Admiral Zumwalt arrived and seconded Captain Hoffman: "This is indeed not an inquiry." We all sat down to talk. Both the Vietnamese and Cambodian governments had accused us of killing several civilian women in the sampan where we saw the paramilitaries. None of us had seen either women or civilians. We were sent back to An Thoi with Captain Hoffman, assigned by the High Command to investigate the incident.

The next day I took Captain Hoffman back to the scene of the firefight. To our surprise the sampan was still there. It had some bullet damage, but not much, and there were no signs of any bodies, and no indication that anyone had died either in the sampan or close by. The sampan itself, oddly enough, was still full of rice, and the rice was lily white. If anyone had been killed or wounded, blood would have stained the rice red. There was no trace of blood. That was the last I heard about that incident.

So how did the Cambodian government know my name?

Many years later at a store near my home in La Jolla, California, I noticed a book entitled *NILO Ha Tien*. The store owner told me that the author, H. L. Serra, lived only a few blocks from my house. I called him up and over lunch he told me about his stay in Ha Tien as Naval Intelligence Liaison Officer. He said all the boat officers were well known by name since Ha Tien was a hotbed of intelligence activity. He referred to it as "a mini Casablanca." I had heard elsewhere that Ha Tien had many spies, but their depth of knowledge was surprising. I guess it just goes to prove the old World War II adage, "loose lips sink ships."

Regarding Henry

W. Henry Inabnett

Radarman Third Class W. Henry Inabnett finished college when he returned from Vietnam and retired from the Naval Reserve as an Operations Specialist First Class. He managed credit unions for thirty-five years before retiring near Austin, Texas.

THE THUMP OF THE LANDING GEAR BROUGHT HENRY TO THE PLANE window where he looked out on white-sand beaches and blue ocean, all of it bathed in brilliant sunshine. Henry had read about the violence in the Republic of Vietnam. He didn't know what to expect, but it wasn't the gorgeous coastline at Cam Ranh Bay.

On that summer day in 1968, Henry knew a bit about the war. But mostly he regarded Vietnam as a potential source of memorable and dangerous adventures. As a boy in northern Louisiana he had led others in exciting expeditions and competitions along wooded streams and lakes behind his house. Many of those boyhood experiences—marked by burning thirst and swimming vast distances—were in his mind now. He learned about the outside world from television. He dreamed of far-off places, and programs like *The Silent Service* and *Victory at Sea* led him to believe the Navy was his surest ticket to adventure.

Henry's father was a civil servant with two years of college, which he had obtained at great personal expense, and he wanted his son to get the degree he couldn't have. But Henry meandered through high school and dabbled in college, always focused on his desire to wander

Henry inspects a fishing boat.
COURTESY OF W. HENRY INABNETT

the world. Naval Officer Training School wouldn't take him because he didn't have the grades, so he enlisted in the Naval Reserve. Three years later he dropped out of college and went on active duty. Soon he was a radarman aboard a Navy oiler operating off the Vietnamese coast, but the only action he saw and heard were nighttime flares and the thump of artillery echoing from distant beaches.

The yearning for action led him to volunteer for Swift Boat duty. He had only a vague idea of what the boats did other than knowing that they worked close inshore, but he knew the boats' specs: they were fifty feet long, traveled very fast, and had twin .50-caliber machine guns in a turret above the pilothouse and a third fifty mounted on top of an 81mm mortar on the fantail. Each boat also carried an M-60 light machine gun, M-16 assault rifles, a handheld grenade launcher, a shotgun, two .38-caliber pistols, and grenades.

Henry first met Lt. (j.g.) John Roland during Swift training at the U.S. Naval Amphibious Base, in Coronado, California. Roland, a U.S. Naval Academy graduate from Georgia, became Officer-in-Charge of Henry's boat. Henry was the radarman, tending the communications gear and the electronics. There was also a quartermaster, a gunner, a boatswain, and an engineman. Near the end of training, Roland was given a choice of where he wanted the crew to be deployed. He picked the Mekong Delta. Later he told Henry he thought the Delta would provide more variety and more interesting missions. He was right.

Up until 1968, Swift Boats patrolled Vietnam's inshore coastline to cut off waterborne supplies to the Viet Cong. But Henry flew south with Roland and the rest of the crew on a different assignment at Coastal Division 13, based in Cat Lo at the northern edge of the Delta. Their job was to work the rivers. This was not Cam Ranh Bay. There was no white sand and no blue sea.

Roland and his crew took over PCF 35. Their primary job was to spend two or three days at a time patrolling river commerce—inspecting shorelines, water taxis, and sampans for contraband and checking for suspicious activities. Henry got to know the Mekong's tributaries like the back of his hand.

On January 28, 1969, PCF 35 left Cat Lo at 0800 on its way to the Ham Luong River. On a previous patrol Roland had briefly probed the Rach Thu Cuu Canal south of the town of Ben Tre, discovering an old metal footbridge in what appeared to be an abandoned stretch of tropical forest. He wanted to explore it further. Seeking another Swift Boat as backup, Roland radioed PCF 100, which was patrolling nearby, and conferred with Lt. (j.g.) Gerald B. O'Grady. Would PCF 100 like to accompany the 35-Boat? It would, O'Grady replied.

The crews went to General Quarters. Henry, the bow gunner, put on his flak jacket and helmet, strapped on a .38-caliber pistol, and gathered up his M-60 machine gun and 3,000 rounds of belted ammunition in reused wooden mortar boxes. He stood in PCF 35's open bow hatchway with only his head and shoulders above the deck. Henry was the first man into the canal. PCF 100 would follow behind.

Henry could hear Roland's footfalls on the aluminum deck as he circled the boat, checking on everybody. It was both a probe and a raid, he told Henry: "When we get in, don't shoot unless we get fired on, or a clear target presents itself," he said. "We'll really shoot it up on the way out." He looked over at PCF 100 and gave O'Grady a thumbs up. "Let's go."

The canal was barely wide enough to maneuver through, with dark water and vegetation that grew right to the water's edge. Henry heard nothing but the rumble of the engines and smelled nothing but sulfurous diesel exhaust. He scanned the thick brush at the base of the palm trees along the canal banks. The boats pushed on until overgrowth in the river and the collapsed metal footbridge blocked their way. A small straw-thatched hut came into view, with an abandoned fire pit smoldering nearby. Roland ordered the helmsman to nose the boat into the clearing. Henry stood up with the M-60 at his hip, turned to Roland, and in a poor imitation of John Wayne inquired: "We hittin' the beach?"

"Yes," Roland said.

Henry grabbed an M-16, dropped extra clips in his pockets, and hooked several incendiary and percussion grenades into his belt. The boat punched the canal bank and Roland, Henry, and engineman Bill Clark jumped from the bow and walked to the hut. There was nothing inside and nothing in the fire pit.

They reboarded the boat for the return trip. PCF 100 was in the lead now, with the 35-Boat following. After getting underway Roland spotted a cluster of huts under some trees, perhaps seventy-five yards from the canal bank. He signaled Henry and Clark to get ready and the trio got off to inspect the huts. They were empty, but there was a dirt bunker on the edge of the compound. Henry tossed a percussion grenade into the bunker. Nothing. Then, after several failed attempts to light the thatched walls of the huts with a cigarette lighter, incendiary grenades were used to burn the roofs and walls.

They returned to the boats and fired aimlessly into the underbrush on either side as they continued out of the canal. Suddenly, Henry saw a cloud of smoke and heard the roar of machine gun fire—no longer random—coming from PCF 100. The boat turned to port toward the canal bank and then suddenly veered away. Then he saw something else.

"Hey, there are two guys in the water!" Henry shouted.

PCF 100 had been ambushed from a firing position near the huts that PCF 35's crewmen had just inspected. The first rocket had hit forward, near PCF 100's pilothouse. Two more hits came from recoilless rifles. More B-40 rockets and recoilless rifle rounds flew overhead and

Engineman Bill Clark on the trail.
COURTESY OF W. HENRY INABNETT

detonated on the opposite canal bank. The 100-Boat's engineman, stationed on the fantail, knew that damage forward had crippled the pilothouse steering, so he used the aft helm to put the boat back on course for the canal mouth. He had no idea that O'Grady and forward helmsman Jim Lloyd had been blown into the water.

Rockets flew over PCF 35 as it approached O'Grady and Lloyd. Henry grabbed the ten-foot-long boat hook and reached for the two men. O'Grady grabbed the hook with one hand and the collar of Lloyd's flak jacket with the other. Henry pulled them alongside, but their flak jackets were so weighted down with water that Roland couldn't bring them aboard. O'Grady grabbed a towline dragging in the water: "Get out of here!" he yelled.

PCF 35 edged forward, but O'Grady couldn't hold the towline. Enemy small-arms fire continued to flash from the riverbank, and Roland ordered the boat to maneuver between the ambush and the men in the water. "Leave us and save yourselves," O'Grady yelled at one point.

Eventually they were hauled aboard, but even then the firefight wasn't over. A shoulder-fired rocket slammed into PCF 35's main cabin just aft of the pilothouse. All the windows were blown out, and Henry saw gray smoke spewing from the openings. The rocket splintered inside, spraying shrapnel that destroyed the radar and radio equipment.

Henry sat in the bow, firing his M-60, surrounded by empty shell casings. As soon as they cleared the canal he went aft to the fantail, kneeling beside O'Grady, whose left leg was burned and pocked with bloody shrapnel wounds from foot to thigh. His left boot was in shreds, and Henry removed it, but left the sock. He bound the leg cautiously with battle dressings. The crew's first-aid training was limited, and Henry didn't want to make anything worse. Roland had tried to radio for a helicopter MEDEVAC before PCF 35 left the canal, but all the boat's communications were destroyed. Luckily, however, there were two heavy riverine craft at the canal mouth. Thirty minutes later the wounded were airborne. Once they were evacuated the PCF 35-Boat crew hosed the blood from the fantail, swept the empty brass over the side, and ate C-rations. Then they returned to Cat Lo. O'Grady and Lloyd were going to be all right.

John Roland was awarded the Navy Cross. Henry and his other PCF 35 shipmates received the Navy Commendation medal with Combat V. Gerald O'Grady got a Bronze Star and a Purple Heart; he spent five months in the hospital and left the Navy with a "slightly shorter" big toe on his left foot.

Henry went home in July 1969, arriving in time to watch the first moon landing on TV from his home in Louisiana. He was twenty-three, and he had found adventure.

Chapter Four

1969

SEALORDS

On November 5, 1968, the Navy formally approved river patrols for Swift Boats. Operation SEALORDS had three goals: stopping enemy soldiers and supplies from entering South Vietnam through Cambodia, "harassment" and disruption of enemy sanctuaries, and "pacification of the Mekong Delta." Admiral Zumwalt had given Swifts license to use whatever tools they had to wrest territory from insurgents who had held much of it for decades.[1]

It was a tall order. The Mekong Delta, a gigantic alluvial fan covering the entire bottom half of Vietnam, had almost no roads of consequence. Instead, there were 4,000 miles of interconnected inland waterways that had been sculpted and improved by the Mekong's inhabitants for a millennium. The delta had mighty rivers like the Bassac, sluice-like estuaries like the Cua Lon and the Bo De, an endless web of navigable streams and creeks, and a lattice of canals large and small connecting vast tracts of tropical forest and swampland. You could go anywhere in the Delta with a boat and get there relatively quickly. Unless you got killed along the way.

SEALORDS made 1969 a deadly year for Swifts. The boats suffered their heaviest losses and endured their greatest defeats, and in the process learned there were things that simply could not be done. But SEALORDS also brought Swifts many of their greatest successes. The boats repeatedly invaded enemy strongholds and shrunk enemy territory. They set up safe havens for war-weary civilians, provided crucial gunfire support for isolated delta garrisons, and brought the South Vietnamese government to places it had never been.

North of the Delta, Swifts working out of Da Nang began making river incursions, while Vietnamese boats increasingly took over Market Time patrols along the central coast. The number of U.S. Swifts at Qui Nhon and Cam Ranh Bay dwindled throughout 1969, and Coastal Division 15 (Qui Nhon) was turned over to the Vietnamese in its entirety in November.

In the northern Delta, Swifts patrolled seventy miles deep into the Ham Luong, Co Chien, and Bassac river systems, allowing the PBRs that had been there for almost four years to move even farther inland to increase pressure on the enemy.

To the west, Swifts began patrolling Bernique's Creek—the Giang Thanh River—to interdict smuggling along the Cambodian border, and raided the Ca Mau Peninsula, the boot at Vietnam's southernmost tip. The Viet Cong had controlled much of this wilderness for years. To the United States and its allies, large pieces of the Ca Mau Peninsula were "free-fire zones," where everyone there was assumed to be an enemy, and every settlement, no matter how small, was assumed to be an enemy sanctuary. In the lower Ca Mau, Swift Boats were at once the hunters and the hunted.

Doing SEALORDS properly—and as safely as possible—required Swift Boats to make significant tactical changes. Not all of these moves were immediately obvious, and crews learned some hard lessons as they refined their techniques.

One change came quickly. Single-boat patrols—the Market Time staple—were a luxury that Swifts could no longer afford. River fighting was close quarters, sometimes at ranges under twenty-five yards, and the enemy's weapons were competitive: .51-caliber machine guns, B-40 and B-50 armor-piercing rockets, 57mm recoilless rifles, Claymore mines, and plenty of AK-47 automatic rifles. Boats got hit and lost communications, suffered engine damage, and took casualties. They needed a backup to provide cover fire, call for help, offer a tow, and MEDEVAC the wounded. During SEALORDS Swifts traveled in pairs at all times, and in flotillas of three or more boats whenever the occasion called for it.

SEALORDS had considerable early success. A string of effective raids into the Cua Lon estuary by the end of 1968 had so disconcerted the Viet Cong that they attempted to block the Square Bay entrance with telephone pole–like logs implanted in the river bottom and crowned with large crosspieces above the waterline. In January 1969, a flotilla of river assault craft picked their way through the rivers and canals of the upper Delta to reach the Gulf of Thailand, then made a short ocean transit to visit Square Bay and the new pilings. Vietnamese troops secured the area while Swift Boats provided cover. Then the heavy boats dismantled the barrier.[2]

Two weeks later Swifts pried open the Bo De side of the estuary. Ten boats, accompanied by U.S. Navy SEALs, Vietnamese shock troops, two Coast Guard cutters, an LST, helicopter gunships, and fixed-wing support aircraft, probed two miles into the river to reach the Viet Cong fortress whose garrison had attacked virtually every U.S. boat that had come into the river. The task force destroyed the entire complex, leveling seventy-four bunkers, seventeen huts, and eleven other buildings, and wrecking twenty sampans and a footbridge.[3]

Late in February, Swifts added another pair of new tactical wrinkles. During ambushes, the usual response was to clear a kill zone at high speed, then counterattack from a distance using mortar and .50-caliber machine gun fire. But on February 28, in the last of eight Swift incursions that month into the Bay Hap River just north of the Cua Lon, the pattern changed.

A three-boat task force probing enemy positions destroyed two earthen bunkers that had been found the previous day, then moved farther upriver. Each boat carried thirty Vietnamese militiamen. Troops on board were a recent innovation, designed to give Swifts the ability to sweep enemy-controlled areas instead of merely raiding them.

But as the task force approached the debarkation point, it encountered heavy small-arms fire. Rather than speed through the kill zone, the boats turned directly into the ambush and beached in the middle of the enemy positions. The surprised Viet Cong stood up and ran, with the troops in hot pursuit. The Swifts moved farther upriver and again came under fire. And again, the boats turned directly into the ambush. PCF crewmen went ashore. The task force killed ten Viet Cong in this skirmish and commandeered twelve tons of rice. The Swifts suffered minimal damage and no casualties.[4]

Other ventures met with mixed results. In a series of river incursions in early March, Swifts patrolling south of Da Nang killed five Viet Cong on the My Thanh River, arrested four others, and destroyed twenty-two bunkers. Six days later, on March 19, PCF 101 was hit with two 75mm recoilless rifle rounds on the Cua Dai River. A fire detonated ammo in the main cabin. A second PCF picked up eleven survivors, but three others spent the night on a river island before other Swifts found them the following day. And, on March 21, PCF 24 was hit with two recoilless rifle rounds and ran aground on a sandbar. Another Swift towed it home to Da Nang.[5]

And there were patrols that ended badly. On February 24, PCF 67, underway on the Co Chien River in the northern Delta, turned into the much shallower Tra Vinh Canal and traveled about two miles before a command-detonated water mine lifted the stern of the boat out of the water and threw two men overboard. The boat picked up the crewmen and made it back to the Co Chien, but the flooding could not be stopped and PCF 67 was beached at a friendly base. Three crewmen were wounded.[6]

Perhaps the most ambitious set of SEALORDS raids began in early 1969 when Swifts began probing the very southern tip of the Ca Mau Peninsula, a notorious Viet Cong stronghold. The first large-scale operation, on February 11, ended inconclusively. Ten Swift Boats carrying Mobile Strike Force Vietnamese troops and supported offshore by an LST, a minesweeper, an amphibious gunboat, two Coast Guard cutters, and Air Force jets conducted a three-pronged probe into the Duong Keo River and nearby waterways. Over eight hours the task force fought two pitched battles, killed two Viet Cong, and destroyed twenty-seven bunkers. But two Swift crewmen were wounded, three Swift Boats were hit with rockets and recoilless rifle fire, and one Swift Boat sank.[7]

Two months later, the Swifts tried again in a massive operation involving thirteen boats and 240 Vietnamese Marines. Intending to trap a pair of Viet Cong heavy-weapons companies in the forest along the Duong Keo, the lead column of eight boats instead was attacked in a vicious close-quarters ambush two hours before nightfall. PCF 43, disabled by rockets and recoilless rifle fire, had to be abandoned in the kill zone. Three U.S. Navy crewmen died in the Duong Keo and thirty-three were wounded in the worst defeat ever suffered by Swift Boats in Vietnam. Two Vietnamese Marines were killed and thirteen were wounded.[8]

Despite this debacle, six troop-carrying PCFs reentered the Duong Keo on May 5 to find and destroy a village reported to be harboring a large number of Viet Cong. The Swifts probed the river in two sections of three boats each. Within a few minutes the first column was ambushed. The lead boat, badly crippled, beached in the kill zone. Meanwhile, the second set of three boats beached below the ambush to drop off its troops, who began to sweep northward despite intense enemy resistance. Boats, troops, and airstrikes killed ten Viet Cong and destroyed ten fortified bunkers. Two Swift sailors died, one U.S. and one Vietnamese, and eight Swift sailors were wounded. One soldier was killed and four were wounded. Two Swift Boats were damaged, one of them very badly.[9]

The May 5 operation was the sort of bloody standoff that came to epitomize Swift Boat river operations. Able to call for aircraft, and, frequently, artillery support, Swifts had the enemy outgunned most of the time and could challenge the Viet Cong anywhere they wished, but they paid a high, and in some cases prohibitive, price to do so. Swifts raided the Duong Keo several times, but they never conquered it.

At the same time, however, SEALORDS in the Ca Mau and the rest of the Delta was pushing the Viet Cong off the main rivers and deeper into the jungle. This gave the South Vietnamese government a foothold in areas where it had never before had a presence. And the Viet Cong could not do anything about it. The next move for the boats was to solidify these gains and carry them forward. The Navy had an idea how this might be done.

Fire Mission

David P. Marion

Army captain David P. Marion left active duty in 1969 and stayed in the Army Reserve until 1972. He went to work for the U. S. Department of Agriculture and retired to College Station, Texas, in 2004.

I ARRIVED IN THANH PHU DISTRICT ON SEPTEMBER 1, 1968, A BRAND-new Army captain (four months in grade) sent as a deputy advisor to Vietnamese militia. Thanh Phu, about forty miles south of Saigon, was a rectangular piece of rice-growing flatland between the mouths of the Ham Luong River to the north and the Co Chien River to the south. To the east, all the way to the South China Sea, were "beaucoup" Viet Cong, who threatened everything else.

The militia, known as Regional Forces/Provincial Forces—more familiarly in U.S. Armed Forces argot as "RF-PFs" or "Ruff-Puffs"—were building a new outpost at the tiny hamlet of An Hoa, about two klicks southwest of a canal where the VC routinely set up ambushes for anyone who came close. We called this spot "B-40 Rocket Alley," and we wanted it back. The Swift Boats, based nearby at Cat Lo, knew the district was a nasty place, and handled it with extreme care. They called it the "Thanh Phu Secret Zone."

The Deputy Province Advisor, a U.S. lieutenant colonel, told me Thanh Phu was low priority. "Don't expect any help to come to you in a firefight," he warned. "We do not have the troops to send." I should be aware of my militia's shortcomings, he said, and "don't get them into anything they can't get themselves out of with what they have. Remember, your RF-PF troops are mostly for defense." He finished with this: "Try not to lose any more hamlets to VC."

That was really reassuring. When I got to Thanh Phu district headquarters, I learned we had about 300 RF-PFs, many of whom were armed with World War II–vintage M-1 Garand rifles and .30-caliber carbines. The local main force VC had AK-47s and plenty of combat experience. But the news was not all bad. I was in great physical shape and brimming with confidence, and my Vietnamese counterpart was a tough customer willing to fight deep inside VC territory. We thought alike. Our troops may have been poorly armed, and some of them were green, but we both agreed we had to push Charlie away from our villages so the mortar and rocket attacks would stop.

In late January 1969 U.S. and Vietnamese intelligence reported increased VC movement around Thanh Phu, heightening my suspicions that a major attack might be brewing near An Hoa. It was the dry season, and there was no water in the rice paddies—perfect maneuvering conditions for VC foot soldiers.

On January 31, Charlie launched probing attacks at An Hoa, testing our defenses and troop strength. Intelligence said more VC were arriving, probably massing for a major engagement. Working from district headquarters, I sent two advisors on February 1 to take an M-60 machine gun and a radio to An Hoa for extra firepower and for direct communications with the other Americans at headquarters. The next afternoon one of the advisors injured his foot and needed to leave. There was nobody to replace him but me. I came in by chopper at sundown.

We had one hundred men on the ground at An Hoa, all of them untested new recruits and all of them armed with outdated weapons. The outpost was half-built with a five-foot wall around it and one circle of barbed wire to discourage bad guys. We had no mines and no overhead cover. From a defensive standpoint we were practically naked. The M-60 covered our right flank, pointing southeast. I found a small hole where a tree had been removed, spread my poncho, and lay down for a catnap.

The VC hit us in a coordinated mass attack at 0115 on February 3. I knew about it immediately when a mortar round exploded with a flash and a loud bang on top of the outpost wall about twenty yards from my hole. So much for the lieutenant colonel's advice; Charlie was trying to overrun us. I hit "transmit" on my radio and called out in plain English: "Fire Mission—Uniform Sierra (U.S. forces) in contact! We need help NOW!"

A voice responded immediately: "This is Perky Bear Hotel." I knew from the call sign that I was talking to a Swift Boat somewhere, but the voice seemed strange. Was it a VC with our radio frequency? I asked the "voice" to identify, and again I heard, "Perky Bear Hotel." I asked again:

"Goddamn it, give me your name," I screamed. "Who are you—in the clear, now!"

"I'm a Swift Boat," Perky Bear answered.

"Roger, Copy," I replied, finally satisfied. "Fire mission, fire mission!" I passed along target coordinates.

But nothing happened. The VC pressed the attack. Vietnamese Army artillery at Thanh Phu headquarters was holding them off, firing on enemy mortar positions and at the infantry trying to reach the outpost. But then suddenly, in the light from a Vietnamese star shell, I spotted a new wave of VC coming at us on the right. I called Thanh Phu for help, but they were too busy to hit a new target. We seemed to be out of options.

Then, like the answer to a prayer, the radio crackled and Perky Bear Hotel came back on the air. They were ready to fire. I sent them the new target. The first rounds landed in the middle of the VC flanking attack, disrupting it and slowing them down. "Target correct," I radioed. "Fire for effect."

"Rounds on the way," replied Perky Bear. Right on the money. I could smell the cordite drifting over the outpost.

"Shift, LEFT FIVE ZERO" (50 yards left), I radioed next, and we began walking the rounds across the VC, then back to the right, then directly toward me. The VC assault faltered, resumed, and ultimately dissolved into several piecemeal attacks. Perky Bear called in that he was out of HE (high explosive) rounds. "Shoot Willy Pete (white phosphorus incendiary rounds)," I said. After a few of these, I radioed "danger close" and walked his mortar rounds practically to the outpost wire.

South Vietnamese troop encampment.
COURTESY OF LARRY IRWIN

At that point, the explosions stopped. Perky Bear came back on the radio. He had a problem, he said, and had to stop firing: "We've done all we can, and we've got to leave." But they had done enough. The effect was devastating. Scattered VC elements came closer, but the M-60 and the RF-PFs stalled and eventually broke the attack. We had held them off, losing three dead and thirteen wounded. ARVN intelligence later estimated a VC battalion of between 400 and 500 troops had attacked us.

I never forgot that night. I served six more months in Thanh Phu and then came home, became a civilian, and went to work for the U.S. Department of Agriculture—but An Hoa for me was always unfinished business. I needed to know who had saved my life and those of the RF-PFs that were with me. I attended Navy meetings and reunions, polled other Navy buddies from Cat Lo, and looked for an after-action report, but I could never find a trace of Perky Bear Hotel or its crew.

In June 1995, I took my twenty-six-year-old daughter, Raye Leigh, to Washington, D.C., for the dedication of PCF 1, to be put on permanent exhibit at the National Museum of the U.S. Navy. The ceremonies and reunion lasted three days, ending on Father's Day. Raye Leigh and I had breakfast that last morning with several Swift Boat sailors, including Wey Symmes and Bill "Hot Dog" Franke, whom I had never met. Franke, as a young ensign, had served as Officer-in-Charge of PCF 56, and Wey was his radarman and leading petty officer.

I asked my usual question about a Thanh Phu fire mission and, as usual, got nothing but blank stares. But when I said "Perky Bear," Wey turned to Bill and asked, "Didn't we do one patrol just before we went to An Thoi?" An Thoi was another Swift Boat base. "Remember that time a round got stuck in the mortar tube?" Bill seemed to recall something like that. And yes, that was the night someone under attack was calling for fire support. "And the guy on the radio kept yelling at me to identify myself."

We compared notes. I went out to my car and got an old map. I showed it to them. They weren't sure where they had been, but they remembered being warned about a collapsed bridge in the narrow waterway leading into the rice paddies, and the bridge was on the map.

It was them. I knew nothing about them, except that they had saved my life, and they knew nothing about me—a disembodied voice on the radio fighting a battle they could hear, but couldn't see. A cascade of emotions and memories came rushing back.

"What took you so long to open fire?" I asked. I had always thought they were north of us on the Ham Luong River, within easy range of our outpost.

But they weren't, they explained. They were on the Co Chien River to the south, and had to drive the boat more than six klicks up the waterway to get to a place where they could reach the VC with their mortar. And leaving the main river at night violated Standing Orders from Cat Lo. This may have been why Bill, an ensign on his first patrol, didn't file an after-action report.

They had to tiptoe into the canal because another boat had told them about the bridge: "If you go balls to the wall, you'll hit it and kill the whole crew," Wey had told Bill. On the way in, they crashed through a log barrier, dodged fishnets, backed out after taking a wrong turn, and then, finally, found a firing position. And everything went fine until the mortar round got stuck in the tube. There was nothing you could do about that. They had to get back to Co Chien before the VC found them. They did not know they had come in through the same infiltration route the VC had used to get in position for their attack.

We finished breakfast and rose to leave. Raye Leigh turned to Bill and Wey. "Thanks for giving me my Daddy," she said. She was born in Texas three weeks after the battle at An Hoa.

Bow Gunner

Joe Muharsky

Radarman Second Class Joe Muharsky spent most of his two years in Vietnam aboard Swift Boats and a destroyer. He left the Navy in 1969 and moved to Mentor, Ohio, where he owned his own air-conditioning business.

EARLY IN 1969, THE SQUADRON ASKED FOR CREWS TO VOLUNTEER FOR duty in Coastal Division 11. Swift Boats had begun raiding enemy strongholds in the rivers and canals of the Ca Mau Peninsula at the southernmost tip of Vietnam. We were bored up north, and river patrols sounded like challenging work. We all voted yes. I heard later that after a while, when "challenging" turned into "dangerous," volunteering ceased to be an option. I could understand that. We were there for the transition.

We had never trained for the rivers. Up in Da Nang we had rain forests and green highlands, but in the Lower Mekong Delta there was swamp, mangrove, and a maze of dirty brown waterways, large and small. Charlie controlled all of it.

At battle stations I manned an M-60 machine gun in the bow of the boat, standing in the anchor locker so I could sweep the M-60 from side to side. The bow gunner was the first person the bad guys saw when a boat came into their territory, and most crews rotated the bow gunner so everyone shared the risk. We didn't rotate, which didn't particularly bother me. Bow gunner was my job.

I don't remember how many rounds were in a belt of 7.62mm machine gun ammo, but it wasn't enough. I got extra ammo boxes and linked 3,500 rounds together in each of two tubs—one for the port side aft and one for the starboard side forward. The M-60 fed from the left, so I'd start with the port tub, and if I had to swing the gun to fire to starboard I could flip the latch and switch belts to the starboard tub. Besides 7,000 rounds of M-60, I had an M-16 at hand with 20 clips of 20 rounds each, a twelve-gauge Remington pump shotgun with double-ought shot, an M-79 grenade launcher, and a .38-caliber Smith & Wesson revolver strapped to my belt. Shoulder-fired rockets were also available.

We had a few firefights, which got us accustomed to the Delta war, or so I thought. Then came the patrols of March 7 and 8, 1969. We were in PCF 5, the middle boat of a three-boat convoy. Our job on March 7 was to pick up some Cambodian mercenaries that the CIA was supposedly paying eight dollars a month to fight for us. We were going to put them ashore where they could find and kill VC.

We entered the mouth of the Bay Hap River on the north side of a large bay emptying into the Gulf of Thailand, right at the southwestern tip of South Vietnam. The river runs west to east and parallel to the Cua Lon River, a much larger tidal estuary that cuts the tip of the Delta at the south side of the bay. We picked up the mercenaries at a village along the Bai Hap along with their two Green Beret advisors—a crusty old sergeant who had spent multiple tours in Vietnam and a lieutenant. The sergeant rode with us. We dropped the troops and the Green Berets off at various points during the day and waited for them while they hunted Charlie.

Nothing much happened, so we proceeded farther along the Bai Hap. I didn't know exactly where we were going, but I didn't like it at all when we turned hard right and headed due south into a tiny canal. Once in the canal we couldn't turn around, even if we had to. We were on a one-way trip to the Cua Lon through enemy-held jungle, with no turning back.

The north end of the canal must have once been a creek. Mangroves brushed the boat as we twisted our way south at idle speed. I could feel my heart pounding in my toes. It seemed like we were there for an eternity before the creek finally opened up into the man-made Cai Nap Canal—a straight shot heading due south as far as the eye could see. We continued to creep along until we spotted a small village of straw huts on the canal's left bank. As we got closer we could see some animals and fresh cooking fires—but no people. Charlie was there, and he obviously knew we were there. One thing I had learned very early was that Swift Boats don't sneak through the jungle. With two General Motors 12V71 diesel engines, even dead slow, you might as well be riding a Greyhound bus.

We were right next to the village when Charlie shot a B-40 rocket from trees bordering a large open field on the opposite side of the canal. The rocket didn't make it to the water; it slid in the mud and exploded on the canal bank, just missing the lead boat. We beached the convoy in front of the trees and raked the area with automatic weapons. Our engineman caught a piece of shrapnel in the biceps of his arm. We thought it was an accident—one of the Cambodians firing an M-79 grenade too close to the boat. Then there were no more rockets and no more shooting. We waited for a bit, then turned our boats around and beached them next to the village. We wasted it with flare guns and automatic weapons, burning it to the ground.

We reached the Cua Lon and headed to a Coast Guard cutter waiting offshore to put us up for the night. Sometime during the day we had taken two suspected VC prisoners—a man in his twenties and an older woman. Neither had papers. That night the Green Berets interrogated the young man on the fantail of the cutter while many of us watched. When he proved unresponsive, the Green Berets hooked a blasting cap detonator to his ears, dumped a bucket of water on him, and shot 2½ amps of current at 60 volts through his head. His body shot into the air every time they did this. Then he shuddered, went limp, and fell to the deck.

Looking back on it now I am saddened that I had no feeling for him at the time. I guess I had taught myself not to feel. Our unit had a casualty rate over 80 percent at that moment, and I think it hurt too much to dwell on it, so we just numbed out. I am not proud of what happened, but I am not ashamed either. The poor bastard was caught in the middle. If he didn't sympathize with the Viet Cong they would kill him; if he did, we would kill him. That's the way it was. Later I could put myself in his shoes and wonder what I would have done to feed and protect my family, but I was nineteen then, and not much given to wondering about anything.

The bow gunner was the most exposed person on the boat. Placing machine guns up forward was not formally authorized. When Swift Boats began patrolling rivers and canals, Swift Boat sailors "found" M-60 machine guns and mounted them on the bow as well as on port and starboard sides of the aft deck.
COURTESY OF JOE MUHARSKY

I don't know whether the prisoner had anything to do with our orders for the next day, but our first reaction when we heard them was, "Are you shitting me?" We were supposed to return to the Cai Nap and play a PSYOPS propaganda tape that told the VC that we were really good guys and that they should come over to our side. Fat chance. I wondered whether the REMF (that's Vietnam-speak for "Rear-Echelon Mother-Fucker") who cut the orders had any idea what we had left behind the day before.

Our engineman had required surgery to remove the shrapnel in his arm, and when I saw the sling he was wearing that morning I knew that he wouldn't be going with us that day. Instead we took a tall friendly guy with us who had only three days to go before he went home. His name was Poole. I never learned his first name, but he knew what he was doing. His job as a fantail gunner was to handle the Honeywell grenade launcher, so named because it resembled an old, boxlike Honeywell movie camera, except it shot grenades instead of film. You turned the crank, and it could spit out thirty-two grenades before the first one hit the ground.

Our wounded engineman and the coasties watched from the cutter deck above us as we loaded up all the ammo we could possibly get on board. The cutter was leaving station that day, so we had to take our prisoners with us. We chained the young man to a fantail stanchion and let the woman sit wherever she wanted. We did all of this in silence. I can't speak for the other two crews, but I know our crew had a bad feeling about this patrol. Even though no one said a word, the glancing looks we gave each other told me that everyone was thinking the same thing.

We were supposed to run the Cai Nap south to north this time, and we reached the Cua Lon in late afternoon. Before we could do anything else, we spotted a VC flag flying from a brick kiln on the riverbank. Charlie had a habit of booby-trapping these little monuments in hope some fool would stop to collect a souvenir. Instead, we blew up the kiln with a trigger-fired 81mm mortar round. Then the Green Beret sergeant and the lieutenant went ashore and blew up other nearby kilns with grenades.

Doing all this took time. It was well after 1700 hours now, and we needed to get to the Cai Nap. We didn't make it. I remember scanning back and forth across the bow, looking for movement—a twig, a leaf, anything that didn't look quite right. I was searching straight ahead when the starboard fantail of the lead boat exploded. A recoilless rifle round blew the starboard engine hatch—a door-sized piece of aluminum—about ten feet into the air, and the engineman along with it. Fortunately, he came down on the deck, badly injured but alive. Then all hell broke loose. All three PCFs were taking heavy enemy fire from both sides of the river. Rockets, recoilless rifles, small arms, and heavy machine gun fire rained down. We kept moving at full speed, about 30 knots, but they didn't stop shooting, and neither did we. Whalen's .50-caliber machine guns boomed from the gun tub over the pilothouse, deafening me almost immediately and making my head feel like it was going to explode.

Mangroves grew thick along the Cua Lon and the enemy was well hidden. I just sprayed the riverbank, hoping to hit something or someone. It did no good to crouch down, as there was no armor on a Swift Boat. I remember seeing one enemy soldier stand up and fire a recoilless round. I pointed my machine gun at him and put him down, but he got his shot off. I noted how I could actually see the rocket coming at us, not in any great detail but as a fast-moving blur. It dipped just before it got to the boat, hit the water and ricocheted over top of us.

Then something else, either another recoilless round or a B-40 rocket, flew in right over my head at a 45-degree angle, punching straight through the center of the pilothouse windshield. It passed between Potter, who was on the helm, and Lt. (j.g.) Salinas and flew out the port door without exploding. These types of duds happened fairly frequently—Charlie's rockets were intended as antitank weapons, and glass windshields and quarter-inch aluminum Swift Boats didn't always provide enough resistance to arm the explosive. Potter was lifted out of his seat by the concussion, but recovered in time to keep the boat from going aground. He drove by looking through the windshield hole, all while wiping away the blood that ran down his face from the glass that was embedded in it.

We lucked out again a short time later when another large round of some sort hit the starboard side of the main cabin, punched through the freezer, came out the refrigerator door, and ricocheted off a fire extinguisher—and didn't explode. So much for the beer we had on ice. Several bullets also found their mark on PCF 5, but so far no one was hit. The boat was beginning to look like Swiss cheese.

By this time my M-60 was getting hot. I started to notice from the tracers that the bullets were no longer traveling in a straight line. The rifling in the barrel was wearing out. Then the gun jammed. I threw open the bail, removed the belt, and banged the stock of my M-60 on deck until both rounds came out. I put the belt back in and started firing again. After a few hundred more rounds, I had another jam. I fixed it, shot some more, and jammed again. Eventually I noticed I had broken the gunstock and that the tracers were looking more like Roman candles, spraying balls of fire in curved arcs that went in every direction. The M-60 had burned out. I grabbed my M-16 and started to fire away with that. I remember thinking how it felt like a BB gun, but at least it shot straight and didn't jam. I knew, however, that 400 rounds were not going to last long, so I saved some and started firing 40mm grenades with my handheld M-79 launcher.

Whalen was firing his twin .50s over my head and Coates had a single .50 on the fantail. Hot brass pooled on deck around the chained prisoner, burning the hell out of his legs. Poole was cranking the Honeywell so fast that he ran out of ammo. The old woman saw this, and she jumped down to the main cabin and rummaged around until she found some rounds for Poole. She carried them up and started feeding him the belts. I guess it didn't matter to her who was who at that point. She just wanted to see her family again.

Then another recoilless round hit the boat. And again it didn't explode. But we'd run out of luck. The round plowed into the aft edge of the main cabin on the starboard side, turning part of the aluminum bulkhead into a hail of shrapnel. A big chunk hit Poole just below the left eye and sliced off a large piece of his face. Coates grabbed Poole just as he was about to fall over the side of the boat. Then, as Poole fell back on deck, he was shot in the leg. He was bleeding badly, but Coates had to go back to his gun. The Green Beret sergeant put his M-16 down, opened a battle dressing, and tied it around Poole's leg. Next, he straddled Poole and bandaged his face. Then he unchained the VC prisoner and made him stand up in the middle of the firefight holding a bottle of plasma while he rigged an IV for Poole.

We endured this for eleven minutes at 30 knots, an extraordinarily long time for a river firefight that covered about six klicks of riverbank on both sides. Intel later estimated that a large enemy force was lying in ambush for us. No shit? Probably an analysis performed by the same REMF who thought up the operation.

Finally the shooting stopped. Lieutenant Salinas stuck his head out of the pilothouse door and looked me over: "Are you hit?"

I couldn't hear him very well because of broken eardrums, but I knew what he had asked: "No," I said. "Is everybody okay?"

"No, get ready to go ashore," he replied. "The 38-Boat is sinking."

Again I felt my heart pound. I now knew the difference between fear and terror. Fear is when you almost get run over by a car and your heart races for a moment, but once the car misses you, it's over. Terror is when the fear has already gripped you for eleven minutes and you know it may get worse. My body tingled with adrenaline. We were not far beyond the ambush, and we had to beach the boats. Was Charlie waiting there, too? Did they know how badly we were hit, and would they double-time it to our position so they could finish us off? By now it was getting dark, which made it even harder to tell what was going on.

I was running on training and instinct now. As we beached the boats, I jumped down into the mud of the riverbank and took up a defensive position with my M-16 and M-79. I didn't know what else to do, so I waited. A few minutes passed, and nothing happened. I climbed back aboard.

"Hey Ski, come here," the sergeant yelled. "I need a shoelace."

I handed him the lace from my right boot and he wrapped it around Poole's leg as a tourniquet. Poole was on morphine now and wasn't crying out in pain anymore. He was staring blankly through his right eye, the only part of his face that showed through the bandages. Some of the mercenaries were also hit, but I didn't pay much attention to them. I was worried about our crew and the crews on the other boats.

Once our situation stabilized I went to see if I could help the others. On the 38-Boat a large-caliber VC bullet had punctured the .50-caliber gun mount and taken off the heel of the gunner's foot. He kept shooting until his crewmates pulled him out of the tub and laid him on the pilothouse deck. The 38-Boat had its windshield scarred by VC rocket fire or bullets, but the helmsman had the presence of mind to blow it out from the inside with an M-16 so he could see to drive. All this while he coped with a sliver of shrapnel in his ass.

MEDEVAC choppers were coming, and so was an airstrike to hit the ambush site. We had to go back the same way we came in. We had a lot of wounded, but not all of them would receive MEDEVAC. If you could fight, you were coming with us. We needed everybody who could shoot a weapon.

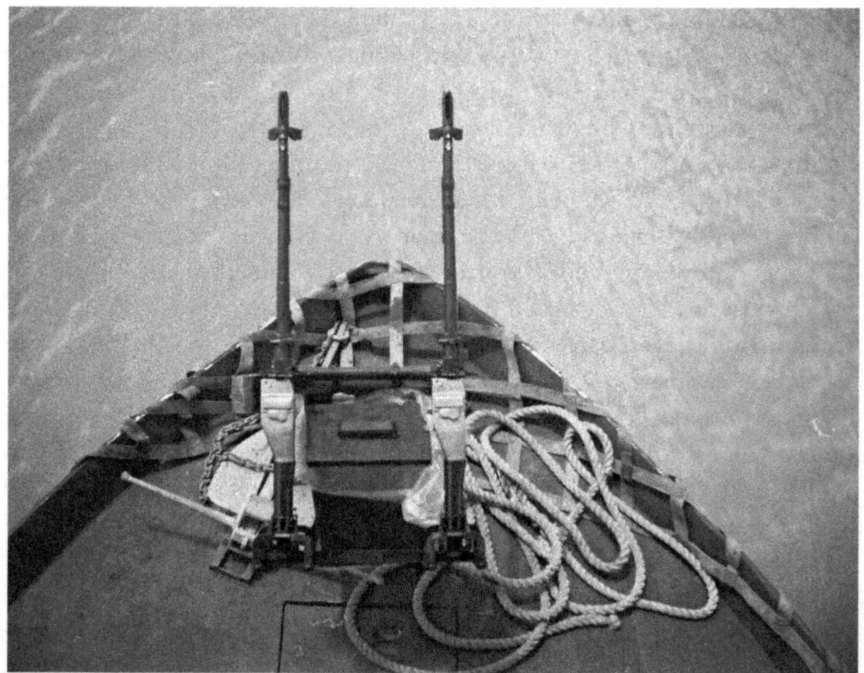

Twin mount of M-60 machine guns.
COURTESY OF JOE MUHARSKY

When I returned to the 5-Boat I decided to knock out our windshield so Potter could see. Instead of an M-16, I used the tool we had for cleaning the mortar—a long metal pole with a steel weight on it. The windshield wouldn't budge, and there was so much spent brass from my M-60 rolling around that I kept slipping and falling. Coates got a broom and started sweeping shells over the side while I bashed away until I was gasping for air. It never broke, but finally it popped inward and landed inside the pilothouse. I threw it over the side.

Everyone on board was busy doing something when the leader of the airstrike called us on the radio, so I took the call. He was sorry, he told me, but "something more urgent has come up and we won't be able to help you out."

"What the fuck is it, the Third World War?" I asked. My heart was hammering again, and my mind was racing until another nearby explosion, oddly enough, settled me down. Time to pay attention again. The next noise was the unmistakable sound of the rotor blades. Slicks had arrived to take our wounded. It's a sound that anybody who ever served in Vietnam will never forget.

I helped carry Poole's stretcher. It was a considerable distance to the choppers and I could hear the pilots screaming at us: "Come on, come on, come on. Get 'em on board!" I was a little pissed. What the hell did they think we were doing out there, having a picnic?

But if you were walking in their shoes, things would look different. They were sitting ducks, either on the ground or hovering. They needed to do their work and get out as fast as they could. We owed them big time. We loaded Poole on the chopper. I put my hand out and he raised his. We clenched fists. "Hang in there, buddy," I said. It was the last time I saw him. I know he survived because years later when I looked for his name on the Wall I couldn't find it.

If my memory serves, ten of the eighteen crewmembers on our three boats were wounded. Those of us who were able climbed aboard the boats and headed south. It was pitch black, and Potter was steering by radar. My body was quivering. I didn't know how far we had to go to get back to the ambush, and I couldn't see anything. We kept going. No shooting.

Then I saw it—could it be? Yes, it was the faint silhouette of the bay where the Cua Lon emptied into the Gulf of Thailand. A few more minutes and we were clear. My fear began to drop away. I could hear nothing but silence and feel nothing but survival.

Duong Keo

Virgil Erwin and Peter N. Upton

Lt. Virgil Erwin left the Navy after Vietnam and retired to San Diego after a career in sales and marketing. He is the author of Cat Lo—A Memoir of Invisible Youth, *which details his experiences as the skipper of PCF 67 and the years following his service as he struggled to integrate back into civilian life.*

Lt. (j.g.) Peter N. Upton left the Navy in 1969, graduated from Boston University Law School in 1973 and returned to the Navy as an attorney. He later went into private practice and opened his own personal-injury firm in central Connecticut in 2004.

WE MUST LOOK LIKE AN ARMADA, LT. VIRGIL ERWIN THOUGHT. THIRTEEN Swift Boats rising and falling in ocean swells alongside the mother ship, the USS *Westchester County*, an LST. She was anchored off the Ca Mau Peninsula at the southernmost tip of Vietnam. The Ca Mau was south of the Mekong Delta, a sweltering tidal swamp crisscrossed with rivers and canals and cloaked in low-lying jungle. It was enemy country. About ten miles from where Erwin stood was the mouth of the Duong Keo River, a nasty little estuary punched into the bottom of the Ca Mau. Intel had reported a heavy-weapons company of Viet Cong guerrillas there, probably augmented by North Vietnamese regulars—seventy-five men or more.

The plan was to raid the Duong Keo that afternoon with 240 marines from the Vietnamese 6th Battalion. The first five boats would drop their marines at the river mouth while the rest of the boats headed upriver and landed theirs. Then the upriver marines would sweep downriver to converge with their mates downriver, trapping the enemy in between. The boats would provide gunfire support and guard the river mouth while Seawolf helicopters blocked a backdoor escape. The Navy called it Operation Silvermace II. It was April 12, 1969.

Erwin, the Officer-in-Charge of PCF 67, watched twenty Vietnamese marines come aboard his boat and look around for someplace to sit without being in the way. Erwin had never been on an op with more than three Swifts. And now thirteen?

"Not a lucky number," said Erwin's bow gunner.

"Should be twelve," Erwin said. "The 43-Boat wasn't scheduled to join us."

Erwin could see Lt. Don Droz, the skipper of PCF 43, arguing with Captain Hoffmann, the Squadron Commander, telling him his boat was okay. But his boat wasn't okay. It was tired, and it needed an overhaul. Captain Hoffmann had decreed that every boat "must be able to maintain 20 knots." Erwin doubted whether Droz could manage it.

But Don was winning the argument. To bolster his case, Underwater Demolition Team 13—ten U.S. Navy frogmen—had gone aboard PCF 43, along with 800 pounds of C-4 explosive, good for blowing up enemy bunkers and ammo dumps. Erwin thought the UDT should have chosen another boat, but maybe Don had encouraged them. Captain Hoffmann had worked with Don in Cam Ranh Bay and Erwin figured he must like Don's professional gusto.

"All right, goddamn it, you can go," Erwin overheard Captain Hoffmann telling Don. "But you drop the UDT guys at the first insertion—then you get the hell out of that river."

Lt. (j.g.) Peter N. Upton, second-in-command of the UDT team, went aboard PCF 43 in midafternoon. He was focused on getting his C-4 secured and settling his men on the fantail for what he knew would be an extremely dangerous trip. Charlie was there in force. They were pros, and they would be waiting.

The boats left the LST at 1630, and an hour later the flotilla gathered about 1,000 yards off the mouth of the Duong Keo, where they formed up in a single column. Upton had his men put on their flak gear and take up battle stations along the periphery of PCF 43's fantail. The boats were supposed to travel fast, but they were all so overloaded that the most they could manage was 15 knots.

Erwin was third in line. It was going to be tricky navigating the shallows and avoiding sandbars at the river mouth. The column slowed, and then slowed again until the boats were just creeping forward. Erwin's nerves were on edge. What a great time for the VC to hit us, he thought—we're groping like blind men with canes, trying to find a way in.

"Lead boat hit a sandbar," said Erwin's twin fifties' gunner, sitting high up in the gun tub. "Next one too."

Now Erwin's was the lead boat. The helmsman picked his way delicately into a wide S-turn and found a channel. "Water just got deeper," he told Erwin. "Twenty feet, now twenty-five, still getting deeper. We're in." Erwin watched the riverbank carefully. Charlie usually hits the second or third boat in line, he thought. Never the first . . . right?

"This is Dipsy-Doodle," the radio suddenly squawked. "First five boats, beach—port side."

"Who's Dipsy-Doodle?" the helmsman asked.

Dipsy-Doodle was Yost, the Officer-in-Tactical-Command of the operation. "Coast Guard commander," Erwin said. "He's a newbie, still cherry. He's on the 31-Boat." All the Swift Boat skippers and crews were veterans of river ops. It seemed strange to Erwin that Dipsy-Doodle, with only a week in-country, would be leading a raid as elaborate as this—and doing it with uncoded messages.

The helmsman spun the wheel and Erwin's boat plowed into the mud on the port side of the river. Four other boats beached, and the marines on all five jumped from the bows, ran to the edge of the tree line, and set up a defensive perimeter. Other marines crossed the clearing and crawled into the woods. No gunfire.

Erwin began to relax, watching as the eight upriver Swift Boats passed by, churning the chocolate-colored water. PCF 43 was last in line, already struggling to keep up. Don had either forgotten, or was simply ignoring, Captain Hoffmann's orders to drop off the UDT guys and get out of the river.

The Viet Cong had plenty of warning that a Swift Boat incursion was coming their way. If the noise hadn't tipped them off, Dipsy-Doodle's messages in the clear left no doubt. And they were ready. About five klicks upriver Charlie had prepared an interlaced network of freshly built bunkers, trenches, and spider hole emplacements buried almost out of sight in thick mangroves. This was their kill zone. Their plan was to trap as many boats as they could in it.

The ambush opened with the explosion of Claymore mines aimed at the lead boat. A fusillade of rocket, recoilless rifle, machine gun, and small-arms fire followed. Every boat in the column was hit immediately, and every boat took casualties. But with an arsenal of .50-caliber and M-60 machine guns, along with more than 150 marines and U.S. Navy crewmen armed with automatic rifles, the boats weathered the initial attack and cleared the kill zone, speeding upstream at full throttle.

All except PCF 43. Upton, on the fantail with his UDT team, immediately saw their predicament. The 43-Boat had just entered the kill zone when the lead boat broke free, closely followed by the other six boats. It was obvious to Upton that PCF 43 didn't have the juice. Suddenly they found themselves relatively alone, isolated in the center of the ambush.

Viet Cong gunners raked the boat with B-40 rockets and AK-47s at nearly point-blank range. One rocket exploded on the fantail, instantly killing the UDT's hospital corpsman. Two other team members were wounded with shrapnel and a third had his helmet knocked off by a shell fragment. A fourth was shot in the leg, causing a clean but gaping wound. Upton had shrapnel wounds in his upper body. He was bleeding, but not seriously hurt.

Then he saw another rocket explode in the pilothouse. The helmsman was knocked unconscious and lost control of the wheel. The boat careened out of control and smacked into the north bank of the river, high and dry in the mangroves, directly in front of the Viet Cong emplacements. Don Droz was dead.

Erwin, marking time downriver, heard the ambush as a set of distant explosions and crackling gunfire. Then came more explosions and constant gunfire. The radio erupted with screaming and high-pitched voices all trying to talk at once. Someone keyed a microphone, but machine gun fire in the background made it impossible to understand the caller. The voice tried again.

"You hear that?" asked Erwin's leading petty officer. "What's happening?"

"Quiet!" Erwin said. "Someone's trying to get through." A boat was calling for help but the signal was weak. Twice he heard "the 43-Boat." No one answered.

"Christ, am I the only one who can hear this?" Erwin made a decision. "Let's go, get 'er underway!" PCF 67 backed into the river and headed upstream at full speed, accompanied by PCF 103.

"Dipsy-Doodle, this is Seawolf 14," radioed one of the Seawolf pilots. "We're orbiting overhead."

"Seawolf 14, this is Dipsy-Doodle. We have some wounded. I want you to MEDEVAC my wounded."

"This is Seawolf 14—we're heavy. We'll have to unload our rockets before we can take on any wounded."

"This is Dipsy-Doodle. Uh . . . understand. Just unload 'em anywhere north of the river."

It was the classic Seawolf trade-off, and Erwin immediately understood that Dipsy-Doodle didn't get it. Seawolves were gunships. They could MEDEVAC two wounded men—three if they left a door gunner on the beach—but they had to get rid of their ammo before they could take passengers. The preferred way to do this was to shoot it at the enemy. Dipsy-Doodle had two Seawolf gunships with rockets and mini-guns on top of the ambush site, but didn't order the airstrike.

On the 43-Boat, catastrophe had produced momentary shock. The remainder of Upton's UDT team and the PCF crewmen had run aground directly in front of the biggest enemy ambush any of them had ever seen. Fortunately, the VC seemed equally amazed, because their attack faltered, giving the 43-Boat survivors invaluable minutes to get organized. Lieutenant Lomas, the UDT team leader, ran to the pilothouse to check on Droz and call for help. A shot of morphine and a battle dressing stabilized Lomas's leg wound. The shrapnel cuts were ignored. To get out of this, the survivors had to fight.

Upton organized a defensive perimeter. Grounding had canted the boat over on its side, making it impossible to use the .50-caliber machine guns. This was bad, but by presenting its hull to the enemy, PCF 43 gave the defenders welcome cover. This was good. Three UDTs crouched on the fantail and maintained constant M-79 grenade fire into the mangroves that hid the enemy. PCF crewmen covered the south bank with M-16s. Two other UDTs took an M-60 machine gun and set up a firing position about thirty feet away from the derelict Swift Boat, using it for cover.

During the prolonged firefight that followed, the survivors had an unforeseen edge. They were out in the open, visible and ostensibly vulnerable, while the enemy was concealed in camouflaged redoubts. This configuration, typical in river engagements, gave the VC the first-shot advantage in slam-bang firefights, but in a pitched battle like this one the balance shifted. The VC had to be very careful that their grenades didn't detonate in the foliage overhanging their own positions. Rockets and recoilless rifles couldn't be used at all. Out in the open the defenders didn't have to worry. They could use everything they had.

And they did. The two sides dueled with hand grenades at a distance of twenty yards. There was plenty of ammo for the M-60 and the M-16s. Enemy fire, though continuous, was relatively ineffective. One UDT member at the M-60 was seriously wounded from an enemy grenade, but a UDT grenade exploded in an enemy spider hole. The defenders, highly trained and experienced, kept a sustained volume of fire on the ambush site for a half-hour, and then longer. The enemy never risked a frontal assault.

Upton soon began to wonder about rescue. Where in almighty hell were the other boats? Rockets had destroyed PCF 43's radio beyond repair and the backup PRC-25 portable didn't have enough power to break through the rest of the urgent traffic on the net.

Downriver, Erwin heard another garbled message on the radio: "50 cal . . . one mile . . . high and dry . . . over."

"This is Dipsy-Doodle—understand one mile from this position," Yost said over the radio. "Which way, and what is it? Over."

The other voice crackled again, unintelligible to Erwin.

"This is Dipsy-Doodle—understand we have the 43-Boat, one mile back, high and dry, is that correct? Over."

"Affirmative," the other voice said.

"Okay, we'll send someone back to tow her out."

Erwin and PCF 103 were minutes from the ambush. A B-40 rocket exploded in the river just behind them, and Erwin's aft .50 gunner opened up. Erwin picked up the radio transmitter: "Dipsy-Doodle, this is six-seven with the one-oh-three. We'll be there in two minutes."

"Six-seven and one-oh-three," Dipsy-Doodle replied, "return and pick up your marines, then come upriver. Insert them short of the ambush."

What? Erwin was astounded. Don was in trouble and Erwin could help. Following this order was wrong. But PCF 103 had already turned around, and discipline in battle was paramount. Erwin ordered his own helmsman to come about. He knew he would live always with the memory of accepting an order that should have been ignored, and that he would always feel guilty for being grateful.

One of the Seawolves came up on the radio: "Fifties, fifties, quad-fifties. Jesus, we're taking fifties!"

"Dipsy-Doodle, this is Seawolf 16," a calmer voice said. "We're taking fire—request permission to unload in that area."

"This is Dipsy-Doodle—we have a boat high and dry, one mile back. Can you provide cover?"

"This is Seawolf 16, roger, I see him—I'm over him now." Crosstalk between Seawolf 16 and another pilot followed. "Okay, let's hose 'em down," one of the pilots said. The sound of miniguns echoed over Erwin's head. Finally.

Upriver, the boats had been badly mauled by Claymores, rockets, and .51-caliber heavy machine guns. On PCF 5, the lead boat, Claymores had decapitated one Vietnamese Marine and cut the legs from another just below the pelvis. A B-40 rocket penetrated the hull of PCF 51, the second boat, as if it were tinfoil, shrapnel exploding in the engine room. The next two boats also took B-40s, and the bow gunners of the next two boats were both shot. Despite the casualties the boats were able to stay together and protect one another as they cleared the ambush.

Only PCF 38, the seventh boat, saw PCF 43 lurch into the kill zone and stall. Tom Gilbert, the 38-Boat's O-in-C, turned around to go help him, but two B-40s hit the boat almost immediately, one in the main cabin, one in the engine room. Steering was lost, the port engine was destroyed, and the rudder was jammed left. Gilbert was wounded, but managed to reach the aft steering controls. The crew tied a tourniquet around his ankle, and he drove out of the ambush once again, with one throttle and jury-rigged steering. It was Gilbert's boat that had tried to summon help over the radio.

Erwin listened to the radio traffic as his boat and PCF 103 raced back to the river mouth to pick up their marines. Dipsy-Doodle was trying to organize a rescue for Don's boat and asked PCF 5 and the skipper of another boat to go back.

"Need a minute," said the O-in-C of PCF 5. He was trying to get his dead and wounded MEDEVACed. The second O-in-C declined—his boat had so many wounded that he didn't have sufficient personnel to man the guns.

Erwin and PCF 103 beached their boats again. His marines were sitting in a large circle, eating bowls of rice. Supper.

"Get aboard, now! Now!" Erwin yelled. They barely looked up, and continued eating. The American marine advisor leaned toward his Vietnamese counterpart. The marines won't move without a direct order from their senior officer, the advisor said. The senior officer was upriver with Dipsy-Doodle.

"Well, call him, goddamn it, call him!" Erwin yelled.

Other boats called Dipsy-Doodle, but the marines wouldn't move. Twenty minutes had elapsed since Dipsy-Doodle ordered Erwin to come about, and Erwin's mood was turning into bitter resentment.

Finally PCF 5 reported getting underway, headed back to help Don.

"Wait," Dipsy-Doodle said over the radio. "I don't want you to go alone."

Upton watched PCF 5 and PCF 31, with Dipsy-Doodle aboard, reenter the kill zone, coming toward them with guns blazing. It was almost dusk, and the 43-Boat's defenders had been under attack for nearly an hour. PCF 31 maneuvered into position adjacent to the wreckage and began loading the dead and wounded. PCF 5 stood off, pouring machine gun fire on the enemy positions. Finally they escaped.

Downriver, Erwin heard Dipsy-Doodle report that they had recovered the wounded from Droz's boat. He needed a MEDEVAC.

"Dipsy-Doodle, this is Dread Advice," said a voice over the radio. "Where do you want me to put down?"

"Come along my port side," Dipsy-Doodle replied.

Oh no, Erwin thought. Dread Advice was a MEDEVAC chopper, not a boat. It needed a landing zone. Dipsy-Doodle had no idea who he was talking to. Fortunately, one of the Swift Boat skippers took over to coordinate the evacuation.

Suddenly, a new voice boomed over the radio, "This is Latch." Latch was Captain Hoffmann. He was aboard one of the Seawolves. At last, adult supervision, Erwin thought. Dipsy-Doodle told Latch he wanted to retreat to the LST. Latch did not agree. PCF 43 was on fire with 800 pounds of C-4 aboard. Don't go near PCF 43. Maybe spend the night in the river? Dipsy-Doodle suggested. "That's right," Latch said. All the casualties had been evacuated, and there was nothing left to do but nurse damaged boats and cope with the psychological consequences of defeat. Hard jobs, both of them, but they could be handled on the Duong Keo for a night.

Twenty minutes later the 43-Boat blew up. When it ran aground the engines were still running, and in the melee no one ever shut off the ignition. Without cooling water the engines ran hotter and hotter until a fire started in the engine room. It was only a question of time before the C-4, the unexploded mortar rounds, the .50-caliber ammo, and the diesel fuel erupted in an explosion that sent flame, smoke, and metal fragments shooting more than 500 feet into the air.

It was a hard night. Upton, upriver with the rest of the 43-Boat survivors, slept fitfully, unable to shed his memories. Downriver, Erwin stared at his marines, wondering how they could be so nonchalant about the day's happenings. This is their country, he thought. I wonder if they care who wins this war, and if they don't care, why should I?

Erwin and his four companion boats got underway just after dawn, finally heading upriver to assist their damaged brethren. As they entered the previous day's kill zone, he saw the melted aluminum skeleton of PCF 43 lying on its side, frames and keel like the ribs and backbone of a beached whale. The marines were sifting the ambush site, looking for bodies.

Above the ambush, the remaining seven upriver boats huddled together. Erwin pulled alongside PCF 51, which had lost both engines from a rocket in the stern. Another rocket in the main cabin had blown out all the windows. The boat was a mess. The 51-Boat skipper, pale and pinch-faced, told Erwin his helmsman was dead. Erwin told him he had seen the remains of PCF 43. "Droz was killed," the 51-Boat skipper said. He turned away. Eventually, the crippled boats formed a column and crept out of the Duong Keo. Erwin and another boat towed PCF 51.

That afternoon, Captain Hoffmann assembled the officers in the LST wardroom to give everyone a chance to speak his piece. When his turn came, Erwin started to describe his frustration with the marines, but he was interrupted.

"I already understand why that happened," Yost said.

The meeting ended then, and the O-in-Cs filed out.

"Got our butts kicked," someone mumbled.

"Lost that battle, but we're winning the war," another voice said.

"Fuck you," said a third.

Rules of Engagement

Rich Kern

Lt. (j.g.) Rich Kern left the Navy in the early 1970s for a career as a freelance wildlife filmmaker based in Miami, Florida.

I HAD DOUBTS ABOUT THE RULES OF ENGAGEMENT ALMOST AS SOON AS I arrived in Vietnam. I was Officer-in-Charge of PCF 64, based in Cat Lo on the northern edge of the Mekong Delta. The rivers, estuaries, canals, and swamps in our op area had a fair share of "VC strongholds," "Restricted Zones," and "Secret Zones," where everybody was supposed to be an enemy and you could pretty much shoot anything that moved, no questions asked.

But you had to be careful with this. Very early experience taught me and my crew that the inhabitants of these "enemy-held" areas displayed a spectrum of political commitments—from those ready to give their lives for Communism, to those who simply wanted to live as their ancestors had lived in the only place they knew as home. The VC typically took over an area and held it by intimidation. Villagers complied under fear of death. The best evidence that an area was really under VC control, we soon learned, was when somebody shot at you.

With that in mind, I was not really prepared for what happened the day I hitched a ride on a single-engine spotter plane for a leaflet drop over Dung Island, a long, narrow wedge that splits the Bassac River—a downstream branch of the Mekong—just before it empties into the

PCF 64 returns to base in the Mekong Delta in 1967. Swift Boats were initially painted official U.S. Navy haze gray when they were used on coastal patrol. When Swift Boats moved into rivers and canals, sailors painted them with camouflage green and black to blend in with the jungle environment. This was the first time since the Civil War that U.S. Navy vessels were painted a color other than haze gray.
COURTESY OF RICHARD KERN

South China Sea. Since Dung Island was a VC stronghold, the drop presented a welcome opportunity to learn more about the bad guys.

We were flying about 500 feet above the island when we spotted a fisherman casting a throw net from his sampan in a small estuary. Suddenly the pilot, whom I had never met before that morning, rolled in and started firing 2.75-inch rockets from a pod under his wing. I could see the fisherman jump from his boat and struggle through the marsh grass as the rockets gouged holes in the mud around him. He staggered into the tree line and out of sight.

This was the air war mindset. On the water things were more personal, but high in the sky the fisherman became a faceless speck. There was no way to hail him with a megaphone, let alone interrogate him at gunpoint or detain him. So you took refuge in the rules of engagement. VC stronghold. Shoot to kill.

I found this disturbing, and even more so a bit later when we got called to MEDEVAC a dozen peasants who had been shot up by a U.S. spotter plane that caught them fishing in a Restricted Zone. There wasn't a soldiering-age man among the wounded—just old men, women, and children. A little girl died in the arms of one of my crewmen as we sped up the Bassac toward the hospital at Can Tho. This affected all of us deeply. It was a terrible mistake. If former President Johnson had spoken often of wanting to "win the hearts and minds of the people," this was not the way to do it.

Our turn came on October 15, 1969, in the "Long Toan Secret Zone"—a coastal area controlled by the VC and forbidden to friendlies. It was located a few miles north of the mouth of the Bassac and about seventy miles from our base at Cat Lo.

One hour before midnight my boat, along with PCFs 25 and 103, crept into the Lang Nuoc River inside the zone. We were late because the 25-Boat had hit a fish trap and because we had to limp along behind PCF 103, the only member of our small flotilla with a working radar. It was dark, and somebody had to be able to see where we were going.

We were on Operation SEALORDS 701. The orders sent to us by encrypted message instructed us to send three boats into the tiny river under cover of darkness and for one boat to exit. Swift Boats were noisy, and there was no way Charlie would miss the fearful racket that accompanied our arrival. But if the two boats in the river parked and shut down their engines, and the third departed with engines rumbling enthusiastically, maybe the VC would think we had all come and gone. The two boats in the river would lie in ambush, while the third would hang out nearby off the coast and await developments. If the VC showed up in the river, we would try to kill them. I was in charge.

We came in at low speed with lights out. Ours was the first boat to be dropped off. We nosed hard into the riverbank and shut down our twin diesels. We were across the river from the mouth of a small canal that emptied into the Lan Nuoc. When we were in place, the other two boats motored another mile upriver. There was nothing special about the Lang

Nuoc. It was a tidal river winding through mud flats in a tropical swamp. It was narrow and dangerous with plenty of cover, about 100 feet wide with a mud bottom, and fringed by low mangroves. In daylight the Lang Nuoc, like the rest of the waterways in the lower Mekong, was the color of chocolate milk. Soon PCF 25 was in place. Then we watched PCF 103 pass by us on its way out.

U.S. commanders had designated the Long Toan a secret zone because the area was believed to be so heavily controlled by the Viet Cong that we should regard anyone operating there as an enemy or an enemy sympathizer. Our rules of engagement for suspicious watercraft were straightforward—command the vessel to stop, and if the boat doesn't stop, fire rounds across its bow; if the boat continues to evade, take it under fire. Comply with these precautions, and a boat commander could attack with a clear conscience.

We settled in to wait in silence, sweltering in our flak jackets and staring at the quiescent river. Saltwater mosquitoes smelled our sweat and harassed us without mercy. After swatting them for two and a half hours, I thought about ending the operation. Our orders didn't tell us how long to wait. Also, the tide was coming in, and we had just floated loose from the riverbank. We were adrift, and I would have to light off the engines to reposition the boat, signaling our presence. Just then, however, my men and I heard the faint putt-putt of a motorized sampan. It was coming down the long, straight canal that met the Lang Nuoc just in front of us.

I couldn't be sure where the sampan was until I found it with our starlight scope, forming in the mist about 150 yards away. It was heading straight toward us, like a wispy phantom. I needed to brief my men on exactly how I wanted them to handle this, but I had left it too late, and the sampan was almost on top of us. I had time to whisper "Don't fire until I tell you. Don't hit the boat unless they're shooting at us," but that was about it. My Vietnamese sailor held a microphone, ready to order the twenty-foot vessel to heave-to. Another crewman was on the searchlight. Our weapons were cocked.

We waited until the sampan was no more than thirty yards away—point blank for our machine guns. At my word the men lit off the engines and flipped on the light. The bright beam caused instant confusion on the sampan. Someone threw something in the water. There were a lot of people in the boat. Within two seconds it had veered toward the canal bank and some of its occupants were jumping out. We had VC, apparently, but no time to think about tactics.

So when I yelled "Fire!" into the sound-powered phones, I could only hope my men would not hit the boat, for there were no shots coming from it. Tremendous streams of .50-caliber and M-60 machine gun rounds skimmed over the top of the vessel and sprayed the surrounding mangroves. Tracers showed me the people hunched down in the sampan. One incendiary round struck a basket sitting high above the gunwale and set it ablaze. A woman straightened up and pushed it into the water with her leg.

It took less than a minute to saturate the area with the machine guns. I ordered the crew to cease fire. In the silence that followed, I began to see movement in the sampan. "Lord, let this not be a massacre," I mumbled under my breath. There seemed to be little hope of that. I was expecting a very ugly scene.

Swift Boats gather at dawn prior to a canal raid in the Mekong Delta.
COURTESY OF RICHARD KERN

We came alongside. I saw six very shaken women and one child—all terrified but all untouched. I was exhilarated. Not a single round had penetrated the crude wooden vessel. I couldn't have been more proud of the skill and judgment of my men. What a performance!

Now for the unfinished business—the men who had leapt from the boat the second we illuminated them. I picked up the radio and called for the other boats. It was about 0130 when crewmen from PCF 25 started searching the mangroves behind the sampan. PCF 103 arrived and nosed into the opposite bank to make sure no one tried a counterattack. I loaded the six women and the child onto the fantail of our boat. The sampan held giant crocks filled with living mudskippers—strange little fish with bulging eyes that scamper over the mud flats on their pectoral fins. We also found sacks of crabs and several live chickens. Evidently the women, living in a restricted zone, were trying to carry their food to some secret market at night.

On the riverbank the 25-Boat's searchers found the mutilated body of a man raked by .50-caliber rounds—slugs far bigger than anything needed to cut down a human. He wore black pajamas and carried a cloth pouch filled with handwritten notebooks, documents, and cash. Two trails of muddy footprints led into the low mangroves. We didn't look for anyone else. Time had passed, and we felt very exposed. Quickly now, we took the sampan in tow, left the river, and turned toward Cat Lo.

Documents marked the dead man as a VC of some importance. On our way up the coast we dropped off the women and their sampan at a Vietnamese base where we learned they were interrogated and eventually released. The women claimed that three VC, whom they said they didn't know, had been in the boat with them. They described them as hitchhikers.

I often wondered how my life would have turned out if we had shot the sampan to bits. The rules of engagement would have covered us—legally. But much later, when I saw veterans who were unable to get their heads screwed on straight years after fighting a war, it was probably because of the endless videotape running in their minds, reviewing again and again the things they wish they hadn't seen or wish they hadn't done. Strong emotions linger long after the fact, and guilt can be a silent killer. Thank God we had been good that night. It could have been very different.

Chapter Five

1969

Pacification

One of the principal goals of SEALORDS was to "pacify" the Mekong Delta, and while Swift Boats had significant success attacking enemy hideouts and pushing the Viet Cong deeper into the jungle, they paid a high price in blood and boat damage for their achievements. And by midyear 1969 they had not pacified anything.

Both to solidify their gains and for purely operational reasons, Swifts needed a more permanent Delta presence, especially in the lower Ca Mau Peninsula. The Viet Cong had overrun the entire region the previous year during Tet, leaving few friendly settlements behind. The Swifts were staging SEALORDS raids from LSTs or Coast Guard cutters anchored in deep water far from the treacherous shallows that dominated Vietnam's south coast. SEALORDS in the lower Ca Mau involved long, tedious transits and prolonged sojourns in hostile country without easy access to fuel or ammo.[1]

So why not build a base in the forest?

Several potential tools emerged during the early part of 1969. In January, Navy riverine units defoliated the banks of both the Giang Thanh River on the Cambodian border and the canal linking Ha Tien with Rach Gia to the south. This was the first time the Navy had used Agent Orange in areas patrolled by Swift Boats. The health dangers of the defoliant were not yet well understood, but as a means of denying cover to the enemy in remote areas, the effect was startling. Trackless jungle suddenly looked like a New England hardwood forest in November—naked tree trunks and piles of dead leaves created a band of open ground 200 yards deep on either riverbank. For the enemy this was no-man's land. Ambushes were suicidal.

Also, emerging evidence suggested that hatred of U.S. forces in the region was far from universal. Local populations might welcome a permanent installation that could provide needed services. Swift Boats and other Navy assets patrolling the relatively populous Bay Hap River region north of the Cua Lon estuary had dropped leaflets and conducted PSYOPS broadcasts early in the year, urging inhabitants to cooperate with South Vietnamese authorities and to show solidarity by displaying South Vietnamese flags on boats and sampans. Some flags began to appear.

Finally, riverine forces provided the necessary technological inspiration. In late 1968 the River Assault Group began "Operation Giant Slingshot" to prevent North Vietnamese infiltration and smuggling from Cambodia to Saigon via the "Parrot's Beak" region north of the capital. The RAG boats and accompanying PBRs needed a patrol staging area, so they towed a set of hollow steel "Ammi" pontoon barges—each one thirty feet wide and ninety feet long—into place and lashed them together, creating an instant naval base, with berthing and messing areas, storerooms, a magazine, an ops center, and even a helo pad.

So the Navy, in May, decided to build a floating base in the Cua Lon estuary. Since it was not on land, it could not be overrun. And with defoliated riverbanks, the enemy could not attack from close range. And if civic action had a chance to succeed, the base would serve as a welcome place to provide medical and dental care and perishable goods that could not be routinely obtained from the Viet Cong.

The Navy called it "Seafloat." Thirteen Ammi pontoons were to be anchored in the Cua Lon opposite the site of Nam Can, the abandoned provincial city that PCF 38 had discovered almost nine months earlier during "Brown's Run." If and when U.S. forces left Vietnam, the Ca Mau was going to need a credible South Vietnamese government headquarters, and this was a perfect spot—next to a former commercial hub with relatively easy access both to the Gulf of Thailand (Square Bay) and the South China Sea (the mouth of the Bo De). The Viet Cong had found Nam Can attractive for the same reasons. Smugglers could reach it easily from either side.

A bit over a month after making the initial decision, the Navy fitted out the first nine Ammi pontoons at the naval base in Nha Be, mounting plywood buildings, stowing cargo, and installing machinery that could be hooked up as soon as the rafts were joined in the river. The pontoons were put aboard three Navy LSDs—floating drydocks—and ferried to the Bo De estuary entrance, arriving offshore June 24. Oceangoing tugs, escorted by six Swift Boats and helicopter gunships, towed the pontoons to Nam Can. They were secured in place with six 9,000-pound, destroyer-style anchors strengthened with concrete piles, massive enough to resist Cua Lon tidal currents that could approach nine knots in either direction. Seafloat officially opened for business June 27, 1969.

The commander of Seafloat came from the U.S. Navy, while the deputy was a Vietnamese officer. The Vietnamese Navy handled most of the intelligence and PSYOPS work, and the U.S. Navy supplied cooks, watch standers, radiomen, maintenance personnel, and logistical services. Seafloat started with a permanent garrison of six Swift Boats. The complement rose to eight and then ten as more Ammi pontoons were added to the original nine. Besides the Swifts, Seafloat also had SEAL, UDT (frogmen), and EOD (bomb disposal) teams, along with ten Kit Carson Scouts (former Viet Cong who had changed sides.) There were no ground forces of any size at first.

The Navy also provided two Seawolf helicopter gunships and a patrol gunboat, and stationed an LST off the south coast to provide additional support. The Vietnamese anchored two large landing craft at Seafloat, a troop carrier and a floating medical and dental clinic. Three weeks after Seafloat arrived, "Hanoi Hannah" took note of its presence in her daily broadcast, predicting the Viet Cong would destroy the base within a couple of days.

But Seafloat did not hear a shot fired for six weeks. In fact, the news was almost all good. The Navy's basic idea, apart from providing a forward military base, was to use PSYOPS—taped broadcasts and leaflet drops—to let people know that better health care and prosperity awaited if they availed themselves of the government services being offered in the middle of the Cua Lon.

The effect was almost instantaneous. Sixty people came forward in the first week. Soon local women were tipping off PSYOPS workers about booby traps. Sampan fishermen warned the Swifts about static ambushes. And when it became apparent that Seafloat was going to stay a while, woodcutters and fishermen drifted into the area to build thatched huts a few miles from the remains of Nam Can. Six weeks after the establishment of Seafloat, this "Annex," as it came to be known, had an ax-sharpening shop, a boat mechanic, and a food store. On August 31, there were 700 people living there, and the population rose to 4,600 by year's end.

The appearance of the Annex and its dramatic growth prompted a surge of South Vietnamese confidence and an expansion of military operations. Beginning in August, companies of Montagnard Strike Force troops began to rotate into Nam Can for one-month deployments. Later arrivals included eighty specially trained Navy Biet Hai infantrymen, a 100-man Vietnamese Special forces unit, additional Kit Carson Scouts, and a company of militiamen. Two Vietnamese Swifts joined the American boats along with ten Vietnamese Navy Yabuta junks, armed with .50-caliber machine guns and 60mm mortars. To carry the additional troops and provide them with gunfire support, the Navy sent a six-boat River Assault Group detachment to Seafloat. Finally, in October, the two navies decided that Nam Can could support a full-scale dry-land naval station after all. They called it "Solid Anchor," and by the end of the year Navy Seabees were building a new Swift Boat and junk base for the Vietnamese.

As the months passed, the Annex developed a thriving trade based on fishing and woodcutting, the lower Ca Mau's two traditional industries. The Nam Can fishermen began exporting fish and charcoal northward via the Cai Nap Canal, and brought home potable water, rice, beer, fabric, and simple household utensils and appliances. On October 4, classes began in a schoolhouse built by Seafloat sailors with desks made out of ammo boxes. In October, a barber began giving haircuts and a restaurant opened. In December, a baby was born on Seafloat.[2]

During the time Seafloat was being developed, Swift Boat operations in the Ca Mau Peninsula underwent something of a change. Swifts were enlisted for PSYOPS patrols, to help with civic action generally, and to escort slower-moving boats bringing supplies into the river. The pace of enemy attacks declined sharply in June, perhaps because the Viet Cong needed time to figure out what to do about Seafloat, but escalated again in July.

And the stakes had risen. Swifts in the Ca Mau and northern Delta routinely carried troops during patrols and were looking for opportunities to use them in more decisive engagements. The Ca Mau boats could now extend their patrol areas because Seafloat offered them a safe place to tie up at night. But trips that went deeper into the hinterland increased the chances of serious trouble. The same held true in the northern Delta and in the rivers south of Da Nang.

Swift fortunes yo-yoed, even as the overall pace of the war gradually slowed. July 1969 brought thirty-nine firefights and other enemy engagements—more than double what had occurred in June. Eight PCFs were damaged and nineteen sailors were wounded. In August, another eight PCFs were damaged in forty-three engagements.

By September the number of hostile encounters plunged to twenty-five, and no boats were damaged; October had only sixteen hostile fire incidents, although two U.S. sailors died and four were wounded. In the Truong Giang River, about seventeen miles south of Da Nang, a U.S. OinC was killed in a prolonged firefight that damaged two boats and caused one of them to run aground.

November brought neither casualties nor damage anywhere. But in December three boats on a civic action mission were ambushed with rockets and automatic weapons on the Dam Doi River, twenty-five miles northeast of Seafloat. Two sailors were killed and five were wounded. The next day troops swept the area and found a bunker complex and campground that could accommodate 300 people. The war was not over yet.

Too Young

Virgil Erwin

Lt. Virgil Erwin's stories, Duong Keo and Irma La Douche, appear on pages 148 and 228.

It is December 1968, the dry season. We're going to the Ham Luong River, deep in the Mekong Delta. Our patrols are three days on, one day off. Longer patrols are more efficient, with more time spent in the rivers and less time transiting to and from Cat Lo. As far as I'm concerned, this is a relief. I must be crazy, but I'd rather risk the possibility of being shot at in a river than the certainty of being seasick and bruised on the ocean. Swift Boats aren't built for storms at sea.

We're a crew of six, preparing to get underway from our base at Cat Lo. I'm the oldest. I turned twenty-four last month, and Taylor, our Second Class Gunner's Mate, is twenty-two. Gnau, my soft-spoken Leading Petty Officer, introduces me to the new guy: "This is Toi, our Vietnamese liaison."

"Good to have you aboard," I say. "Have you been to the Ham Luong? Do you know the river?"

"Yes, I know the river—a little." Toi is maybe twenty-three, but he looks to be eighteen. He fits right in with the rest of us, as far as age is concerned. Other than that, he's an outlier. He's barely five feet tall and thin, as if he never gets enough to eat. He has a nice smile and his uniform is spotless, a reflection of the pride he must feel for the Vietnamese Navy. Pride in our navies is perhaps the only thing we can openly share.

He looks good, while we're getting pretty scruffy. We're all taller than he is. And after six months patrolling in Vietnam, our smiles are becoming sardonic—not so "nice," if they ever were.

"OK," I say to Moison, our Boatswain's Mate, with a measure of reluctance. "Cast off, time to go to work." Moison is really easygoing, a trait I envy. I'm three years older than him but I haven't managed to perfect his relaxed poise.

After three hours we reach the Ham Luong and begin winding our way upriver, inspecting sampans and junks. We're supposed to control the rivers, inspecting sampans like traffic cops, as if we were stopping drunk drivers and looking for booze: "License, registration, and open your trunk please." The tedium is unending. I remember my dad saying war is 90 percent boredom and 10 percent unadulterated terror.

Rivers are forbidden to anyone at night. As curfew approaches, fishermen begin returning from the sea. Suggs, our engineman and self-appointed chef, has crammed the freezer full of steaks. Suggs is a bit overweight, reflecting his menu choices. He notices some of the sampans have live lobsters. These are high on my hierarchy of need. Suggs and Toi team up. While Toi translates, Suggs haggles.

"Steak for lobster, one for one," Toi suggests.

It's a deal. Suggs keeps the lobsters alive in the clean bucket until dinnertime. The other bucket is our toilet. No one wants to use the head, which is below decks in the crew's forward berthing space. It's a real bad idea to be indoors when Charlie is firing B-40 rockets that penetrate our thin hull and detonate inside the main cabin.

Taylor, the gunner, has the watch. He is squatting on top of the pilothouse, scanning the river with binoculars. He has a deep bronze tan and looks like a middleweight boxer. I have never seen him smile. He expresses a burning hatred for the VC, and constantly encourages me to be more aggressive. He suggests we set up night ambushes. Maybe it's the bodies we've seen floating in the river, bound to stalks of bamboo, that have inspired his black mood. I wonder what this war is doing to him.

"Skipper," Taylor calls out, "there's a large junk comin' upriver."

"OK, standby for board and search," I say to the crew. It's not an enthusiastic command, but one of routine. I don't feel we're accomplishing anything, searching junks and sampans. Out of 300 searches this month, we've found only two suspected VC—one with too much money, and the other with a large stash of medical supplies.

As we close on the junk, Toi calls out over our loudspeakers, *Lai dei, lai dei*—"Come here, come here."

The old junk is over sixty feet long, easily ten feet longer than our patrol boat and bigger than any vessel we've searched. Her brown weathered sails are furled and she's slowly making way with the putt-putt sound of a small diesel. A Vietnamese sailor tosses a line and we tie up alongside. An old man appears to be the captain. Toi asks for identification papers while Taylor and Moison leap aboard to begin a search. I stand near the aft helm, watching the old man. He's barefoot, wearing baggy black shorts that cover his knees and a filthy shirt three sizes too big.

Hoffman, our radarman, is crouched on our cabin top, a pack of cigarettes rolled up in the sleeve of his T-shirt. Suggs is in the bow and Gnau is on the fantail, so he has an unobstructed view of the junk. All three have M-16s, safeties off, and all are focused on the junk's crew. To protect Taylor and Moison, they won't hesitate to shoot.

"Skipper," Taylor yells, "I've found something!" He waves to Toi and me to follow him. There is a dark mahogany cabin at the stern of the junk, wide with a low ceiling. We bend down to enter. There, lying on a woven mat, is a young girl with a frail, delicate face framed in silky, coal-black hair. Thin white linen is draped from her chest to her ankles. She seems sedated, not reacting to our presence, her eyes as if in a trance. No tears. Just black pupils staring at nothing.

Brown stains are seeping out through the linen. Toi gently lifts the cloth. Her burns shock me. Her flesh is grotesque—tortured designs in shades of gray, with thin white streaks of tissue drawn taut like violin strings, stretching her young breast into unimaginable distortions, a startling contrast to her pale angelic face. Her chest, stomach, and legs are oozing yellow pus. I have never in my life seen anything like this. A putrid odor makes me gag. I know it's a sign of infection, maybe gangrene. I fight the urge to vomit.

"Toi," I say, "tell the captain we're taking her to the hospital in Ben Tre. Taylor, get our stretcher."

Taylor starts to leave and then pauses. "Mr. Erwin, this isn't our job. We'll be out of our patrol area for the rest of the day." Taylor's formality is a sign. Whenever he disagrees with me, he addresses me as "Mr. Erwin."

"Taylor, get the stretcher!" I repeat. Taylor bolts from the cabin, kicking the door, his body language conveying fervent disagreement. He's furious, and I can hear it in his voice as he yells at Moison to search the cargo hold and barks at Hoffman to get the stretcher.

The captain of the junk squats next to the girl, and I kneel on the other side. As Toi translates, the captain becomes agitated, speaking fast and loud.

"He's refusing to let her go," Toi says. "He thinks we believe this girl is Viet Cong—thinks we are going to put her in prison." Toi pauses and then says, "Mr. Erwin, she might be Viet Cong, wounded in some battle."

"For crying out loud, tell him this girl is going to die if she does not get to a hospital! Tell him she's not going to prison. Ask him if this is his daughter." I watch the old man's eyes as Toi translates—I can tell when he hears my question. The old man looks at me and nods.

"Why is he refusing my help?" I ask Toi. "This is his daughter—a hospital can save her life."

Toi translates, but the captain just stares at me without responding. I wonder if he cares. I've seen evidence of the brutality of the VC, killing innocent civilians. I've heard the Vietnamese don't care about their children, that their culture is different. I now think it's true. I believe the years of war have made the Vietnamese callous to human suffering, an entire country just trying to survive, the task too overwhelming to worry about the life of one child. They can always have more.

Hoffman crawls into the cabin, pulling the canvas stretcher behind him. The father is startled, rising up to his feet, yelling, screaming at me with a vehement protest, spittle flying from his mouth.

There's no translation necessary. He's four feet away, his feet and arms spread, muscles tense—his whole posture says he's ready to fight, to sacrifice his life to prevent me from taking his daughter. I'm armed with a .38—the father with nothing but his body.

"He doesn't trust you," Toi says, "fears he'll never see her again."

Why is this father against me trying to help? I wonder if we did this to his daughter with napalm, or if he believes we did it. There's that possibility.

Taylor comes back into the cabin with our medical kit. Toi translates as Taylor gives instructions for the burn cream, the sterile gauze, and the morphine. The father begins to relax. I am amazed, even more impressed that Taylor, our twenty-two-year-old hardass, has such detailed medical knowledge and is willing to use it with such a gentle touch and without recoiling at the ghastly wounds.

Taylor turns to me and whispers, "Junk's clean, no weapons, just fish and rice." He pauses, and then says softly, "Skipper, please, let 'em go."

How can I—how can we—make this decision? We're not that much older than this girl.

Hoffman and Taylor look at her, and then back at me, waiting for a decision.

I want to help this girl—she's close to death. In my gut I want to save her life, but all I can say to Taylor is, "OK, let 'em go."

The junk pulls away from our side, and I watch it motor upriver. Nobody says anything. Even later we don't talk about it. I wonder about Vietnamese values, about love for their children. Maybe I've been wrong—maybe they're just like me. I wonder what poison I've taken to fall under this prejudice. Maybe I created this image for my own self-preservation, the concept that no one will mourn if I kill someone. I'll be off the hook, no bad memories for taking a life.

I don't think the young girl will live. In my mind I still see the father cradling her in his arms as she closed her eyes. I don't care if she is VC—she's too young to die.

Seafloat

Jim Corrigan

Jim Corrigan was separated from active duty as a Quartermaster Second Class in April 1971, and married his fiancée five months later. He became a CPA and retired to north Florida after a thirty-year career as chief financial officer and chief executive officer of large hospital systems.

In the spring of 1969 the Navy decided to build a floating Swift Boat base in the mangrove swamps at the southern end of the Mekong Delta. I was in Cam Ranh Bay at the time, a Third Class Quartermaster serving an extended Vietnam tour as a watch supervisor at Coastal Surveillance Force headquarters. We ran the Navy's Market Time operations—tracking seagoing traffic along the Vietnam coast and staying in touch with five divisions of Swift Boats and a fleet of P-3 surveillance aircraft.

The boss was Capt. Roy Hoffman, an aggressive commander who spent a great deal of time out of the office riding Swift Boats, particularly in the Ca Mau Peninsula in the far south, a Viet Cong stronghold for years. Things had gotten worse since the Swift Boats had started raiding in the Ca Mau rivers and canals in the latter half of 1968. There were a lot of ambushes and firefights, and crews were taking casualties.

The Ca Mau was remote—a logistical nightmare. The Navy had no bases, and Swifts had to nest alongside LSTs anchored offshore in the South China Sea and stage their raids from there. It was hard to get quick air support, medical care, or evacuation—as I well knew, since I was often the one trying to find help.

Middle of Seafloat base with U.S. Navy Seawolf helicopter setting down on the fuel barge landing pad.
COURTESY OF GERALD CORRIGAN

The solution to these challenges was Operation Seafloat: nine floating steel barges, each ninety feet long by twenty-eight feet wide, to be towed into the Bo De River from the South China Sea and then to the middle of the fast-moving Cua Lon estuary, opposite the derelict town of Nam Can. There the barges, commonly known in the Navy as "Ammi pontoons," would be strapped together and anchored to form a floating base, an instant Navy presence.

Seafloat needed eighty people as a permanent garrison, split evenly between Americans and Vietnamese. The call went out in the spring, and I volunteered. I had unfinished business, and Cam Ranh, with its beautiful half-moon beach, the world-class bay, and aquamarine water wasn't the place to complete it. For personal reasons, I needed to be in a combat zone.

I had once been a reluctant soldier. I turned twenty in 1967, a bad year to be out of high school and not in college. Many of my friends were getting drafted and joining the Army or the Marine Corps. They were going to Vietnam. I wanted nothing to do with Vietnam, so when I received my draft notice, I practically ran to the Navy recruitment office. They signed me up and decided to make me a quartermaster.

I was studying at QM school in Newport, Rhode Island, and going home to Long Island almost every weekend to see my friends and family. Then on October 17, 1967, one of my best friends, Marine PFC Peter Penfold, who had just turned twenty himself, was killed in Vietnam when his armored vehicle took a direct hit somewhere near the DMZ up north. I was shocked and devastated. Decades later tears come to my eyes as I write this.

I went to the funeral along with Peter's other two best friends—two brothers, both marines, both in dress uniform, and both going to Vietnam. My first cousin, just drafted into the Army, was going to Vietnam, too. My girlfriend, Roseanne, flew in from college to be there. The next day I told her that since I had finished first in my QM school class, I could pick my duty station, and I chose Vietnam. I had lost my friend, and I wanted to get even. I was angry and confused, but there was no changing my mind. To make it right I had to go to Vietnam like the rest of my friends.

At Cam Ranh Bay I made many friends, and we had good times, so much so that several of us extended for six months. The buddy thing was important, but the Navy sweetened the deal by offering a free round-trip ticket anywhere in the world and thirty days leave before you had to come back. So I went home and had a great time. Roseanne and I started talking seriously about getting married. I also saw the antiwar movement up close for the first time. I was angry with everyone involved in it. I defiantly wore my khaki jungle shirt and hat all around town. We had 500,000 servicemen in Vietnam. They needed support, not demonstrations.

When my leave was over I went back to Cam Ranh. It was easy, but it was also boring and frequently tedious—and I wasn't doing anything for Peter. Seafloat was the opportunity I was waiting for, so when it came around, I grabbed it. Besides working in the Seafloat command center, I found out that I would also be part of "Operation Duffel Bag"—planting sensors around Seafloat to detect enemy movement. I trained for several weeks and then I went south to Nha Be Naval Support Base south of Saigon. No more softball games, no more surfboard, no more cookouts.

At Nha Be over the next few days the rest of the American volunteers trickled in, and we got to work helping teams of Seabees complete the construction and assembly of Seafloat. There were six main pontoons to be lashed together, three abreast. They had wooden structures built on top of them to serve as barracks, officers' quarters, a mess hall, a command center, and various offices and work areas. We put the buildings together and equipped them with everything from ammo to mosquito nets.

Pontoons and plywood were colored dark brown, and all the windows had blackout canopies that rolled down at dusk. The roof of every building was made of a heavy metal designed to protect against mortar rounds. Pontoons facing the riverbanks had waist-high redoubts that were three feet wide and filled with sandbags.

The last three pontoons had nothing built on them. One was a helo pad and the others would serve as a mooring dock for the Swift Boats and other riverine craft. When the pontoons were lashed together and anchored in the Cua Lon, Seafloat would look like a big fat capital letter "T" from the sky above.

As soon as we finished Seafloat's berthing spaces, we moved aboard. The beds were spring frames with air mattresses, really uncomfortable, so a few days before leaving Nha Be a few petty officers, including me, raided the transient barracks and stole some padded mattresses. If anybody suspected us they never said anything. When it comes to creature comforts in the Navy, almost anything goes.

The food on Seafloat was great, and we ended up eating in the mess hall. We had fans and big refrigerators and freezers, with electricity supplied from several gas generators. Showers weren't much, just lukewarm water in 55-gallon drums perched atop a wood frame. The head was even less: wooden seats with holes in them sitting over open water.

We drilled all the time. We loaded and unloaded ammunition, and then did it all over again. No one explained why this was important (the Navy never explains anything) and we thought it was just busy work to keep us from getting drunk and raising hell.

On June 24, with no ceremony to speak of, Seafloat's nine pontoons were individually towed to the middle of the Nha Be River by several tugboats and pushed into the bellies of three Navy LSDs—floating drydocks. We got underway, heading south to our rendezvous point at the mouth of the Bo De River.

It didn't take long, and by dawn the next day the LSDs were disgorging their cargo. Each pontoon, fully outfitted with its buildings and supplies, had two line handlers to help the tugs rig their tows. I was on the barracks pontoon, and it was the most nerve-wracking phase of the trip. We only had five feet of free deck space and no railings. The pontoons bobbed like corks in four-foot swells beneath an overcast, gloomy sky, and within minutes we were soaked from the spray, skittering along the slippery metal decks in our orange life jackets. Thank God everything inside was well secured.

After the tugs corralled the barges and formed up in a line, we began our slow trip to the river mouth. The color of the ocean changed from gray to mud brown as we got closer to shore, and I swapped my foul-weather gear for a flak jacket and an M-19 grenade launcher, the latest model, which spat grenades like a burp gun. Other soldiers were scattered among the pontoons, armed with M-16s, and, in a few cases, M-60 machine guns.

We had a big escort. My personal diary counts ten Swift Boats, two Seawolf helicopter gunships, a couple of OV-10 Broncos for close air support, and a 165-foot patrol gunboat, armed with a 40mm cannon. Supposedly Phantom jets were on call if we needed them.

Between choppers and boat engines we were making a lot of noise, but to me it felt like I was traveling in slow motion in eerie silence. Thick jungle cloaked both sides of the Bo De. Steep mud banks dropped down to muddy water, gray beneath the overcast. I stared intently at the shoreline, trying to imagine how anyone could walk through the foliage. Nevertheless, I felt like eyes were watching us every second.

We reached the Cua Lon and then Nam Can. There was nothing much left of the town, long abandoned by the Viet Cong and the villagers. The U.S. Army had staged an offensive there afterward, and when they left, planes saturated the site with Agent Orange, defoliating both sides of the river to a depth of several hundred yards. By the time we got there, Nam Can was nothing but a mud flat with pools of standing water that harbored some of the scariest snakes I would ever see.

The tugs dropped enormous concrete anchors at the four corners of Seafloat, and expertly maneuvered the pontoons into position so they could be lashed together with thick steel cables. Over the next few days, divers installed underwater barbed wire fencing to protect the base from sapper attack and water mines. Generators were lit and communications were established. The galley served meals and the helo pad had its first landings. Swift Boats tied up at the pontoons while other Swifts patrolled the area.

A major task in Seafloat's early days was to take control of our perimeter, with the long-term objective of making it possible for the local Vietnamese to return to Nam Can. On our third day in the river, I went ashore with a small party to explore what was left of the town. We found the perimeter of the old Army camp and accidently tripped a wire that ignited a flare, a security warning from long ago. Back in the tree line we found a straw hut recently and hurriedly abandoned, with a cooking fire still burning in a clearing in front of it. A short distance away we found a camouflaged sampan hidden in the mangroves. We suspected a booby trap, so we left it alone. Later another team investigated further and blew it up.

Swift Boat patrols and SEAL team operations began immediately. PCFs captured more than two tons of VC rice. Charlie attacked another Swift with B-40 rockets. SEALs killed two of the enemy in a

The booby trap that did not detonate.
COURTESY OF GERALD CORRIGAN

firefight. And, on Seafloat, we began to fish floating signs out of the water daily: "Your mission will fail!" the inscriptions read. "We will blow you to small pieces!"

Soon after that we started Duffel Bag operations. We hung special sound buoys in trees along trails. They ignored jungle noise, but could pick up human voices or conversations and let us listen back in the command center. At ground level we planted infrared sensors to detect body heat, and also metal detectors.

We installed our first sensors shortly after our arrival, and kept at it periodically, many times riding Swift Boats into the canals. Since I weighed only 145 pounds I became Duffel Bag's "monkey," the one who climbed the trees and rigged the sensors. I was unarmed when I did it, which didn't bother me in remote areas, but made me extremely nervous when we were bugging VC campgrounds and bunkers.

And there was one other thing. In early July, I had just started to climb a tree when hundreds of large, red army ants swarmed my body, stinging unmercifully. They invaded my clothes, my ears, my cuts, and even my nose. I finished installing the sensor and bounded down the tree so the rest of the team could slap and swat me clean. Everybody had a good laugh, but on future climbs I made sure to tape my neck, wrists, and boots.

After the first couple of weeks, the novelty wore off. We had fired off a lot of ordnance to demonstrate our firepower so Charlie wouldn't attack Seafloat, and it seemed to be working. But by mid-July Swift Boats were taking rocket hits on a fairly regular basis, and we had casualties. We started to get nervous. One day our Duffel Bag team was cruising along a canal just north of Seafloat when we tripped a booby trap and a grenade leaped into the air, hovering for an instant three feet above us. I waited for the explosion, but it never came. The grenade dropped harmlessly into the water, bobbing up and down. One of my teammates picked it up. "US Army" read the inscription. A tripwire set by friendlies long ago. Now a waterlogged dud. Thank God!

The next time was no joke. Duffel Bag was hitching a ride with a Swift Boat nighttime patrol that was broadcasting shrieking PSYOPS tapes into the jungle in hopes of getting local people to abandon the VC, surrender, and get a fresh start. We planned to stop along the way at an important river-canal intersection and plant a couple of sound buoys.

At first it went well. With the PSYOPS tapes providing a noise screen, our boat nudged into the bank undetected and dropped us off. We planted the first buoy easily. For the second one, we decided to find a more secluded spot. The PSYOPS noise faded away, leaving an eerie stillness. After thirty yards we reached level ground.

There was a good tree to my right, and I moved toward it, intending to climb. But as I reached its base, a shaft of moonlight rebounded from a sheet of metal or glass right in front of it. I took a closer look. It was the glass cover of a large Claymore mine and it was aimed right at us, only inches from my feet. It was huge. We used a red-lens flashlight to check the rest of the clearing. Claymores rimmed it. We were standing in a minefield.

John Wayne would have pulled a knife, dropped to his knees, and calmly probed the ground in front of him as he crawled to safety. Not us. I picked up my sound buoy, we called our PCF, and then we ran straight back—exactly straight back—to the boat, which had already started its engines. We jumped aboard and left. "Not to worry," the Explosive Ordnance guys told us the next day after investigating. The Claymores were command-detonated and not trip-wired, they told us. All we needed to do was crawl behind them and cut the wires. You bet.

By the time my tour finished in August, there were still no buildings or people in Nam Can. A trickle of folks had started to come in for medical attention, but that was the best we could do. I calculated that I had planted over fifty sensors in three months, but I have no idea whether they did any good. I can recollect only one incident when three sensors were set off in perfect sequence and our mortars fired at the coordinates of the last contact. A team checked for damage the next day, but evidence was sketchy.

I guess on one level, Seafloat was a typical Vietnam experience: You went there, did something you thought was tremendously important, and then you came home and never needed to think about it again. But on a personal level it meant everything to me. I felt I contributed, and I felt I could stand tall with my close friends who also served in Vietnam. All of us came back, and all of us became grandparents. I tell Peter about this whenever I go to Washington. You can find Peter Penfold at the Wall, on panel 27 East, line 35.

Death in the Family

Robert Hunt, Charles Janner, and Reynaldo Lopez

Quartermaster Second Class Bob Hunt retired from the Navy as a chief quartermaster in 1983, earned a master's degrees in business management and public administration, and taught elementary school in Chicago and Los Angeles before retiring to Post Falls, Idaho, where he became State Commander for Disabled American Veterans.

Gunner's Mate Third Class Charlie Janner left the Navy in October 1971 and went back to his job with Union Carbide Chemical Company, retiring in April 2000 to travel widely and return home to Texas City, Texas.

Engineman Second Class Rey Lopez left the Navy in 1970 and became an air-conditioning technician in his hometown of San Benito, Texas.

LT. (J.G.) KEN NORTON WAS A GOOD GUY. HE WAS AN ACADEMY GRADUate, regular Navy, and at twenty-five, he was "older" than the rest of the crew. He had a good sense of humor and didn't sweat the small stuff, but he came from a destroyer, so he knew his business—fair, but no patsy. The best kind of officer.

QM2 Bob Hunt met Mr. Norton and the rest of the crew at Swift Boat school in Coronado. Bob was twenty-three and had spent a year in Vietnam on riverboats. He volunteered for a second tour to be Leading Petty Officer on a Swift. The boat had two gunner's mates, Texan Charlie Janner and John Michels from New Jersey. Another Texan, Rey Lopez, was the engineman, and Radarman Harvey Miller was from Maryland. Bob liked Mr. Norton from the start. So did the others.

During training the crew studied engines, seamanship, gunnery, communications, and electronics—and the Vietnamese language and culture. Everybody learned to do everything, and gradually each man found his favorite spot. Bob, being the quartermaster, drove the boat. Mr. Norton, like a lot of Officers-in-Charge, liked to sit in the pilothouse doorway, next to the helmsman, the radio, and the charts.

The crew arrived in Vietnam in the summer of 1969 and was sent to Coastal Division 12 at Da Nang. After a couple of shakedown cruises, they took possession of PCF 61 and went fifty miles south to Chu Lai, at the mouth of the Cua Dai River. They would be doing both coastal and river patrols.

It was a bad time in the war. Families in the States were watching troops getting shot up on television every evening and trying to get information about loved ones any way they could. The squadron told everybody to write down the names of "important" people they knew. Bob had a low threshold for chickenshit. He listed two "uncles": Gen. William Westmoreland, the commanding general in Vietnam, and Sen. Henry M. Jackson, chairman of the Senate Armed Services Committee.

But Vietnam was no joke. During one of PCF 61's first patrols, Bob was trying to get Gunner's Mate Michels to keep the twin fifties pointed at the beach, especially when the boat was close in, like it was on that day as the crew was pulling up VC fishing nets just beyond the surf line. Every time the boat came about, Michels had the guns pointing out to sea. Finally, Bob climbed on top of the pilothouse to explain himself "more forcefully," as he put it, and when Michels didn't respond, Bob slapped him hard.

Mr. Norton saw this, and didn't like it. He was about to say something when an enemy machine gun opened fire from the beach. Suddenly everyone knew what to do. They found out that day that most firefights didn't last long, but were very intense while they did. Once "the adrenaline kicked in," Charlie Janner said, the crew kept firing until the enemy machine gun fell silent. Michels never again pointed the fifties out to sea.

For much of the time, Vietnam for the crew of PCF 61 was almost a series of snapshots—shared experiences to be recalled over a beer late in the evening. There was the time they saw the battleship USS *New Jersey* firing at inshore targets with 16-inch shells that looked to Charlie like Volkswagens in flight. And on beautiful days at sea, traveling at high speed, Mr. Norton and Harvey Miller would sit in the bow with 12-gauge shotguns, taking potshots at flying fish as they leapt from the water. No one could recall if they ever hit any.

There was the time the crew beached the boat on a sandspit to go for a swim, get some sun, and eat fresh bread from a local French bakery—and then all of a sudden incoming mortar rounds started falling. Mr. Norton used the radio to yell for a cease-fire, but no luck, so they had to get underway and skedaddle. They learned later it was South Korean "friendly" fire, but they never found out where the Koreans got the coordinates.

Sometimes it seemed like almost everything was a narrow escape. One day, Mr. Norton stopped the boat near a small village on the banks of a narrow river—just a collection of about twenty huts with palm roofs—and went ashore with Bob and Miller to have a look around. All three wore cut-off greens and cloth boonie hats and carried M-16 rifles. They didn't bother with flak vests because nobody was there.

At least that's how it appeared initially. Each of the huts had a cooking brazier in front of it, and several of them were hot and smoking. Plates were strewn around the fires, many holding half-eaten food. "Shit, shit, shit!" shouted a voice inside Bob's head. Maybe 100 people—unfriendly people—had been eating a meal moments before the arrival of PCF 61. Very carefully the three-man recon team sauntered back to the boat, climbed carefully aboard, and abandoned the "abandoned" village at full throttle.

Then there was the time Bob got two boxes of tear gas mortar rounds from the Americal Division. That plan was to drop a couple of rounds on the dunes above the beach to flush the bad guys from their bunkers. Unfortunately, the boat turned sharply in choppy seas and Bob went sliding over the deck with the firing lanyard in his hand, triggering all sixteen rounds in one box. Then the boat drove right into the cloud. Mr.

Norton came out of the pilothouse, red-eyed, choking and coughing. He grabbed the second box and hurled it into the ocean.

PCF 61 also learned about the uncertain seaworthiness of Swifts. During the monsoon, the combination of a rain-swollen river and ocean tides turned the mouth of the Cua Dai into a violent "sea-saw" with enormous swells, so bad that sometimes the boats couldn't reach the sea. Charlie had the helm during one episode. With Mr. Norton coaching him, he turned the boat 180 degrees without getting pitch-poled—flipped end over end—and then surfed home, taking care not to capsize in following seas. Another time Bob skidded down a forty-foot wave wall, punched the boat nose-deep into a trough, and catapulted from the helmsman's seat into the overhead, knocking himself unconscious. Mr. Norton grabbed the wheel while the rest of the crew tended to Bob.

Every crew had to train the Vietnamese sailors who would eventually take over the boat. Most were summarily conscripted Saigon street "cowboys" with little interest in military service. Leading Petty Officer Hunt had to keep PCF 61's recruits in line, and when they ran and hid in the main cabin during a firefight he grabbed one of them and "smacked him" in the face. Bob thought they'd be more inclined to fight if they feared him more than the enemy. Mr. Norton warned that they might jump him to get revenge. "They don't have the guts," Bob said.

Frustration mounted. Several times during firefights Bob jammed a rifle into a VN sailor's hands and put his arms around him—"like you do when showing a girl how to shoot." And once, when all hands were needed to unload a truckload of ammo, two of the Vietnamese went to dinner while the third sat on the toilet, claiming to be "lovesick."

The final confrontation came before a patrol in mid-September that the Vietnamese said was "too dangerous." Bob confronted them with a .45-caliber revolver, intent only on impressing them with the seriousness of their refusal. "I grabbed the closest one with my left hand with the intention of throwing him toward his clothing locker," he said. But when the muscles in his left hand tightened, his right hand reacted in sympathy and he shot the crewman in the elbow and in the side. The impact knocked him back twenty feet.

Bob rushed to the sailor to stop the bleeding, cursing him as "a chickenshit, yellow-bellied coward," hoping the sailor would be "mad enough to kill me," so he wouldn't go into shock and die. The sailor told Bob the Americans were "so hard" and the Vietnamese were soft. Bob told him he was "full of crap." The North Vietnamese were hard as nails, and "there wasn't a nickel's worth of difference between them." The sailor spent six weeks in the hospital. Six weeks after that he was transferred to the Vietnamese Army. And six weeks after that, he was killed in action.

Mr. Norton immediately reported the incident to the division commander in Da Nang. The rest of the Vietnamese sailors had mutinied and were singing Buddhist death chants in the Chu Lai barracks. The Division Commander came down from Da Nang and told Bob to sleep in the brig for his own protection. The door was open.

The next day, filled with remorse for what he had done, Bob was taken to Da Nang for Captain's Mast, where he pleaded guilty to assault with a deadly weapon. He told the Division Commander he would accept any punishment without appeal. Rather than rule on the case directly, as was his prerogative, the DivCom ordered a Special Court-Martial—more formal and more serious than Mast, and a vivid demonstration to the Vietnamese of how the American military justice system worked. Bob had a pretty good idea his Swift Boat days were over.

On October 7, 1969, PCF 61, accompanied by PCF 69, went on patrol in "Long River," a Cua Dai tributary and a VC stronghold that included the hamlet with the half-eaten meals. The task was to cripple the VC food supply by tearing up fishing weirs and long lines, and sinking sampans.

With Hunt in Da Nang waiting for his court-martial, Charlie Janner had been driving the boat, but Mr. Norton sent him to the fantail on that day because the aft .50-caliber machine gun wasn't working properly and he wanted Charlie to check it out. Mr. Norton took the helm. The two boats went up Long River and turned around. It had rained off and on, and Rey Lopez, on the twin fifties above the pilothouse, could see the river was high because of the wet weather. For reasons that the rest of the crew never understood, Mr. Norton and PCF 69's OinC had decided not to shoot their way downriver, which was the usual practice. You expected the bad guys to be waiting for you on the return trip. If you shot at them, they'd keep their heads down.

The river was narrow, and Rey could see a dogleg right a little bit farther on. Turns were bad in a narrow river. The enemy could set up on the riverbank opposite the turn and hold you in his sights as you came straight toward him. He didn't have to lead you. Sure enough, from the fantail Janner spotted puffs of smoke from rocket launchers coming off the riverbank, and heard the rat-a-tat of at least one AK-47 assault rifle. The rockets missed, but the AK stitched a line of holes the length of the pilothouse.

Up in the gun tub Rey returned fire, but as the boat passed through the turn it gave a sudden lurch to the right and then headed at full speed toward the riverbank opposite the ambush. Rey slid to the bottom of the gun tub where he saw Mr. Norton slumped over the helm with one hand locked on the throttles. Rey moved to loosen his grip and pull him free, but the deck was slick with blood and covered with empty .50-caliber brass and ammo belt links that rolled under his boots every time he took a step. By the time he succeeded in lowering Mr. Norton to the deck, the boat had driven high up onto the riverbank and stopped with its screws fouled in mud and mangroves.

Mr. Norton was wounded badly. One bullet hit him in the left armpit and exited through his chest. Another apparently ricocheted off the steel helm and buried itself in his forehead. Rey leaned out the port door and yelled to Janner and Michels for help. The three of them managed to haul Mr. Norton out the starboard door. Rey went aft to check the engines and plug AK-47 holes below the waterline. Janner and Michels tried more first aid, but it wasn't doing any good.

The firefight continued sporadically, and the crew used up all of its ammo except mortar rounds. A MEDEVAC helicopter arrived but had no place to land, and the boat couldn't get off the riverbank. The portable radio was shot up, so the crew had to call base ops to get them to tell PCF 69 they needed help.

The other boat quickly returned but couldn't get close enough to PCF 61 to pass a towline because the water was too shallow. Rey, with enemy fire continuing from the opposite bank, jumped into the water and swam a line to PCF 69. But the tow couldn't break PCF 61 loose. It was too far aground. Janner and Michels brought Mr. Norton to the fantail, and Rey made a second trip to PCF 69 to carry him to safety. PCF 69 took him to a clearing where he was MEDEVACed. But Mr. Norton was dead.

Extra boats arrived later and eventually were able to pull PCF 61 back into the river. Janner remembered nothing else from that moment until the crew left Chu Lai and went back to Da Nang, where Ken Norton's brother, Chuck, an army officer in Vietnam, came to collect Ken's stuff and accompany his body home for burial at sea.

The crew broke up after that. Bob Hunt was still in Da Nang when he heard about Mr. Norton's death, the worst news in a month of terrible news. At his court-martial Bob was reduced in rate to QM3, but he stayed out of jail. The result was more than fair, he remembered: "It was assault, and I was lucky." Unknown to him at the time, his division commander had negotiated a pretrial agreement: Hunt could either be reduced in rate or fined, but not both, and could not to be punished in any other way.

The consequences of what he had done filled him with shame. The "real" punishment, he said later, was to be "separated from my crew, what was left of it." Then there was the humiliating irony: he committed a crime and got to go home to safety. "It felt almost cowardly to leave," Hunt said. And there was the guilt of knowing that Mr. Norton was sitting in his seat the day he was killed.

The rest of the crew dispersed to different boats. They all served with distinction. Charlie Janner, deeply affected by Ken Norton's death, wouldn't talk about it for years, but he eventually tracked down several members of PCF 61's crew and in 2009 represented them at a memorial service at Honoraville, Alabama, home of Ken's brother Larry. Charlie showed slides and told the story of October 7, 1969, the first time Norton's family had ever heard the details.

Rey Lopez was awarded the Silver Star for jumping into the water to carry the towline to the second Swift Boat and diving under the boat to clear the engine cooling water suction. He regarded Ken Norton as "the best officer I served under," and credited him with saving the lives of the rest of the crew that day by turning away from the ambush and keeping his hand on the throttles even as he died.

Bob Hunt, who eventually rose to become a chief quartermaster and later worked as an advocate for disabled veterans, keeps a file folder in a cabinet next to his computer desk. "The folder is simply labeled 'Ken Norton,' and it is pretty much empty," he said. "But while the file is empty, my memories are full."

WIA

Patrick L. Evans

Lt. Patrick L. Evans practiced law in upstate New York from 1975 to 2015. He never again had an infection in his wound site, but deafness from gunfire advanced over the years and an old knee injury plagued him.

We had good intentions—take a three-boat patrol up the Dam Doi River to a tiny hamlet where a new Vietnamese mother lay ill, unable to feed her infant because of trouble during childbirth. We had a couple of cases of condensed milk for her.

Nobody could remember the last Swift Boat patrol to the Dam Doi. It was December 5, 1969. We were based at Seafloat, a relatively new complex built atop steel pontoons anchored in an estuary about fifteen miles west of the river mouth. The Dam Doi flowed down from the northeast and was hostile territory. We set out under blue skies and a hot sun. I was Officer in Tactical Command and PCF 56, my boat, led our small armada. A Vietnamese Swift followed me, and PCF 50, skippered by Lt. (j.g.) Shelton White, was third. The trip upriver came off without incident. We traveled to the Dam Doi, turned into a narrow creek, found the woman, and left the milk. The creek was so narrow that instead of looping around, we simply reversed course for the trip home. PCF 50 now led and we were last.

All seemed peaceful back on the Dam Doi, but that didn't mean anything. We went full speed. In Vietnam, you usually got where you wanted to go. Coming home was the problem. Charlie wasn't stupid. He knew when you were near.

The first rocket shot out of the jungle and exploded in the water ahead of PCF 50. It was apparently a signal, because the entire south bank immediately erupted with automatic weapons and rocket fire. Everybody on our boats returned fire, but we were caught in the kill zone. PCF 50, badly mauled, cleared the ambush downriver. An antitank rocket smacked into our boat and the engines died. The Vietnamese boat was also hit, causing it to slew off to port and run aground.

I felt a stinging sensation high on my left thigh. I put my hand down and pulled it back. My fingers were bloodied to the third joint. Odd, I thought. I had a hole in my body the size of a tennis ball yet I felt no pain.

Mel Lien, my Leading Petty Officer and helmsman, tried the ignition and, much to our amazement, the engines fired up. He pushed the throttles forward, intent on escape, and passed the Vietnamese boat, still stalled on the beach. I was dizzy. I first sat down behind Lien, then I lay down. I told Lien we'd have to turn back to help the Viet boat. He wanted to discuss it. I repeated myself over the roar of the guns. He wheeled us around and we returned to the kill zone where we sat motionless, firing away until the Vietnamese boat backed off the riverbank.

Our boat had been incredibly lucky. I was the only one wounded. PCF 50 and the Vietnamese boat were another story. When we stopped at the mouth of the Dam Doi I saw Shelton White standing on the fantail of his boat, his face anguished and covered with blood. I was horrified at the gore and the bodies lying on deck.

The Viet boat didn't stop at the river mouth. Instead, it raced directly back to Seafloat. Later I learned that it lost two sailors and an American advisor. I was told the advisor bled out on the run home. I always wondered if he would have lived if the VN OinC had known we were waiting at the river mouth for help. By that time, I was pretty much out of it.

At the mouth of the Dam Doi my crew lowered me from the boat and into the arms of sailors who put me in a Seawolf helicopter. Bleeding and groggy from morphine I sat in the open hatch, squeezed between other wounded, my legs dangling in space. I hooked my right foot behind my left to keep my left leg from swinging around in the slipstream. It hurt.

The next thing I remember, I was lying on a pad of some sort in the open air on Seafloat, filled with morphine, my thoughts eddying back and forth. I thought about how badly we had been hit and how lucky I was to be alive. I had been in firefights before, but nothing with the fury and firepower of this ambush. I kept thinking about the attack, convinced I had done right by helping the Viet boat, but wondering if I could have done more—for them and all of us. I never saw or spoke to Shelton White again, but I'll never forget the look on his face.

The other feeling I had was completely different, but just as powerful. I'd worried all my life whether I could face danger and not flinch, and I had passed the test. Hard as it was to admit, especially with the carnage that surrounded me, I felt a deep undercurrent of pride and satisfaction—and a huge sense of relief.

MEDEVAC choppers loaded me up with the rest of the wounded and flew me north to the Army hospital at Bien Hoa. Medics lowered me onto a gurney with little wheels, and Vietnamese orderlies pushed me toward the triage area. I weighed over 200 pounds, and when the wheels slipped over the edge of the sidewalk, I thought we were going down. Eight or ten concerned faces appeared above me as the orderlies struggled to hold the damn thing up and push it to the door.

A surgeon strode through a room full of soldiers and sailors. I remember he looked me over and yelled out "Seventeen!" I had sixteen guys ahead of me, but I thought of March 17, St. Patrick's Day—my patron saint. Things would be okay. The yelling and clamor of the triage area drifted away as the drugs took over, and I went under.

I awoke between clean sheets in the quiet of a darkened Quonset hut, drugged and comfortable with air-conditioning humming in the background. Very nice. Safe and sound. Then I felt a large bandage on my left shoulder. Shoulder? I came in with a hip wound! "Bandage on my left shoulder," I thought. "Oh Christ, the Army operated on my left shoulder! Oh, no." I was still dazed, but I knew where I had been wounded. What had gone wrong?

I panicked. A medic passed by the foot of my bed: "Help, my shoulder, my shoulder!" I croaked. He turned, gave me a friendly smile, and strolled casually up to my bed. He stopped and reached for my shoulder.

"No, no, don't!" I wanted to say, but no words came out. He grabbed my bandage, ripped it off, and reached in with a big grin, pulling out a handful of shrapnel that the doctors had dug out of my hip. They had taped it to my shoulder for a souvenir.

I kept it together after that, and things improved. Because the surgeons had cut from fragment to fragment, the wound site was a jagged open hole, a zigzag almost a foot long. The theory was to let it heal by "secondary intention"—let it close by itself. Twice a day someone flushed the wound with hydrogen peroxide.

After a couple of days at Bien Hoa, I was flown to another Army hospital, and a few days after that I went to the Army hospital in Cam Ranh Bay, which was also the headquarters of Coastal Squadron One—the Swift Boat command. It was good to see friends. I learned that forty-five minutes after I set out on my last patrol, the squadron had sent orders detaching me from Seafloat and sending me to Cam Ranh for a staff job as an inspection officer. I was one of the senior Swift Boat officers in-country at that point. "We're holding the job open for you," a friend said. "Get well soon."

They asked me what happened, and I told them about the firefight. They said Lien and I were both written up for Navy Commendation medals. It was a modest award, and I was furious. I still am, even as I write this many decades later. I had seen senior officers get Bronze Stars for nothing at all.

The long gash in my hip was slowly drawing together from the bottom up and from the middle outward. Attendants poured hydrogen peroxide into the wound two or three times a day—in one side and out the other. It still didn't close entirely, and nobody knew why. I wasn't worried, believing it would all work out.

I lay in a Quonset hut divided by an aisle with about twelve beds on a side, most of them filled with marines. Over the next few days a half-dozen marines came in with self-inflicted wounds to the foot—between the big toe and second toe. Simple wounds to get off the front lines for a while.

Cam Ranh was a quiet, peaceful place. It was here that I joined the community of war wounded. We were a closed group, isolated in our own self-centered world where we looked out for ourselves and our comrades and no one else. It was strange when somebody came to our ward suffering from something like appendicitis or pneumonia, just as it was odd to hear about a relative who was ill or had died in the States. Their sickness was not our sickness, and their battle was not our battle. They were on the outside. We were on the inside. The world may have been doing its thing—miniskirts, hippy-dippy long hair, acid rock, demonstrations and peace marches—but it didn't involve us, so we were oblivious.

The doctors at Cam Ranh were hugely disaffected. They wanted only to go home and wouldn't talk to the enlisted patients. This really pissed me off. I told one doc I had been a premed in college and was going to med school when I got out of the Navy. Since I was the only officer in the ward, the doctor talked to me—about my condition and about everyone else's. The doctor would tell me about the guys and then leave. The others would limp or wheel over to my bed, and I'd brief them on their condition. It took me a good long time before I was able to see the humor in the movie *M*A*S*H.* or its subsequent TV series. Being nonchalant about treating war wounded wasn't funny.

As for my own treatment, I never got an answer about what was happening to me—just shrugs. I was frustrated because I expected to heal up soon and return to my new duties on squadron staff. But I wasn't healing. Eventually the hospital concluded that I'd have to go stateside, a decision made over my objections. I'd already passed on two division staff positions and an R&R to get the squadron job, and I didn't want to give it up.

Too bad. On Christmas Eve, I was flown to the U.S. naval hospital at Yokosuka, Japan. It had the largest claw-footed bathtub I'd ever seen. What a Christmas present! I felt better. I lay in the clean hot water and smiled. Safe at last, and on my way home. Later that night, my roommate got me ready for midnight Mass. A wounded Marine pilot's sister was visiting and pushed my wheelchair. She and others had smuggled booze into the ward, so we all got drunk. I sat in the wheelchair rolling my head back, trying to nestle into the bosom of the first American girl I'd seen in nine months. It didn't work.

I blended smoothly into my new community. One morning my roommate rushed in: "Come on, you've gotta see this," he yelled, and wheeled me into "boys' town," where a half-dozen junior officers bunked together. A crowd had gathered, and we pushed to the front. There a marine officer sat in bed while corpsmen carefully removed bandages from his chest and left shoulder. He had a four-inch square hole in his flesh. We could clearly see his pectoral muscles.

He was waiting for a skin graft, and the corpsmen were examining his wound. But nobody seemed to care about that. Instead, everyone started yelling. I didn't get it, but then I did. The marine crossed his right hand over his left wrist, and flexed his pectoral muscles. You could see the red meat moving. It looked like sirloin that was alive. He turned left and right so everybody could see. We cheered madly. We were alive! God bless us all!

New Year's came and went. I was more mobile, but still stuck in a wheelchair most of the time. I flew home the second week of January, lying in the third bunk off the deck of an enormous slow-flying C-130 rigged like a hospital ward. I was at eye-level with the stewards and nurses. In bed with constant feminine care—that's the way to travel. We stopped in Alaska, and the crew lowered the belly ramp to give us some fresh air. The cold rushed in, lifting my spirits immediately. American air smelled different—and wonderful.

We landed at Andrews Air Force Base, outside of Washington, D.C. A single elderly woman representing a local VFW post met us as our gurneys rolled into the terminal. She gave us each a small medal and thanked us for our service. That was our welcome.

A day later I was in St. Albans Naval Hospital on Long Island outside New York. At this point doctors were still flushing my wound regularly with peroxide, and I still had two holes that wouldn't close. I was walking around more, but I had no physical therapy. I did deep knee bends and stretches on my own. As before, no one seemed to know or care about my condition.

One day as I was walking, I felt a wrenching deep in my hip. I asked about it. No reaction. The doctors just wanted to know when the two holes closed up. I came to believe that wrenching my leg had opened an abscess in the scar tissue, but I ignored it at the time. This was a mistake.

My roommate was a marine returning for a follow-up operation. For some unknown reason he had tried to unscrew the cap from a white phosphorus incendiary grenade, and it went off in his hand, burning up a good part of it. His remaining fingers could close enough to lift a quart of beer, but the doctors were going to break his thumb again in hopes that he could hold a champagne glass.

Then there was the fellow with the all-body spica cast that ran from his armpits to his toes with an aluminum rod between the thighs to support it all. We took him with us one Tuesday night when we snuck off to the Officers' Club. Somebody's girlfriend had a Volkswagen Beetle with a sunroof, and we were able to stand our spica-ed friend up in it, drive him to the O-club and lean him against the bar. He began drinking. Nonstop. He slid a bit to the left, but nobody noticed. He kept drinking. He slid a little farther. And finally, he went down with a crash while a half-dozen drunken invalids tried to get out of his way. Medical staffers rushed over to pull him up, but he refused all help. "Just turn me over on my stomach," he said. "I can get up on my own," he yelled again and again.

He started doing violent push-ups, but couldn't get enough momentum to change his center of gravity. The rest of us stood around laughing, until finally, to keep him from doing real damage to the cast, we convinced him it was all right for him to accept help—from us. We propped him back up. He kept on drinking. Insiders take care of their own.

Eventually my wound closed and I began walking without a crutch or cane. My first time out of the hospital, I went into Manhattan to visit my college fraternity at Columbia University. There were still a few guys I knew, and we stood around the bar telling stories. Suddenly, a young woman from Barnard College ran up screaming: "Motherfucker baby killer, goddamned homicidal maniac!" Spit flew from her mouth as she raged on and on. Quickly, two or three guys grabbed her to keep her from hitting me. They dragged her downstairs and threw her out the door. As she departed she yelled one final insult: "I bet you even like John Wayne!"

In early February 1970 I got orders to Naval Headquarters Staff, Washington, D.C., at the old Washington Navy Yard. I was ready for full duty. Over the next year and a half I held a variety of administrative jobs: District Enlisted Housing Officer, correction officer, and, finally, legal officer for the command.

As correction officer, I babysat a division of sailors either serving sentences or awaiting trial. Most were mentally defective, psychologically disturbed, or simply evil. Some were not. One kid, a seaman apprentice and antiwar activist awaiting trial for treason, had, among his other sins, mocked L. Mendel Rivers, chairman of the House Armed Services Committee. A team of twenty-five FBI agents was looking to send him to Leavenworth forever. This and similar persecutions left a sour taste in my mouth.

During that time I was getting back in shape. I ran regularly, and played handball and then volleyball. The social life of Washington was great. There were a couple of Swift Boat drivers there and we partied hard.

One day, I felt my wound site burning. Looking at it, I saw it was red and swollen. Back at my desk, I mentioned it to my office mate, and suddenly I was shaking, with sweat pouring off me. I lay down on the floor. The next thing I remember was waking up in Bethesda Naval Hospital. Over the next year and a half it happened four more times: localized heat, wild systemic fever, collapse, Bethesda. I don't ever once recall being picked up by the ambulance. The fifth time it happened, my temperature spiked, I passed out, and when I awoke in Bethesda my entire left side was paralyzed and I couldn't talk. I'd had a stroke. All I could do was blubber nonsense.

Doctors rolled me off for a brain scan and gave me some tranquilizers. I dozed through the night. The next morning broke bright and clear. I could talk and feel. Everything was normal. After a week or so, I was released on a Saturday morning. I rushed over to American University to take the law boards. I did really well in the morning session, but passed out in the afternoon.

I decided to leave the Navy. Besides growing dissatisfaction with my jobs, I was worried about my health. The worst attack was the last, but I didn't know that at the time. It was time to go. Before I took action, however, I was lucky enough to bump into our chief medical officer, a pleasant white-haired old captain. He inquired about my plans, and I told him I was resigning.

"No you're not," he said. "I'm going to get you a medical discharge." And he did. I was released on temporary disability at half-pay, and the Veterans' Administration covered all my law school expenses.

In the fall of 1971, I entered Union University's Albany Law School, and in 1975 I passed the New York bar. By 1978 I was practicing on my own when the Navy advised me that my temporary disability status would be challenged and that I should appear at a hearing at Great Lakes. My assigned counsel told me that since I hadn't had a relapse I could be pronounced fit and ordered back to active duty—even sea duty. Like any good lawyer, I settled for a small cash payment and an honorable discharge. So ended my Navy career.

Chapter Six

1970

Doing the Best You Can

Swift Boats at the beginning of 1970 appeared to be in better control of their war than at any time since the eclipse of the North Vietnamese trawlers two years earlier. SEALORDS had cleared the enemy from large swatches of the Ca Mau Peninsula, forcing them to withdraw to strongholds deep in the forest. Firefights and ambushes had declined, and civilians could move about the region with relative ease. Seafloat was a resounding success, fostering the growth of a substantial settlement where none had existed before, thereby giving local people a chance to earn a living.

Up in the northern Delta, Swifts had joined with PBRs and RAG units to choke off the flow of supplies and men along the Cambodian border. A second detachment of Swifts policed the border from a makeshift forward base at Ha Tien.

The northern Delta could be dangerous and deadly, but, as at Ha Tien, it could also be tedious work: there were endless board-and-searches of river sampans and small junks during the day, coupled with post-curfew "night ambushes" in which crewmen waited in mosquito-infested mangroves for smugglers and infiltrators to try an illegal crossing.

But cracks began to appear in this happy façade. In 1970, the Navy had two goals that were not always compatible: to consolidate and continue the gains of SEALORDS, and to implement "Vietnamization," President Richard Nixon's plan to extricate the United States from the war by turning it over to the South Vietnamese government and armed forces. To do this the Navy planned to disband the U.S. Swift Boat command by the end of the year.

Unmistakable signs soon emerged that neither the U.S. nor the Vietnamese Navies had a great deal of confidence in Vietnamization. The U.S. Navy was having difficulty finding boat officers. A plan to make fresh-faced ensigns into Swift OinCs was implemented and quickly abandoned. More experienced officers were needed, but "lifers"—academy graduates, ROTC officers, and other regular Navy types—were looking elsewhere. Swift Boats were not a growth industry, and Vietnamization was an escape hatch, not a winning strategy. Career officers apparently were looking for something with a more optimistic future.

As the year began, the new officers—these would be the last U.S. OinCs ever to serve on wartime Swifts—were, with almost no exceptions, reserve lieutenants junior grade who had decided to finish their three years of active duty in Vietnam. They were motivated by a variety of reasons. Boredom with fleet life ranked high, as did simple curiosity. Some were ideologically committed, while others volunteered only to decide later they had made a terrible mistake. Regardless of motive, they were just as competent as their predecessors, but without illusions. The end of 1970 was the end of the line: no more boats, and no victory.

The Swifts viewed their Vietnamese counterparts with suspicion. In the early days the Navy encouraged Swift crews to get to know local folks, take the time to learn about the Vietnamese culture, and encourage the Vietnamese Navy. SEALORDS had changed all that. Swifts in 1970 planned their own operations, and while Vietnamese boats might accompany them, the Vietnamese took orders from their ops staff and the U.S. boats took orders from American staff. At ground level, the two navies never really knew one another.

In what contacts they had, the U.S. crews found their counterparts to be competent but reluctant to take risks, and thus perhaps not to be trusted. Had they analyzed the relationship in detail, the Americans would have realized that the only thing they had in common with the Vietnamese Swifts was the hardware. The U.S. crews were like children in a playground. They were blessed with formidable nannies: air and artillery support, repair shops, and a stable government. When it got dark, they went home. The Vietnamese could rely on none of these things.

They were already home and forever saddled with whatever happened. Vietnamization meant early departure for many U.S. crewmen. For the South Vietnamese Swifts, Vietnamization meant nothing but uncertainty.

After six months in the rivers, crews realized that even the hardware had a new set of shortcomings. Swift Boats were not as "swift" or maneuverable in shallow water. Screws and rudders had no protection against river vegetation. A lot of drive shafts broke. Mud clogged cooling water systems, which could cause engine burnout.

Crews did what they could. They tied the exhaust flaps with fishing line to stop them from clattering so the boats would be quieter. They "up-armored" to get a modicum of shrapnel protection by hanging old flak jackets from guardrail wires and stealing sheets of Kevlar wherever they could find them. But the boats—Mark I's, except for five new Mark III's that had arrived at the end of 1969—were old and beat-up, and nothing was going to restore lost youth. PCF 50 was hit with a rocket in December 1969, then with a Claymore in early May 1970. Ten days after that a homemade Viet Cong "launch bomb" blew a five-foot hole in the port side, and the boat had to be hoisted aboard a barge to get it out of the Cua Lon.[1] Nonetheless, the Navy overhauled it at Cat Lo and turned it over to the Vietnamese later in the year. And there were plenty of boats either just as tired or even worse off. The last of the original rationales for Seafloat was to provide a "safe haven" for Swifts during the monsoon. By 1970, this was no afterthought.

Intelligence gathered at Seafloat from captured documents indicated that the lower Ca Mau Peninsula, contrary to the relative calm in late 1969, was a hotbed of insurgent activity. Large chunks of territory were controlled by the Viet Cong, with company-sized insurgent units providing muscle. The enemy was interested in attacking Seafloat but had not yet done so, probably because of aggressive patrolling ashore and in nearby rivers and canals. The population at the Annex held steady, around 4,000 civilians.

It turned out that the intelligence was right. The Viet Cong may have withdrawn from the Cua Lon, but they had not left the Ca Mau Peninsula. On January 16, Swifts inserted a thirty-man Vietnamese reaction force, along with U.S. SEALs and an ordnance disposal team, to sweep the Cai Ngay River, deep in the forest northeast of Seafloat. The troops found grenade booby traps, land mines, and an electric wire leading from the river to an abandoned bunker complex thirty yards away where the enemy had set up a static ambush. The EOD team cut the wire lead and looped a line around a heavy object resting on the bottom of the canal. A Swift Boat hauled the object onto the riverbank: It was an unexploded U.S.-made 750-pound bomb rigged as a battery-detonated water mine.[2]

Three months later, on the night of April 21, four enemy swimmers attacked Seafloat. Sentries spotted bubbles in the water around 2205 and saturated the area with concussion grenades. Five hours later, at slack water, three more swimmers were spotted snorkeling toward the pontoons. All three were killed. On April 24, Navy frogmen found the bodies of the first four swimmers. One man carried 250 quarter-pound blocks of TNT interspersed with plastic explosives. The other three had Soviet grenades, time-fuse pencils, blasting caps, and nylon line to secure the mines to the pontoons.[3] Together they carried enough explosives to sink the entire base.

In mid-May a squad of SEALs and Kit Carson Scouts surprised seven armed insurgents in a sampan hidden in a mangrove swamp five miles east of Seafloat and took them under fire. Swift Boats later extracted the squad, which had apparently intercepted the lead elements of a company-sized enemy force attempting to cross the Cua Lon. Eleven insurgents died in the firefight.[4]

On May 30 two Swifts investigated a canal where Seawolves had attacked and destroyed three camouflaged sampans. The Swifts salvaged 165 Chinese, American, and Viet Cong grenades and fuses, along with automatic rifles, rocket launchers and rockets, homemade launch bombs, and equipment for a machine shop and foundry.[5]

All this suggested that the Viet Cong, far from backing away from the Ca Mau, were returning to areas they had abandoned in 1969. SEALORDS had clearly hurt them, cutting back their supplies of sophisticated Soviet bloc equipment, but they were compensating by making their own guns, ammo, and explosives, and getting an occasional helping hand, perhaps, from imported North Vietnamese talent—the snorkelers?

Just as the enemy was ratcheting up, the U.S. Swift Boat force was shrinking dramatically. Da Nang closed down in February and Cam Ranh Bay followed soon after. At the beginning of March there were sixty-three U.S. boats left. On June 23, Secretary of the Navy John Chafee visited various bases and turned over 273 riverine combat vessels—including thirty-six Swifts. "The Vietnamese Navy takes over today the major combat role in its own waters," Chafee announced at the ceremony. "And, with the turnover next December of the final 123 combat boats, the U.S. Navy will relinquish all surface combatant responsibilities in Vietnam."[6] At the end of June, there were fifty-two U.S. Swift Boats left at Seafloat and in the northern Delta. Vietnamization was half over.

The Original Arnold Horshack

Paul D. Johnson

Engineman Second Class Paul D. Johnson left the Navy after Vietnam and served for thirty years as a Chief Engineer for the U.S. Merchant Marine. He worked for Washington State Ferries and retired in Seattle.

I MET UP WITH ARNOLD HORSHACK IN 1969 WHEN I GOT ORDERS TO PCF 12, stationed at An Thoi. Horshack and I came aboard about the same time. We were the whole crew at that point, as the previous bunch had all gone home. Horshack (not his real name, but close) had already spent several tours in Vietnam. He was a skinny little guy, maybe five foot seven with black hair, a short scruffy beard, and a beaded necklace with a peace medallion that attracted quite a bit of hostile attention from the higher-ups. Horshack didn't care. I soon learned that Horshack didn't care about a lot of things, most of them having to do with discipline.

He was the only guy I ever met who claimed that he never went to Swift Boat school. Instead, he told me, the Navy sent him to An Thoi from boot camp. When he arrived no one knew what to do with him (his words to me). Finally, the Executive Officer sent him to an LST off the coast of the Ca Mau Peninsula that was serving as a forward base for Swifts to refuel and resupply. He was supposed to fill in as a relief crewman for those who went on leave or R&R, or who went home. After three months of this without a break he noticed that regular PCF crews had to deploy only for thirty days before returning to An Thoi for rest and boat maintenance. Nobody was saying anything to Horshack, so he caught the next boat back to An Thoi to find out what was up. The next day he showed up at the ship's office and asked to see the XO, who took one look at Horshack and let out a gasp. "Where the hell have you been?"

"I've been right where you sent me three months ago. I need some time off," Horshack said. "What gives?"

The XO ran to the radio room. "Have you sent out that MIA report on Seaman Horshack yet?" he shouted. "Well, if you have, please stop it and change the seaman's status to present and accounted for!"

And now we're together on the 12-Boat. Eventually, the rest of the new crew shows up and then we're underway for Ha Tien, a port town on the river that separates Cambodia and South Vietnam, near the Gulf of Thailand. Our base is a couple of barges tied up next to some disheveled buildings. Charlie has been using the area forever to smuggle troops, ammo, and supplies into Vietnam. We're supposed to stop him.

At dusk the first day we travel upriver for a "night ambush," a fairly simple op in which we are supposed to find a convenient tree, tie up, kill the engines, douse the lights, and wait until bad guys try to cross the river from the Cambodia side to Vietnam. Then we grease them.

We set up, and I'm on watch with Horshack in the bow, trying to keep the mosquitoes from eating me alive on a dark, muggy night. Then Horshack notices something on the riverbank and calls to me to look. I don't see anything.

"There's a trail in the bushes," he says.

"Big deal," I say.

"I'm gonna see where it leads."

"You're crazy."

He lowers himself to the riverbank, swinging hand-over-hand down the mooring line. Then he disappears into the jungle. I tell the boat officer. He says, "Why didn't you stop him?" Sure, you bet. I return to the bow all alone, hot, sweaty, and swatting the mosquitoes. I wait for what seems like most of the night before I hear a voice from the darkness.

"Hey, Johnson, can you give me a hand?"

"Where have you been?" I ask.

Swift Boats nested at Ha Tien base.
COURTESY OF LARRY IRWIN

"Here take this, and be careful. It's live." Whereupon Horshack hands me a nasty-looking pancake-shaped thing with spikes sticking out of it. It's a land mine.

"Set it down and help me with the rest," Horshack says. "I've got five more."

"What the hell have you been doing?"

"Exploring the jungle."

I remind him that we aren't supposed to go off on our own.

"Don't worry so much," he said. "Nothing happened, and everything is okay."

Then the sun comes up and it's time to get back to Ha Tien. We're going full speed because it's harder for Charlie to hit us when we're traveling fast. Horshack is the bow gunner, but pretty soon he's back on the fantail with a land mine. There isn't enough room up forward for him, his mines, and his machine gun. He decides he has to do something with his mines, so he sets one down on the fantail and walks back to his battle station to get the rest.

Before he returns with the second one, the first one is sliding around the deck every time we careen around a river bend. I am beyond upset. I tell Horshack he's got to secure his trophies. He piles them in the center of a mooring hawser laid on deck in a circle. Now any incoming can obliterate us with one lucky shot—with me first!

Eventually we slow down and I call Ha Tien and tell them I've got a buddy with Explosive Ordnance Disposal. Can he meet us?

The EOD is standing on the fuel pier when we come alongside: "What's the big deal?" he asks.

I point to the land mines. The EOD is a warrant officer and a pretty crusty guy, but his eyes almost shoot out of their sockets. "Where in the hell did you get those?"

Horshack is summoned to explain. He retells his tale, with new details. After he jumped off the boat, he followed the trail he had seen for a quarter mile until it dead-ended in a main road of some kind. That was far enough, he decided, and so he turned around.

On his way back along the same road, he noticed some spikes sticking out of the ground in the middle of the trail. He had seen a lot of war movies and decided this must be a land mine. He took out his trusty KA-BAR knife and started probing the mine to locate the edges. Once he accomplished this (like in the movies), he dug the mine out and lifted it from the ground. Then he spotted another one. And another. Eventually he reached the boat with an armload of six. The fact that he had traversed the whole minefield without triggering anything does not seem to concern him.

The EOD guy listens to all this and scratches his head. He doesn't know what to make of Horshack.

"Somebody get me an empty pallet board," he finally says. "Has anyone got some parachute cord?" One sailor brings him a shot line. The EOD guy ties one end of the line to the pallet and lowers it over the stern of the boat into the river. He lies flat on the deck while we hold his legs.

"Carefully hand me one of those land mines," he says. He puts the first one in the center of the pallet and adds the rest one by one, carefully arranging them so the pallet doesn't tip over. Then he slowly lets the line out until the river floats the pallet and its cargo downriver about 300 yards. He calls for a marksman to take an M-14 rifle, find a high spot, "and, when I call out, shoot the pallet."

At this point there's a big audience. The sailor with the M-14 shoots and misses. Then he misses again. But the third time: *Boom!* It was great theater, like Charlton Heston parting the Red Sea in *The Ten Commandments.*

Then the EOD guy turns to me. Time to cut me a new you-know-what for bringing six live land mines out of the woods, driving them down the river, and having them on the fantail when we tie up to the fuel barge. I remind him that Seaman Horshack is the one who did it. He doesn't care. "Don't do it again," he tells me.

"Yessir." What else can I say? I hand him the bottle of Jack Daniel's I've got stashed in my seabag.

Horshack, of course, skates—beaded necklace and all.

The 12-Boat

Paul D. Johnson

Engineman Second Class Paul D. Johnson's story, The Original Arnold Horshack, appears on page 206.

During my year in Vietnam, from May 1969 to May 1970, I spent about eight months based at An Thoi, a small island in the Gulf of Thailand. It was not unusual to serve on several boats during a tour. Some were swapped out at overhaul. Others just required different crews due to end of tour, R&R, sickness, wounds, or, in some cases, death. Some boats remain etched in my memory, like the 12-Boat. Let me tell you, it was no prize.

I was all alone and unassigned at the time, as was PCF 12. I have always felt this was not a chance meeting. Another guy who was in similar circumstances was Gunner's Mate Horshack, a stranger to me at that moment, but soon to be a valued colleague in misfortune.

I'm in the engine room and Horshack is on deck, so we divide up the jobs to get the old girl in shape. I change the oil and filters, strip the fuel tanks, and check for spare parts and tools—details that always seem to haunt me later if I let them wait. My credo is to trust no one. When you have the time, the parts, and the repair shops, you do the work.

Horshack is doing the same thing topside—checking mooring lines and supplies of toilet paper and food, and making lists of what is and isn't on board. Then we turn to the practical: Does the stove work? Do we have a gun tub cover? Radios? Check. Then we look at the guns, ammo,

Swift Boat returns to An Thoi.
COURTESY OF LARRY IRWIN

spare barrels, grenades, and mortar rounds. It's best to inventory the ammo locker for quality and toss anything that looks dicey—just like Mom used to do in the refrigerator back home.

The rest of the crew shows up. We decide to take this baby for a test drive. It doesn't go well. At full throttle, the rudder wants to be between four to six degrees to starboard or the boat won't go straight. I speculate that someone had the rudders off and didn't realign the linkage. I also discover that the port engine is misaligned and the packing gland that encases the port shaft is all messed up. It's worn on one side and the shaft is running in an uneven orbit, doing a kind of horizontal hula. Good Lord.

We decide to have the tender pick her up so we can get a look at the outside of the hull. But as soon as we maneuver the boat beneath the crane, I hear groaning from the tender's crewman: "Oh, no, not that pile of junk again," he says. Another said, "Call the welders and tell 'em to bring their MIG (arc) welder. They're going to have a long day."

"So, okay guys," I ask. "What's the big deal?"

I learn that during its last patrol, our pride and joy was traveling on one of the rivers at full speed when some VC on the riverbank detonated a water mine close by. It was about the size of a fifty-gallon oil drum. So the boat, weighing twenty-seven tons and moving at twenty-three knots, suddenly leapt between six and nine feet into the air. I'm getting the picture.

I seek out some sailors who know something about this. One seaman tells me he was riding on the bow of the boat directly astern of PCF 12. One moment he was looking at her butt end, he said, and the next moment he was staring at the hull six feet in the air with both screws still going full speed. The force of reentry ripped the port engine from its foundation and tipped it over on its side. Soon the starboard engine stopped. In the end, the rearranged mess of 12-Boat had to be towed out of the river by other Swifts. Thank God no one was killed, but several crewmen went to the hospital and were subsequently reassigned.

The engineman working at the base at An Thoi was one of the crew. He tells me he can no longer ride the boats because he has broken several vertebrae. When the mine went off, he says, he soared into the air along with everyone and everything else. He landed on the fantail on some ammo cans, and all kinds of ammo and other stuff landed on top of him. As he lay there, he felt something warm and wet on his face. He reached up and discovered his entire upper body was covered with liquid. His thick glasses had shattered and he couldn't see. He started hollering that he was shot and dying, but when rescuers arrived they didn't seem particularly concerned—he was covered with motor oil from a busted jerry can.

Everyone on the boat was injured, but some fared worse than others. The gunner manning the twin .50-caliber machine guns in the forward gun tub went up in the air along with his weapons, his gun ring, his counterweight, and the cans of ammo that surrounded him. He did a front flip and landed upside down in the tub, his feet sticking up in the air, his arms pinned by belts of ammo wrapped around him like fouled fishing line. Rescuers had to de-link the ammo by hand to get him free. During the firefight he was defenseless and unable to move, his legs kicking in the air like a trapped squirrel as bullets whizzed through the gun tub without hitting him. This sort of horrid experience can provide years of nightmares.

We finally get to look at the boat out of the water. It's not a pretty sight. All of the hull plates are punched inward like upside-down soup bowls. From the lazarette to the forward end of the main cabin, all of the hull plates have this concave appearance. There are cracks everywhere. The rudders are in their correct positions as near as we can tell. We speculate that the keel is bent, even though we don't have the equipment to measure it.

We now turn our attention to the port engine. It's in a sad state. I ask if anything can be done to fix the alignment. There's not much hope, I am told, unless we take out the engine and build a new foundation. This would require a trip to the yard at Cam Ranh Bay, which ain't gonna happen. The machinists do what they can, but it's not much. So we go on patrol and try to take it easy. We could run full speed, but the port shaft was never properly aligned, so we had to apply right rudder constantly. It was one sad ride. After a couple of months of this, our whole crew got pulled off and a bunch of fresh-faced rookies took over. And they were the ones who got to take the 12-Boat to Cam Ranh. I guess they wanted to make sure the old salts stayed in the combat zone.

I have come to the conclusion that the 12-Boat's sad story is one of command hubris. The powers that be did not want to scrap the boat and credit the opposition—whatever happens, don't put one in the enemy's win column. And if mechanical failure aboard this crippled lady causes heartache or loss of life, one merely has to fill out a casualty report to explain it all away: "Lost at sea with all hands aboard." But never: "Lost to enemy action."

So welcome to the fray, young men. Line up like the cannon fodder you are, and accept your fate. Those on high can take comfort knowing that they will neither suffer from our mistakes nor will they be required to learn from them. *C'est la guerre.*

Hearts and Minds

Tom Byrnes

Lt. (j.g.) Tom Byrnes retired from the Navy as a commander in 1988, worked briefly as a realtor, and then became a gentleman farmer in Jacksonville, Florida.

HOW DO YOU CONVINCE PEOPLE OF A DIFFERENT RACE, WHO DO NOT speak your language, who cannot read, and have absolutely nothing in common with you, to give up their allegiance to your enemy and support you instead?

I had no idea, but the U.S. Navy supposedly did, and for ten months it trained me to become a Psychological Operations Officer. I found out a lot of stuff about Navy organization and enemy propaganda, but I didn't learn anything about how to win new friends and influence people. Probably just as well.

I reported to the CO of the Coastal Surveillance Force at Cam Ranh Bay in December 1969. I was supposed to become the PSYOPS Officer for the Navy's exotically titled Seafloat Mobile Advanced Tactical Support Base. "Seafloat" was a group of steel pontoons cabled together and anchored in the middle of the Cua Lon River, home to about one hundred U.S. Navy and twenty Vietnamese Navy personnel. It was at Nam Can, in the Ca Mau Peninsula, at the very southern end of South Vietnam. There were anywhere from twelve to fifteen U.S. Swift Boats stationed there at any one time. The idea was to establish a Republic of Vietnam presence in what was essentially enemy territory.

Seabees and civilian contractors were building a permanent base on the riverbank across from the pontoons.

My immediate difficulty was that the Surveillance Force CO didn't need a PSYOPS Officer at Seafloat. He needed a Logistics Officer at Cam Ranh Bay, so I spent three months handling shipping containers and sending .50-caliber ammo to Swift Boats. Then, one day, word arrived that Seafloat's PSYOPS officer, a friend of mine, had been seriously wounded on a helicopter reconnaissance flight. I was shocked, and then shocked again an hour later when the CO told me to pack my gear and head south. My only weapon was a KA-BAR knife. When I first arrived at Cam Ranh there weren't enough guns to go around.

I reached Nam Can at dusk one day in early May 1970 aboard an Army Chinook helicopter. It didn't want to stick around, but a very large johnboat took me to Seafloat. The next morning I met the three quartermasters who were my PSYOPS team. I found that we had plenty of people ready to help us, but nothing for them to do. We could drop leaflets from helicopters, except we didn't have any leaflets. We could ride boats into the Nam Can forest and nail posters to trees, but we didn't have any posters.

I messaged my PSYOPS support officer in Saigon and asked him to send me anything he could. Within a couple of days several thousand colorful leaflets arrived. The message made no difference to me. I couldn't read it, and most of the local population was illiterate. But it was something tangible that people could hold. They could hand it over to us, like a "Get Out of Jail Free" card, or failing that, use it for toilet paper.

Besides leaflets, two "Beach Jumpers" also showed up, bringing a portable 1,400-watt battery-operated broadcast system. Beach Jumpers were experts in "cover and deception"—fooling the enemy about our true objectives. They taught us how to operate the broadcast system and left us a copy of "The Wandering Soul," a newly developed PSYOPS tape about a Viet Cong guerrilla lamenting his decision to support Communism. We were to learn quickly that there was nothing deceptive about "The Wandering Soul."

I took my men aside and outlined our plan: We would first test out "The Wandering Soul" on a Swift Boat, then try it on a helicopter to see which worked best. We didn't listen to the tape and weren't particularly interested in what it said. We couldn't understand it anyway. I talked to some of the Swift Boat Officers-in-Charge about a short nighttime op to test the gear, but there were no takers. Their reasoning made sense: Make noise at night on the river, draw gunfire. In desperation, I went to Seafloat's Swift Boat Coordinator. Somehow he got a boat to take us.

It was pitch black when we powered up the sound system. Then I hit "Play." Instantly, every hair on my body stood at full attention. The loudspeaker bellowed out the beginning of "The Wandering Soul," and even though the language was Vietnamese, we got the message. The spooky wails and echo-chamber effects, rapidly changing in amplitude, nearly drowned out the dreadful screams of the "dead" Viet Cong soldier calling out to his living daughter not to make the same mistake he had made. Every person on the boat rushed to shut the speaker system off, but we weren't fast enough. Within fifteen seconds gunfire was crackling from a nearby Regional Force/Popular Force militia encampment—friendlies. We slipped into the middle of the river where the current was running fastest and drifted silently and ignominiously past the militia outpost to safety.

Embarrassed and contrite, I quickly reviewed the action in my mind to determine what had gone wrong. I figured out that Swift Boats work best when used in one of two ways: in stealth, by hiding along a riverbank until the enemy rounds the bend and runs into them; or in an open show of force, like when they escort a tug and barge down the center of the river daring anyone in the area to take it on.

Stealth and "The Wandering Soul" obviously were not a winning combination. Instead, we decided to use the tape during or immediately after firefights. The noise could disrupt enemy verbal communications, instill fear, and enhance the effect of mortar fire on enemy positions. Eventually, we also obtained a "laugh box" tape with a particularly sardonic and annoying recording that the Swift Boats played for one or two minutes at the end of a firefight as they drove away. Not your usual studio laugh track.

It was also obvious that no helicopter could circle an enemy position long enough to play "The Wandering Soul" without getting shot down. So, in the air, we decided to use short recorded broadcast messages to convince the Viet Cong to come over to our side. The idea would be to get Viet Cong who had "rallied" to the South Vietnamese government to make tapes to encourage their former comrades and neighbors to surrender. Unfortunately, nobody had ever surrendered.

Over the next few months my team spent the daytimes either dropping leaflets from helos or working with villagers in the town of Ham Rong, building a school. Occasionally we rode Swifts on indigenous troop insertions, either tacking 8×11 posters to trees in the backwaters of tiny canals, or serving as "hired guns" to help protect the boat. We also helped with tug and barge escorts and accompanied Swifts on night ambushes.

Being out on the rivers was no worse than being back at the pontoons. Seafloat was the high-value target on the river, and the enemy tried incessantly to sink it. Swimmer-sappers on opposite sides of the Cua Lon would each hold the end of a rope attached in the middle to a large explosive charge. They would float down the river and try to snag the charge on Seafloat's anchor chains. The current would draw the ends of the rope and swimmers together so they could tie off the rope ends with enough slack to position the charge directly beneath Seafloat. The key was to make the charge explode before the current changed direction.

Seafloat protected itself as best it could. There were four sentry positions, one at each corner. Each sentry would throw a concussion grenade every two minutes. The detonation would drive the air from swimmers' lungs and force them to the surface. Any swimmer that surfaced died instantly. In the months I was there, one swimmer was shot by a sentry and another drowned beneath the pontoons. No swimmer was ever captured alive.

In July, I left Seafloat for R&R in Hawaii, but on my layover in Saigon I heard unbelievable news. A whole village of 150 people had given themselves up to Seafloat forces as I left the base. I was incredulous. I had hoped to get some *hoi chanh*, "ralliers," at some point, but it had never occurred to me that there would be so many. The ralliers included the local Viet Cong tax collector and his two bodyguards, all three of whom had probably been shooting at us a week earlier. Now they were neighbors. I later asked the tax collector why he had become a Viet Cong: "There was nothing else to be," he said.

Seafloat in the lower Ca Mau Peninsula summer of 1970. Seafloat was meant as a temporary base to reestablish a presence after the Ca Mau Peninsula was overrun during the Tet Offensive. In the background, construction is underway for a permanent military base.
COURTESY OF JOHN W. YEOMAN

My attitude toward the enemy changed. While there were certainly hardcore Viet Cong in Ca Mau, most of our ralliers were just poor, uneducated people who wanted to be left alone. Like the tax collector, they had only two choices: be a Viet Cong or be dead. I contacted Saigon and set up transportation for the ralliers to go to a reeducation camp. Before they left we made about a dozen short audiotapes in which they appealed to relatives to join them. We played these whenever we could get a helo, and people responded almost immediately. Seeing a Swift Boat, they would wave the leaflets we had dropped. Once they came in, we made new tapes and began the cycle all over again.

It wasn't long before I heard from the Ham Rong villagers that the Viet Cong had offered cash rewards for me and my three team members. My bounty was 100,000 piasters (about $20,000) and the team members were 20,000 piasters (about $4,000) each. The Viet Cong called me "the man who eats baby livers." This quickly fell out of fashion, since no one ever saw me eat a baby's liver, but I toyed briefly with the idea of changing my call sign to "Babylivers." In the end, I decided to stay with "Heartsactual," since it was known to everyone on Seafloat.

The *hoi chanh* were coming in regularly from the western side of the peninsula, but we had nothing working from the east or south. The previous year, Swifts had fought a vicious, deadly engagement in the southern Duong Keo River. In late June, they had fought another one in the same general area, so we knew there were a lot of people there, and they weren't friendly. We worked the area with leaflets and our homemade helicopter tapes, but only got shot at for our troubles. It was time to try something else.

So, about 2100 on one fairly dark night in August 1970, we left Seafloat aboard a 36-foot Vietnamese Navy Yabuta junk, traveling about twenty miles east to the mouth of the Duong Keo. We hoped to capture a departing Viet Cong sampan and get its occupants to tape some surrender appeals that we could broadcast by helicopter—if we could find their village.

We ran the bow of the junk onto the riverbank at 0100. There were nine of us—four Vietnamese and five Americans. Everyone understood the plan, except that the junk captain apparently had no intention of shutting off the engine while we lay at ambush. We talked it over very intensely. In the end, the captain killed the engine.

But not soon enough. About an hour later two helicopters—U.S. Navy Seawolf gunships by the sound—approached. I wasn't worried. Our position was marked on the big area chart in the Seafloat Operations Center. Then I heard a sudden change in the chopper noise. The Seawolves were starting a dive. I grabbed my radio handset: "Seawolf, this is Heartsactual, are you on a firing run?"

I instantly heard their transition to level flight. They were indeed on a firing run, one of the pilots said, and they were loaded with 2.75-inch folding-fin flechette rockets, each one of which held 2,500 two-inch steel darts. A U.S. Army Mohawk infrared surveillance aircraft had observed a "hot spot" over our area—probably the junk's diesel engine. I never found out why no one bothered to check the ops chart.

Our adventure had started badly, and it got worse. Less than twenty minutes after the Seawolves had passed, we heard many diesel engines rumbling towards us. Swift Boats. Now what? I didn't know about any Swifts in the area. I didn't know whether the Swifts knew about us. And I didn't have their radio frequency. I told the others to be quiet. If we were spotted I would call out to the Swifts. We waited. Everyone was terrified.

Within seconds the boats passed us. We breathed a sigh of relief, but clearly it wasn't our night. I suggested we wait for the Swifts to round the headland just west of us, and then light off our engine and follow them home. The captain agreed. Everyone was happy.

Not so fast. Just after the Swifts turned, Charlie took them under fire. The Swifts returned fire, roaring through the ambush at more than thirty knots. Our immediate problem was the hail of bullets passing over the headland and coming toward us. Small-arms rounds plunked into the water nearby, but the .50-caliber rounds flew past us, among them tracers that looked like big orange basketballs.

They missed us. I sat down on deck with my back leaning against the wooden cabin. Suddenly, something struck my helmet on the left side, almost knocking it off my head. I looked up and saw an orange wink right in front of me. Someone was behind a small bush on the riverbank shooting at me, and a piece of the junk's wooden hull had glanced off my helmet. I saw two more orange winks before I was able to bring my M-60 machine gun to bear. I fired almost 200 rounds into the bush before I regained control of myself. The shooter was blown into the water, and I was shaking but unhurt.

And that, finally, was all. We crept around the point, then roared after the Swifts at our top speed of about four knots. The river gods helped out with a following current of two or three additional knots to push us home.

Thirty years later I found out that the shooter that night in the Duong Keo didn't quite miss. My wife noticed dark objects right under my beltline at the small of my back, apparently deep under the skin. Over the years they had migrated close to the surface, and she started digging them out with a needle. They were wood slivers, and she was still finding them in 2015.

Our efforts on the western side of the peninsula continued to bear fruit. Small numbers of people appeared on the riverbanks, normally with leaflets in hand. Others probably bypassed us and went directly to Ham

Rong. Seafloat, on the other hand, was doing badly. Too many concussion grenades had opened cracks in the pontoons. We pumped every day, but couldn't stay even. On September 15, 1970, everything on Seafloat was moved to "Solid Anchor," the base on the beach. We expected Charlie to mine Seafloat that evening since there was nobody around to throw concussion grenades, but it didn't happen. Within a few days, tugs arrived to haul the pontoons away.

The U.S. Swift Boats left Nam Can on October 1, 1970, and were replaced by Vietnamese Swifts. My team lingered on, along with some new U.S. Navy arrivals who provided base defense and logistical and operational support. I started to feel that our days of accomplishment were ending.

I had a hard time convincing the new Vietnamese Swift Boat coordinator to allow my team on their boats. On our first tryout, riding as hired guns, we were just turning off the Cua Lon into a canal when the gunner on top of the pilothouse opened fire with the twin fifties. The op was compromised, and we quickly headed back to Solid Anchor. The next time I tried to go on patrol, the Swift coordinator turned me down: "the spirit of flotation has left my boats," he said. I stuck with Seawolves and leaflet drops. There were shrinking numbers of ralliers from the west, and nothing from the east.

My relief, a Navy lieutenant, arrived at the beginning of December 1970. I briefed him on our activities. We had 823 ralliers at that point. The next morning I took him on a Seawolf recon flight. As we overflew the mouth of the Duong Keo I spotted a man down below: "Look at that Viet Cong trying to chop down that tree by swinging his AK-47 stock at it like an axe," I said.

He didn't care. "I'm a Naval Academy graduate," he replied. "Getting killed in Vietnam won't help my career. I'm going (to Saigon) to become the admiral's aide."

I left Nam Can for good an hour later. I gathered my team to say good-bye. They were probably going to be on their own and shouldn't rely too much on the lieutenant, I said. Indeed, I learned later, the lieutenant became the admiral's aide. Actually fighting the Vietnam War had apparently become unfashionable even in the Navy.

What the Hell Am I Doing Here?

Ted Kenny

Lt. (j.g.) Ted Kenny was in the U.S. Navy Reserve from 1967 to 1970 and served on a Swift Boat in 1970. After separating from the service, Kenny pursued several careers, serving as vice president of an investment firm, working in custom home construction, and serving as vice president of sales at IDEX Microsystems, after which he returned to the brokerage business and ventured into commercial real estate. In 2012, Kenny retired with his wife to Colorado.

WHAT THE HELL AM I DOING HERE? I HAVE ASKED MYSELF THIS QUESTION several times during my life. I remember asking it on more than one occasion in the surface Navy, and probably daily in Vietnam while on a floating beer can called a Swift Boat.

I have always loved the water. The year was 1967 and most everyone was serving whether they wanted to or not. The Navy was a natural for me, and it became even more imperative when I reported to my induction physical at Fort Hamilton in Brooklyn. The standard "turn your head and cough" and "bend over and spread your cheeks" routine suggested to me that the Army was not the way to go.

But real fear reared its ugly head when a fellow inductee had an eye exam. The medic shouted over to the sergeant that this guy couldn't see out of his left eye. The non-com barked, "Can he see out of his right eye?" "Affirmative," came the reply. He passed the physical. Oh my God, I thought. They are taking any warm body.

During this time, I was waiting for orders to Navy Officers' Candidate School in Newport, Rhode Island, and it was a race to the finish. I won. I raised my right hand and joined the Navy at the very moment my Army induction notice was being delivered to my parents' house. Thank heaven for small favors.

My first two years as a line officer were uneventful and even afforded me spare time in one of the country's best cities, Boston. My ship was in the yards and I decided to put off reading Tolstoy's *War and Peace* in favor of cavorting from one end of town to the other. The XO actually told me once that he was grateful I had duty every four days so my liver could have a rest.

While in Boston I met the cutest gal, who would eventually become my wife. She was living with four girls I went to Georgetown with. It was love at first sight, but I couldn't go quietly. We had not just a lover's quarrel but a full-blown breakup before I left.

The plot thickened. Enter Stage Right, my Detailer—the guy in Washington who allegedly looks after you when you need new orders. "Where would you like to go?"

"Just get my ass out of here," I said.

"East Coast? West Coast?"

"Just get me out as fast as possible." Long deliberation and thoughtful reasoning were not always my MO.

Six weeks later I had made up with my wife to be, and the phone rang in the ship's office. "It's for you Mr. Kenny." Uh oh, the Detailer! He told me I was going to Coastal Squadron One. Hmm, I thought, staff duty. How nice. I asked about the location of this outpost.

"In-country, Vietnam."

"Oh. Just what am I going to be doing?"

"You will be the Officer-in-Charge of a PCF."

"What's that?"

"Look it up in *Jane's Fighting Ships*," he said, and hung up.

So, as you see, I didn't quite volunteer. On the other hand, I truly felt that if a guy with a wife and kids was over there, it wasn't my time to bail.

Fast-forward to a Flying Tiger 707 coming into Cam Ranh Bay, 1970. We had left Seattle in late afternoon and followed the sunset across the wide Pacific. The plane's running lights were darkened, and I was now farther from home than I had ever been.

As we taxied to a halt, I could feel the oppressive heat even in the middle of the night. Inside the terminal we were briefed, and I noticed a chap of Asian descent darting to and fro with an Army-issue nine-volt battery strapped to something. Holy shit! He's got a bomb, I thought, and I haven't even been here thirty minutes. Of course, it was a transistor radio tuned to Armed Forces Radio.

So I started my tour. I had 365 days and a wake-up to go. I began by making many startling discoveries that weren't particularly combat-oriented. I found that the beaches were vast and unspoiled, and that Saigon still had most of the trappings of a slightly seedy, delightfully wicked French colonial port city. Vung Tau, on the sea at the northeast corner of the Mekong Delta, was in many ways a resort. You would do fifty or sixty days in the jungles and canals and then have a wonderful dinner with a vodka and tonic.

Seafloat—our Swift base on floating barges moored in the middle of an estuary deep in the Ca Mau Peninsula—offered a totally different reality. Agent Orange rendered lifeless anything from the shoreline inland for 100 yards. There was no hustle and bustle. We owned 500 yards of water and wasteland in the middle of nowhere. The other side owned the rest.

The Brown Water Navy was an apt description for where we were and what we did. The region's prolific tide changes reminded me of a toilet being flushed. The banks oozed mud and you shook your head as you watched one villager brushing his teeth, another washing clothes, and a third taking a dump within shouting distance of each other. I sure hope they switched sides when the tide turned.

I was twenty-four years old and known as "Captain," "skipper," "boss," or "Ted" depending on who was talking. I was responsible for five crewmen and a 50-foot boat. There were no watches. I was on all the time. The guys were great, but I was the man. If I caught a catnap, I was inevitably jolted awake when the engine speeds changed a mere 50 rpm. Guns. Positions. Radios. Code books. Keeping everybody up and alert. Ain't nobody but me holding this thing together. You can train all you want, but the most amazing and challenging part was making split-second decisions. You tried to skew the odds, but you realized if you screwed up there wasn't much latitude. You had a bit of a swagger. You were a Swiftie. But you tried to keep your emotions and arrogance in check. We were playing for keeps.

There were hijinks, of course. Some planned. Some embarrassing. One colleague and his crew had fallen asleep when their boat plowed through some guy's hut from the bedroom to the living room. Although funny at first, the reality of invading these people's world was sobering. Sometimes you just couldn't make it right. And their lives were changed forever. I felt for the villagers who had probably traveled to a city maybe once in their lives, even though it may have been only ten miles away. You got the feeling they didn't care if we were VC or American, they just wanted to be left alone.

There was a camaraderie among officers and crewmen that can't be duplicated. We lived on boats, barges, and barracks, ate crappy food, and laughed and kept each other safe. Arguments were rare. We maintained a fast pace, performing several patrols in a twenty-four-hour period, and time passed quickly. The scariest part was that it really did become our home. You fell into a rhythm, a routine. You haven't lived until you've showered with ice-cold water provided by a cistern. There were so many mosquitoes it sounded like JFK airport at night.

Every so often you had "merry-go-round watch," where one boat circled the base and a nest of moored Swifts and other gunboats. We continually dropped concussion grenades on our loop to ward off sappers, all while gunners from the base were firing .50-caliber rounds into the woods to keep them low. We dealt with it. Life's a bitch, and then you die.

So many years have passed and the memories have become foggy. We always err on the plus side and embellishment seems to be the order of the day. But my thoughts aren't on this rice paddy or that one. I can't remember the names of the rivers and checkpoints. To this day, I have no affinity for guns or high-capacity magazines.

I think I have earned the right to speak of war as a horrendous waste of money and men's and women's lives. Not as a Vietnam veteran against the war, and not as a pacifist—just as a thinking person who looks at the facts and draws an obvious conclusion about the futility of such folly, as the few pursue power and domination. And then, once again, I have to ask, "What the hell are we doing here?"

Irma La Douche

Virgil Erwin

Lt. Virgil Erwin's stories, Duong Keo and Too Young, appear on pages 148 and 170.

WE HUNT THE VIET CONG AT NIGHT IN THE RIVERS OF THE MEKONG Delta near Vung Tau. They wait patiently for us in mud bunkers and blinds for a chance to ambush us with rockets, as if we were mallards. We risk an attack to get them to tip their hand, so we can blow them out of their bunkers.

It's May and the southeast monsoon has arrived, with endless days of torrential rain. I am the skipper of PCF 67. The hot, humid air is unbearable. Our mattresses are vinyl-covered, and gross pools of sweat collect in the depression my body creates. My green fatigues are like damp dish-towels and Gnau, the quartermaster, tries to dry paper charts limp with mildew. Gunner's Mate Taylor bitches about keeping his guns and ammo dry, and he bitches about trying to catch the Viet Cong.

"Let's set up our own ambush," Taylor says.

"Where?" I ask.

"Some canal, hide in the bushes. Gotta get creative." He points to a small canal on the damp chart. "Here," he says.

Gnau looks at the chart. "Don't know about this," he says, shaking his head. "Pretty tight." The canal looks narrow, but I think Taylor's idea is worth a try.

"OK, we'll do it tonight," I say.

There's no moon as we patrol the winding Vam Co River, but even though it's invisible, the lunar gravity has pulled brackish water upstream from the bay of Vung Tau. The combination of rain and tide has raised the Vam Co nine feet; the riverbanks and rice paddies have disappeared underwater.

Our Decca radar is incredibly acute at capturing the sharp image of anything floating on a smooth river—a clump of vegetation, a swimmer, or a VC sampan. But it is useless for navigation tonight. The swollen Vam Co no longer resembles the chart, and our radar can't tell us where the river is deep.

"Slow to five knots," I tell Hoffman, my helmsman. He watches the fathometer, feeling his way over the dark river bottom. We creep into the canal Taylor suggested. Hoffman kills one engine, but the clinking metal flap covering the exhaust pipe still makes too much noise, like a clapper ringing a dinner bell for the VC.

The water level in the canal is so high that tree branches, normally above Taylor in the gun tub, are pushing in through the pilothouse door, creating a floral arrangement on my chart table.

"Shut 'er down," I say to Hoffman.

"Lasso that branch," Gnau tells Stancil. Stancil is the youngest man aboard, still too young to drink, and probably the brightest engineman I have ever met. We sit patiently buried in trees along the bank, watching for VC. Taylor peers through the green light of the night scope. I take turns with Hoffman watching the amber sweep of our radar.

Muggy heat suffocates the pilothouse. Rank odor leaks from my sweat-soaked flak jacket, as if some decaying rodent was inside. I have my face buried in the boot covering the radar, the inverted rubber cone hiding its light. The small opening stinks with sweat from my face. It seems like hours have passed. I fight fatigue, shaking my head like a Labrador retriever stepping out of a lake.

"Something's coming," I say softly.

"What?" Hoffman asks.

"Sampans. One, two . . . a whole string of blips," I say. The wet hair on my neck is electric.

"Sampans, get ready," Hoffman whispers to the crew over his phone.

"Wait!" Taylor says, "I see 'em in the scope. It's a Mobile Riverine Force, HOLD YOUR FIRE!"

"Shit," I say, "What if *they* fire? Turn on the running lights."

Hoffman flips a switch and little red, green, and white lights sparkle around the gun tub. I make a radio call on the only common frequency I can think off.

"This is Elbow Golf six-seven. I have running lights on, M-R-F unit approaching me. Acknowledge."

"Roger, see ya. Out." The radio voice is so casual, like not a care in the world. Thank God they answered my call.

Goliath monsters emerge from darkness. They're painted black-olive-green. These Mobile Riverine vessels look like Civil War monitors with huge gun barrels. They're sheathed in welded rebar armor and they're so low to the water that their bow waves are a bare ripple. The canal is narrow and I stand on the gunnels as they creep past our port side, a mere ten feet between us. The only sound is a deep-throated rumble, like a grizzly sleeping in a cave.

I don't see any faces. Where is the driver; where are the men? It's as if these are ghost ships. They keep coming and coming, passing in a slow, single-file formation. One after another they pass, and not a voice is heard, not a "howdy," nothing.

"Doubt we'll see any Viet Cong tonight," Taylor says.

"Not with that flotilla around," Gnau says.

I don't go to sleep, but my pucker factor drops several notches.

Morning light captures rivulets of water draining from the bank. The moon-driven tide has ebbed. Our bow line to the tree branch is nearly straight up and Taylor stands on top of the pilothouse to untie it. We leave the canal in the same direction as the silent armada last night and enter the Vam Co. I'm eager to be relieved from patrol.

"River's at least nine feet lower than last night," Gnau says. Rice paddies are still draining and are now covered in rich, savory mud. We're driving downriver at twenty-five knots and I spot an apparition, like a painting by Salvador Dali. It's a distorted image, but I know what it is—a Swift Boat in a rice paddy, easily fifty feet from the river and nine feet higher than the water. It's sitting in the mud like a cake decoration. It's both comical and obscene, bringing a chorus of sorry laughter from my crew.

We look at this pathetic sight, a beautiful gunboat built for speed, now mired in mud. Hoffman maneuvers our bow into the bank. It seems odd to stand on top of the pilothouse in order to be eye level with the Swift Boat skipper who's knee deep in muck.

"Need any help?" I ask. I laugh, looking at this stranded sailor on the side of the river highway, as if he's blown a tire and doesn't have a spare. He's Ensign Doug Martin. He smiles, but I can feel his embarrassment. I see a water buffalo grazing near the bow of his boat and the local militia standing in the distance, a defensive perimeter guarding PCF 98. The militia soldiers are smoking cigarettes and laughing.

"We had a blip on the radar," Ensign Martin says, "thought it was a sampan. Maybe our radar was on the wrong scale. We were going pretty fast."

Without him telling me more, I can visualize the scene, his face in the boot of the radar scope, the image of the river looking narrow and normal. A flip of the range dial would have alerted him, would have told him that something was wrong with the banks of a small river now seeming to be over a mile wide. Checking the range dial would have told him the rice fields were flooded.

"I guess the blip you were chasing last night was that dangerous and ferocious water buffalo," I say to Martin. We both look at a young boy leading the buffalo away.

"VC buffalo for sure," Taylor says.

"Tax collector," Gnau adds.

Going aground is not uncommon for Swift Boats. In some cases it reflects bad navigation, like the time I hit a shallow reef. In other cases, it's inexperience or aggressive behavior. Last night, I suppose, it was all three.

"How is he going to get his boat back in the water?" Stancil asks.

"Won't be easy. Almost fifty-thousand pounds," Moison says. Moison is a Boatswain's Mate, absolutely the best at driving our Swift Boat.

"Maybe wait for another high tide?"

"Won't be enough," Gnau says.

The Vietnam mud is notorious. The Viet Cong build bunkers along the rivers, constructed of massive tree trunks, packed and covered with this mud. When it dries the bunkers become virtually impenetrable. Fifty-caliber machine guns and flamethrowers have little effect. But the Mobile Riverine Force offers a unique solution to the ensign's dilemma—they have "Irma La Douche." The name is a play on words: *Irma La Douce* is a movie about a Paris prostitute who has a passion for everything that makes life worth living. Someone changed *Douce* to *Douche*.

Irma shoots water. It's an incredible weapon—a water cannon. Irma has two massive pumps that suck water from the canal, each through a six-inch hose. The pumps blast a stream at 3,000 pounds per square inch through a two-inch titanium nozzle. The cannon dissolves mud bunkers as if they were sandcastles on a beach. The water's velocity can rip a man in half.

Irma is called to the frontline to save the stranded Swift Boat. The cannon carves a trench in the mud below the stern of the boat and a steel cable is attached to her stern. Irma pulls with twin diesels, while a constant stream of water lubricates the channel, breaking the suction as the Swift Boat is inelegantly pulled backward into the river. The sight does not become the lady, a graceful Swift Boat with a passion for life, being dragged by her derrière through mud as if punished for adultery.

We head back to Cat Lo. I can't wait to get to the Officers' Club. I have a great story to share.

Chapter Seven

1970

Turning Out the Lights

On March 6, 1970, during a Giang Thanh River patrol along the Cambodian border, PCFs 9 and 96 came under attack by an enemy rocket team hidden in underbrush along the riverbank. PCF 9, hit once, returned fire and escaped the kill zone with minimal damage, but PCF 96 was holed three times, once near the waterline, and the entire crew had shrapnel wounds. Still, by keeping the throttles wide open, PCF 96 was able to raise the bow high enough to prevent flooding and get out of trouble.

The ambush was the worst of several attacks by a North Vietnamese "hit team" tasked with harassing and destroying as many border-region Swift Boats and PBRs as it could. But it was also the hit team's last attack. PBR crewmen investigating the ambush site found several enemy dead and recovered the team's launcher. It was locked and loaded with a Chinese rocket.

For the tiny Swift garrison at Ha Tien and the PBRs farther upriver, the rocket team had provided a deadly interlude in the ordinarily sleepy routine of Bernique's Creek. Swifts had come to regard Ha Tien almost as in-country R&R—time off from the nerve-racking patrols at Seafloat.[1]

There was a lot more to come on the Cambodian border. SEALORDS was squeezing enemy supply lines, and pressure increased as 1970 advanced. Coastal Division 13 moved from Cat Lo on the South China Sea coast up the Mekong River to Sa Dec, deep in the northern Delta, but much closer to the frontier and to enemy smuggling routes. Swifts, PBRs, and RAG units had the entire border covered from Ha Tien to the Bassac River, a major arm of the Mekong.

Led by Prince Norodom Sihanouk, Cambodia had remained nominally "neutral" during the war, but had allowed the North Vietnamese to run their supply lines through Cambodian territory. Growing resentment toward the Vietnamese led the Cambodian National Assembly to depose Sihanouk on March 18 and replace him with army general Lon Nol. Civil war broke out immediately. Sihanouk, exiled to Peking, allied himself with the North Vietnamese and Cambodia's Khmer Rouge Communist insurgents.

On May 1, the U.S. Army First Cavalry Division crossed into Cambodia to join South Vietnamese troops already fighting the North Vietnamese there. The "Cambodian Invasion" lasted until late July, with U.S. troops withdrawing June 30. Its military success remained in dispute long after the war ended. While it undoubtedly dealt a heavy blow to North Vietnam's logistics, the confusion it caused improved the chances of the genocidal Khmer Rouge, the eventual winners in Cambodia. It also brought a fresh wave of antiwar outrage in the United States.

For the Swifts at Ha Tien, the invasion prompted an unnerving new development. Crews on the Giang Thanh hunkered down, watching helplessly as artillery shells and mortar rounds arced over their heads in ugly duels between Cambodians and Vietnamese on either side of the river. These clashes were fueled not necessarily by politics, but by ethnic animosity and pent-up hatred caused by the Vietnamese using Cambodia as both a staging area and a refuge. Now it was payback time. The Cambodians did not care who got hurt as long as they were Vietnamese. The Vietnamese returned the favor.

During the first week of the invasion, the Sa Dec boats continued regular patrols along the tributaries of the Mekong. But upriver in Cambodia, the enemy captured Neak Loeung, a key commercial hub where Route 1, the main highway connecting Saigon with the Cambodian capital at Phnom Penh, crossed the river.

On May 9, an enormous flotilla of Vietnamese Navy ships and boats crossed the border, intent on securing the river between the two capitals and rescuing thousands of ethnic Vietnamese who had fled to Cambodia to escape the war and who now feared for their lives. Seven Sa Dec Swifts joined the column. They were to guard the ferry crossing at Neak Loeung once Vietnamese troops had cleared the area of enemy troops.

Opposition, however, was practically nonexistent, and the Swifts took control at Neak Loeung without incident. For the next six weeks, until they withdrew to South Vietnam, the Swifts watched the Vietnamese Navy evacuate refugees from Cambodia. Nearly 20,000 fled between May 10 and May 20 alone. By August, South Vietnamese ships had rescued 81,790 people—more than 20 percent of the estimated 400,000 ethnic Vietnamese who had been living in Cambodia.[2]

In the lower Ca Mau Peninsula, the pace of enemy attacks slowed at midyear, but those that occurred were both audacious and professional. The days of hit-and-run firefights were over for both sides. The enemy was shooting straighter and hitting more targets, but the Swifts and RAG boats were hitting back with reaction troops whenever an ambush occurred.

On June 9, the Viet Cong attacked PCFs 93 and 96 from the bank of the Cua Lon west of Seafloat, normally a relatively peaceful stretch of river. A rocket hit PCF 93 on the port side amidships, wounding two crewmen with shrapnel. PCF 96 took a rocket at the waterline below the port pilothouse door, wounding the OinC. The PCFs beached in the middle of the ambush and mortared the kill zone while Seawolves mounted an air strike. Two more Swifts arrived with troops who swept the area, recovering six firing tubes and a B-40 rocket.[3]

In July and again in August, the USS *Canon*, the 168-foot patrol gunboat assigned to Seafloat, was hit by a total of nine rockets. The first attack wrecked the port engine, forcing the *Canon* to beach on the Bo De River. The second attack wounded half the ship's complement—including the captain—and damaged the gunboat so badly that it had to be repaired first in Cam Ranh Bay and then in Guam.[4]

Sapper attacks continued at the Seafloat anchorage. On July 6, a water mine blew a twenty-by-seventeen-foot hole in the USS *Krishna*, a repair ship anchored just west of the pontoons to provide maintenance for the Swifts and RAG boats. Damage-control teams stopped the flooding by listing the ship to starboard. One Swift Boat crewman was killed in a boat moored alongside.[5]

On July 30, just after midnight, a mine blew up the starboard side of a Vietnamese Navy amphibious ship being used as a clinic. The boat capsized and sank by the stern within minutes. Swifts moored at Seafloat scrambled to pick up patients, visitors, and crew as they swam away to escape the wreck.[6]

And on August 18, the body of a dead sapper washed ashore at Solid Anchor on the beach next to Seafloat. The swimmer's chest had been crushed, probably by the impact of a concussion grenade tossed in the river by Seafloat sentries to deter—or kill—enemy swimmers. The dead man was tied to a wooden box filled with 118 pounds of TNT and buoyed by a partially inflated rubber bladder.[7]

Despite the attacks, the news from Seafloat was not all bad. On July 8, three sampans containing twenty people came alongside a pair of Swifts to announce their wish to leave their hamlet deep in enemy territory south of the Cua Lon and seek refuge at the Annex. That afternoon a squad of Kit Carson Scouts visited the village and found fifty-four more people ready to switch sides. The hamlet's Viet Cong leader had left the village that morning when he realized he had lost control of its inhabitants.[8]

Throughout July and into August, refugees streamed into Seafloat. Between August 23 and August 29 alone, 313 people abandoned Viet Cong–held settlements in the Ca Mau backwoods. At that point the Annex had a population of 5,200 and was growing at a rate of 10–15 percent per month.[9]

Even with these successes, Seafloat's days were numbered. After fifteen months of concussion grenades, the pontoons' metal skins were springing leaks. The shore facility at Solid Anchor was almost finished, and, on September 15, everything moved to the beach. Three days later tugs arrived to tow away the derelict base. U.S. Swift Boats fought on in the Ca Mau Peninsula for a few more weeks.

Vietnamese fortunes declined precipitously. The enemy attacked Solid Anchor thirteen times in September, damaging three Vietnamese Swifts and sinking two Vietnamese riverine craft. Six sailors were wounded and eight others were lost and presumed drowned. The other nine riverine units assigned to Solid Anchor could not get underway because of mechanical problems.[10] On the central coast just south of Qui Nhon, sappers in early September mined a Vietnamese Swift lying at anchor, blowing the bottom out of the boat and killing a crewman. On October 20, a Viet Cong company annihilated the PBR pontoon base at the Ong Doc River mouth just up the Gulf of Thailand coast from Solid Anchor. And on November 2, two Vietnamese Swifts foundered and sank in a storm during transit from Solid Anchor to Cat Lo. The crews were rescued.[11]

The Navy turned over twenty-four Swift Boats to the Vietnamese in September and October. Coastal Division 11 at An Thoi, the original U.S. Swift installation established in 1965, shut down. The last of the north Delta boats left Sa Dec and returned to Cat Lo where they were joined by the remaining Ca Mau boats.[12]

By the end of October, only fourteen U.S. Swifts remained in Vietnam, participating in "Operation Blue Shark," the Brown Water Navy's last hurrah in the Delta. Blue Shark, using Swifts, PBRs, and RAG units, had a diverse menu of missions, including board-and-search, interdiction, and SEALORDS-style raids, but the Swift Boats' main task was to probe particularly nasty areas around the mouth of the Mekong River.

Unknown to the crews, many of these raids were diversionary, focusing enemy attention while SEALs searched for hidden Viet Cong prison camps. They did not find any. Four U.S. Swifts, by contrast, discovered a large cache of enemy arms and ammo in the Than Phu Secret Zone in November and fought a vicious encounter there. Ambushed on the way in and on the way out, two Kit Carson Scouts were killed and three Swift crewmen and two more Scouts were wounded. This turned out to be the U.S. Swifts' last firefight.[13]

On December 1, 1970, the Navy turned over the remaining U.S. Swift Boats in a simple ceremony at Cat Lo and closed down Coastal Division 13 and Coastal Squadron 1. Crewmen who were "short" went home early. The rest stayed on as advisors—a new role for them, but an old role for the Navy in Vietnam.[14]

The strategic status quo had not changed between 1965 and 1970. The North Vietnamese and Viet Cong still controlled vast territories in the Mekong Delta, and the Brown Water Navy and its Vietnamese Navy allies had not been able to dislodge them. The difference in 1970 was that the South Vietnamese Navy had 40,000 men and 1,500 ships and boats, including over 100 former U.S. Navy Swift Boats. Maybe the Vietnamese, like the Americans, could at least fight the enemy to a draw. Or maybe not.

Cambodia

Bill Rogers

Lt. (j.g.) Bill Rogers returned from Vietnam in October 1970 and married his wife, Jan, on Thanksgiving Day a month later. He left the Navy as a lieutenant in December 1972, and with Jan opened an employment business in Tacoma, Washington. He retired to Gig Harbor, Washington.

AT LONG LAST WE SPOTTED THE WHITE BOW WAVE OF OUR RELIEF BOAT as it sped upriver toward us. Our Swift Boat, PCF 54, had been on station as a border guard for eight long days, anchored near the small Vietnamese village of An Phu, where the Bassac River flows southward out of Cambodia and into the Mekong Delta. We were out of food, low on fuel, and bored out of our minds from sitting in the hot sun day after day with nothing to do.

Of all the jobs we could be assigned, this one was the pits. We were six young guys on a powerful Navy patrol boat, armed to the teeth and ready for action. But instead of making war, we were anchored at a small river crossing, checking the occasional sampan for contraband and trying to find something to beat the boredom. At night we cruised slowly up and down the river on one engine to conserve fuel. At dawn we threw the anchor overboard and began another day of broiling in the tropical sun. We hated it.

The arrival of the relief boat meant that we could return to our base for a shower and a decent meal—our first in more than a week. But it was not

Lt. (j.g.) Bill Rogers administers first aid to young Vietnamese refugees.
COURTESY OF WILLIAM ROGERS

to be. The boat pulled alongside just long enough to deliver several cases of C-rations and a Marine Corps sergeant dressed in starched fatigues. The boat then abruptly departed.

We stood there on the afterdeck watching the relief boat disappear downriver, feeling deeply frustrated and wondering what had just happened. We turned to the sergeant. He looked to be about mid-thirties, a little thicker in the waist than most marines, and very out of place in his creased uniform. We were all shirtless and dressed in cut-off shorts and flip-flop sandals. As Officer-in-Charge, all I could think of to say, with great emphasis, was "Sergeant, what in the hell are you doing here?"

He was just as bewildered as we were. "I don't know, sir," he replied. "I was on Okinawa yesterday. I was told to grab my seabag and report to the flight line. They put me on a flight to Saigon, a helo to the Delta, and a boat to here."

"But why here, sergeant? There are no Marine units anywhere in the Delta. What's your MOS [Military Occupational Specialty]?"

Marine Corps sergeant (left) and U.S. Navy intelligence officer (right) in a Cambodian village near the Neak Loeung ferry landing gather intelligence on the whereabouts of the missing ferry.
COURTESY OF WILLIAM ROGERS

"I'm a linguist, sir. I spend my days on Okinawa listening to radio intercepts."

Suddenly I had a very creepy feeling. "What language, sergeant?"

"Cambodian, sir." And with that we all looked at each other and mouthed the words, "Oh, shit!" It was instantly obvious to us that the Navy planned to send us into Cambodia, and we wanted nothing to do with that.

For years Cambodia had been a sanctuary for the North Vietnamese Army. It was at the southern end of the Ho Chi Minh Trail that brought men and matériel from North Vietnam. The NVA used Cambodia—supposedly a neutral country—as a staging area for operations in the Delta and a safe haven where its troops could withdraw for rest and resupply after a battle. Given a choice, we would definitely prefer boredom on our side of the border. But someone else was doing the choosing. That evening we received a coded message ordering us to abandon our post without relief and return immediately to our base.

The YRBM-16 (Yard Repair Berthing and Messing) was a big floating repair facility that could house and feed a crew while their ship was undergoing repairs. For Vietnam YRBMs were outfitted with a rooftop helicopter deck, medical facilities, and a beer barge moored alongside for entertainment. They could be towed wherever they were needed. Ours was anchored thirty klicks south of us near the city of Chau Doc.

It was after dark when we arrived, and it was obvious that something big was underway. We were instructed to refuel and rearm immediately and get ready to head north. When we had completed our preparations, I took a few minutes to write to my girlfriend, Jan, a registered nurse in San Diego:

> *[T]omorrow at 0500 we are going north deep into Cambodia. The details are secret (although you'll probably hear them on the news), however, we will be going about 30 miles into Cambodia to capture a key ferry crossing. There will be 8 American Swift Boats, 13 VN swifts, 8 armored river boats and other support craft. So you can see it is a rather big operation.*
>
> *I think we'll be gone about a week but no one knows. And needless to say there won't be any mail.*
>
> *We really don't know what to expect but of course we're a little nervous. But don't worry, we'll have plenty of support all the way and the Mekong is a wide river.*

Our orders were straightforward. We were to charge up the river as fast as possible and capture the ferry crossing near the small Cambodian village of Neak Loeung, where the main highway from Saigon crossed the Mekong River on its way to the Cambodian capital of Phnom Penh. We were to secure the ferryboat and keep any bad guys from crossing the river. Very simple, except for the distinct possibility that we were going to be ducks in a shooting gallery. All the NVA had to do was line up along the riverbank and fire away as we passed by. None of us slept very well that night.

We got underway at dawn the next morning, May 9, and formed up with seven other Swift Boats from Coastal Division 13 just south of the Cambodian border on the main branch of the Mekong. At 0700 we pushed the throttles all the way forward and headed north in single file at twenty-eight knots. We didn't know what to expect, but we were prepared for the worst.

Maybe it was the presence of the helicopter gunships escorting us, or maybe the ample warning that we were coming in force, but there was no shootout. The river, which was over a mile wide at the border, was totally empty of traffic. For thirty miles, the only humans we saw were two bloated bodies floating face down.

As we approached our objective, a flight of six UH-1 helicopters passed over us in a V formation heading to the ferry crossing to drop off an assault force of Vietnamese Marines. They landed about twenty minutes before we got there and set up a secure perimeter. Like us they arrived without incident. But the ferryboat was nowhere in sight. So we moved back into the middle of the river and lined up about 600 yards apart to prevent anyone from crossing. The next day I was able to post another letter to Jan:

> *We are about 25 miles into Cambodia now, anchored in the Mekong. A Navy Chaplin stopped by a short time ago to see the crew (it's Sunday) and [he] will be returning down river soon. So he will mail this for me.*
>
> *Well over 100 boats and ships of all sizes came across [the border] after us . . .*
>
> *No one knows how long we will be here but I would guess four or five more days. But you never can tell.*
>
> *Anyway, I just wanted to let you know that everything is back to normal. Sitting at anchor is just as boring in Cambodia as it is in RVN [the Republic of Vietnam].*

American vessels were prohibited from going past Neak Loeung, leaving the Vietnamese Navy to handle everything to the north. As we rode at anchor it seemed like the entire Vietnamese Navy passed in review. Everything that could float, from slow-moving armored riverine vessels to large World War II–era LSTs, was heading upriver to Phnom Penh and beyond.

Neak Loeung ferry landing.
COURTESY OF WILLIAM ROGERS

Their objective was to rescue and repatriate ethnic Vietnamese. Over the years, about 400,000 Vietnamese had migrated up the river and into Cambodia to escape the conflict in the lower Delta. They were now in mortal danger.

Two months before our arrival, Cambodian army general Lon Nol had deposed Prince Norodom Sihanouk as head of state and allied himself with U.S. forces. Sihanouk, the architect of Cambodia's tenuous "neutrality," set up a provisional government-in-exile and allied himself with Cambodia's Khmer Rouge Communist guerrillas. Any pretense of peaceful coexistence between ethnic Cambodians and Vietnamese evaporated.

On April 15, the Khmer Rouge had rounded up 800 Vietnamese men in the village of Churi Changwar, tied them together, executed them, and dumped the bodies into the Mekong River. More atrocities followed. As we watched from our anchorage, the huge Vietnamese flotilla made repeated trips northward, its vessels returning fully loaded with refugees. A Vietnamese Navy LST passed us carrying what looked like thousands of people. Smaller vessels carried a few dozen.

Throughout May and June there was fierce fighting going on in the Cambodian interior as U.S. and Vietnamese forces fought to clear the NVA from their sanctuaries. Over 800 Vietnamese and 300 U.S. sol-

A Vietnamese Navy LST evacuates several thousand Vietnamese refugees from Cambodia.
COURTESY OF WILLIAM ROGERS

diers died in those two months, but the area around the river remained strangely quiet. We took advantage of this to hunt for the missing ferryboat. A U.S. Navy intelligence officer and his two Vietnamese bodyguards came aboard, and five of us, including the Marine sergeant, set out to comb the villages in the vicinity of the ferry crossing.

The villagers—ethnic Khmers who were shorter and darker than the slim Vietnamese we were accustomed to seeing—were a little wary at first but in no way threatening. We eventually had several long conversations with them. And, of course, the kids warmed up to us right away. After a while we were walking about almost casually with little thought of security. I later looked back on that day with amazement. Within five years that area would become part of the infamous killing fields where the Khmer Rouge systematically slaughtered over a million people.

Despite our best efforts we were unable to locate the ferry. But a few days later it was spotted from the air. It had been scuttled in the river, and a Vietnamese Navy salvage boat raised it. It was repaired and put back in service.

We stayed in Cambodia through the end of June, moving back and forth from the YRBM-16 to the river crossing. There was constant military activity inland. Landing craft moved many tons of ammunition and supplies up to Neak Loeung. We were kept busy boarding and searching the houseboats and sampans that flooded southward filled with Vietnamese refugees. The lucky ones had built their houses on rafts so they could quickly float away to safety. Others crammed their families into the small sampans and escaped with almost nothing.

American news organizations had few reporters in Cambodia, so they struggled to make sense of the conflict. Some photos appeared in U.S. publications showing scores of bodies tied together floating on the river. And headlines reported that "neutral" Cambodia was being invaded to clear out the NVA sanctuaries. But the thing that most surprised us—and which went almost totally unreported—was the visceral hatred between Vietnamese and Cambodians. It had been festering for centuries and had once again erupted with murderous intensity.

We met one very brave American who wanted to see for himself. He was a freelance photographer, alone and armed only with two Nikon cameras. He wanted to get close to the action, and the only way for him to do that was to hitch a ride. I thought he was crazy, but we took him aboard and dropped him off on the riverbank several miles north. As we departed I took a photo of him standing alone, barefoot and holding his shoes in his hand. I never saw him again and always wondered if he survived.

Life soon returned to normal on that part of the river. My Marine Corps linguist returned to Okinawa. Boredom also returned, as we were again tasked with boarding and searching the many sampans and houseboats that passed by. On May 28 I wrote:

> *We are anchored on the Mekong in Cambodia—about 15 miles upstream from the border. Doing the same old thing—checking sampans. For the first week or so there was practically no civilian traffic on the river. But they've found out that we won't shoot them, so business is back to normal. Many . . . many sampans moving on the river.*

A U.S. Navy salvage boat lifts the sunken ferry.
COURTESY OF WILLIAM ROGERS

> *Times are tough, love. The AC generator died two days ago. The beer is warm, the coffee's cold and no tape recorder [for sending tape-recorded letters]. I can see asking a guy to die for his country, but this . . .*

Almost two months after it started, the Cambodian incursion ended on June 30, with all vessels moving back across the border into Vietnam.

Rescue on the Mekong

Senyint Chim

Cambodian Senyint Chim eventually settled in San Diego, California, where he married and started a family. He became a middle school math teacher for the San Diego Unified School District. His mother and two brothers were executed by the Khmer Rouge government of Pol Pot. Four other brothers also died. Two sisters eventually joined him in the United States.

In May 2011, I had the honor of addressing Swift Boat veterans of the Vietnam War in San Antonio, Texas. I formally thanked the sailors who saved my life more than forty years ago. Two years later, I spoke to them again at their Swift Boat reunion in San Diego, California, relating the story of how I came to the United States from Cambodia.

During the first years of the war in Vietnam, Cambodia was officially neutral, favoring neither side. However, the Communist Vietnamese used my country as a haven to transport men and matériel as they pursued their revolution in South Vietnam. This was silently approved by the government in Phnom Penh and our chief of state, Prince Norodom Sihanouk. On March 18, 1970, Prince Sihanouk was forced out of office and a pro-U.S. government led by Lon Nol took power.

Shortly afterward, the Communists—a group that included the North Vietnamese Army, South Vietnamese Viet Cong, and Khmer Communists—took over the area surrounding my village, Trapeang Svayplous, on the Mekong River. I was living in Phnom Penh at the time, where I was a student at the only school teaching English as a

After Senyint Chim's rescue, he stands (second from left) with Lt. Cdr. Jack A. Herriott (far left) and Lt. Giles Whitcomb (right). Others pictured (back row, left to right): "Mossey," Lt. William Powell, John D. Leisenring, Chau Le, "Fuzzy," Bill Reese, Lt. Cdr. Rick Lippincott (kneeling), and James Riemer.
OFFICIAL U.S. NAVY PHOTOGRAPH

second language. When I heard about the takeover of my village, I returned home to try and persuade my mother and siblings to get away. Most chose to flee, but my mother refused to abandon our rice mill, which was the family's main source of income. I stayed behind to help her and my youngest brother.

As we went about our daily activities, I helped run the mill, all the while keeping my eyes and ears open to see how the Vietnamese Communists ran the village. My mother went off to visit different officials of the Angka Leu, the Khmer Communist high command. She told me I was not to charge those people who brought rice to our mill in big oxcarts because this rice was going to feed the troops. I reluctantly complied, and this kept the Communists from interfering with our operation.

Meanwhile, most of the villagers around my age were being pressed into joining the revolutionaries. I avoided recruitment by offering my

English translation skills to the North Vietnamese officer in charge of the village. Shortly after their arrival, the Communists set up a command post on the east bank of the Mekong River not far from my house. I watched them attack Cambodian Navy patrol boats, one of which they sank. Later, I went to the same North Vietnamese major and requested permission to go to Phnom Penh, pretending I wanted to visit my ailing sister. The major approved, but he reminded me that I must return in one week because I still had my mother and brother there. I understood this to mean that if I failed to come back on time my family would be in danger. The major gave me a note granting safe passage through Communist-held territory.

On April 21, 1970, I made my way to Phnom Penh, passing through both government and rebel security checkpoints. As soon as I arrived in the city, I went to see the commanding officer of U.S. Naval Intelligence and described to him in detail the Communist presence in my village.

I returned home one week later, as I had promised the Vietnamese major. That night, the Communists took control of nearby Neak Loeung.

PCF 56 (fifth boat from right), commanded by Lt. (j.g.) Clayton Howze with Quartermaster Second Class George Nelson as leading petty officer, was the boat that saved Mr. Chim.
COURTESY OF H. CLAYTON HOWZE

Senyint Chim held this sign to get the attention of a passing Swift Boat.
COURTESY OF EDWIN L. SPRATT

Four days later, government forces launched a retaliatory attack, targeting the rebel base in my village. Like the other villagers, I was forced to find safety in a bomb shelter. The Communist command post near my home was destroyed and my house was hit as well.

It soon became clear that an informant had betrayed me to the rebel commander. Some of the villagers warned me, and I knew my life was in danger. I felt confident they would not try to capture me in public because my family was respected in the village. However, this would not stop them from trying to take me at night.

I was frightened but kept my wits about me. On May 8, I took a chalkboard and wrote out an SOS message in English: *I WANT TO GO WITH YOU. I HAVE SOME NEWS TO TELL YOU. I AM CAMBODIAN. I WANT TO GO WITH YOU.* I set the board on the roof of my house in the hope that it would be spotted by one of the American helicopters flying back and forth. For the next two days I stayed in open places where no one could grab me and take me away. At night I slept in the homes of two Vietnamese friends where I felt I would not be found.

By May 10, I was still anxious. That evening I tried to behave as though nothing was wrong as I went out to the river to bathe. A neighbor girl on her bike stopped and told me I should leave, saying it might be my last night. She stealthily pointed out that I was being watched by armed men, and urged me to "go away, fly away!"

After thanking her, I went into my bomb shelter where I had set up an altar with my father's ashes. There I burned three incense sticks, lit a candle, and prayed to my father to help me escape this crisis. Then I went back to my house and pulled down the SOS sign. As I carried it toward the river, I saw a beautiful sight—two U.S. Navy Swift Boats with American flags waving! A Vietnamese neighbor boy named Nghia came and asked what I was doing. He noticed the writing, but fortunately he could not read English.

A South Vietnamese sailor on one of the two boats was scanning the village with binoculars. Suddenly, he pointed in my direction. I raised my sign and waved it in the air. He lowered his binoculars, wiped his eyes, then looked at me again. He went away and soon returned with a tall white man, whom I later identified as Clayton Howze, the Officer-in-Charge of PCF 56. The man went on the radio and both boats were placed on alert, the crews taking their positions and donning helmets and flak jackets. They did not know if it was a trap. Using the boat's loudspeaker, the officer told me to swim over to the boat.

Accepting the invitation, I removed my student ID from my wallet and quickly undressed. I wrapped a neck scarf around me as a loincloth, as if I were going for a swim, and then handed my clothes to Nghia and asked him to give them to my mother. As I was about to enter the river, Nghia said that someone wanted to talk to me.

I ignored him and began to swim toward the patrol boat with my ID in my mouth. Rebel soldiers were watching from the bamboo groves on the shore, but they did not dare shoot at me for fear of starting a firefight with the Swift Boats, whose .50-caliber machine guns were trained on the shore. I was a poor swimmer and when I got about ten meters from the boat my energy flagged and I called out for help. One American sailor dove in to assist me while another went in after my ID card, which had fallen out of my mouth when I yelled.

Once on board, I stood shivering and asked for a shirt and pants. The sailors gave me a light blue shirt and a pair of pants too big for me. Talking quickly, I told the crew that I was in danger and the Viet Cong wanted to capture me. I added that I had information I wished to share with their commander. Not long afterward the crew took me to see Lt. Giles Whitcomb, a Naval Intelligence Liaison Officer. The lieutenant spoke to me in both English and French. After reviewing the Communist activities in my village, Lieutenant Whitcomb introduced me to his superior, Lt. Cdr. Jack A. Herriott, the Officer-in-Charge of the Fourth Riverine Intelligence in Vietnam.

And so began my involvement as an operative for the Cambodian intelligence services. I provided information on the local political and military situation in Cambodia, and, after one year, I joined the Cambodian Navy, eventually realizing my dream of coming to the United States through the Navy Exchange Program. I have lived here ever since, earning bachelor's and a master's degrees, finding work in education, and raising a family. For my survival and the better life I found in the United States, I am truly grateful to the American sailors aboard PCF 56 who came to my rescue.

"What Are They Going to Do, Send Me to Vietnam?"

Lou Marucheau

Lt. (j.g.) Lou Marucheau left active duty in October 1972, joined the Naval Reserves, and, after a six-month stint of active duty during Desert Storm, retired from the Navy as a commander. He obtained his law degree from the University of Denver in 1977 and practiced nearly forty years as an environmental and mining lawyer before retiring in Denver in 2015.

We didn't sweat the small stuff, and we didn't worry about military formalities. We wore what was comfortable and didn't need laundering—everything from cut-off fatigue greens to Vietnamese tiger-stripe camo uniforms. We grew beards that were probably a lot longer than what Admiral Zumwalt intended (and definitely not appreciated by the Army lieutenant who told me, "Shave it off or you don't go on R&R"). We didn't wear rank insignia officially, because the VC might use it to target officers. As Officer-in-Charge of a Swift Boat, I was indeed a lieutenant junior grade—but to be honest, I didn't think Charlie was taking a special interest in me. I didn't wear rank insignia mainly because I rarely wore a regulation uniform.

And then there was the big stuff. I had been in Vietnam for almost a year, operating briefly along the coast but mainly in the rivers and canals of South Vietnam, living with four or five other guys aboard a fifty-foot aluminum boat. We were subject to getting shot at or sapper-attacked

Lou Marucheau. COURTESY OF LOU MARUCHEAU

by the enemy any time of the day or night. Without a second thought I would risk my life, and those of my crewmates, to protect or rescue fellow Swift Boat sailors, American advisors, or other allies who needed help. And I expected them to do the same for me. The trust was reciprocal and unequivocal.

Respect for authority was a different matter. In the military, doing what they tell you is a big deal, but the people doing the telling, for the most part, weren't doing the doing. Swift Boat officers tended to interpret orders in their own way—or ignore them altogether. Some OinCs wouldn't conduct Harassment & Interdiction (H&I) fire on civilian targets, such as temples, unless they had specific information about why it was a good idea. To question an action would be deviating from the military norm, but we reasoned, "What are they going to do to me, send me to Vietnam?"

In September 1970, about a month prior to my scheduled DEROS (Date of Expected Return from Overseas), I was OinC of PCF 45, operating out of a Vietnamese junk base near the town of Long Phu on the lower Bassac River. My boat was one of three Swifts conducting "Blue

Shark" operations—raids, probes, and troop insertions mostly around Dung Island and the Long Toan Secret Zone, significant VC strongholds.

With PCF 48, we had just completed an insertion and extraction of Vietnamese "Ruff-Puff" militia (Regional Forces/Popular Forces) on Dung Island's main canal. We had been ambushed three times that day, and we needed to refuel. We set off on the Bassac the next day, headed upriver to Binh Thuy.

Suddenly both of the engines on my boat stopped dead, and we were adrift. The boats were old and showing the mileage, and mysterious ailments were not a rarity (like discovering after exiting a firefight that the engine compartment was filling with water—the engine-cooling water discharge line had broken). Losing both engines, however, was as bad as it could get without encountering hostile gunfire, and my heart

Port main engine with aft deck hatch cover removed.
COURTESY OF LOU MARUCHEAU

RVN Coastal Group 36 base at Long Phu. Swift Boats used these remote bases to reprovision, refuel, and rearm.
COURTESY OF LOU MARUCHEAU

sank. The Bassac was particularly dangerous because of its fast-moving current, accelerated at that time of year by the southern monsoon. We immediately threw out our anchor, which bit deeply into the river bottom. PCF 48 came to help and ended up towing us to Binh Thuy. We came alongside the repair ship USS *Krishna*, anchored in the middle of the Bassac River. *Krishna* did repairs and maintenance on both American and Vietnamese boats.

There was nothing exotic about our casualty. While deployed at Seafloat, a floating base at the southern tip of Vietnam, we had gotten river water mixed in with our fuel. The constant use of concussion grenades to protect Seafloat from NVA sapper attacks had opened leaks in the fuel barge. When we got down to the bottom of our fuel tank, the water went into both engines, blowing all the injectors, instantly shutting down both engines, and, most important, wrecking the port engine altogether.

I went to *Krishna*'s repair office. Their people wouldn't be able to get to us for a while because there was a long queue, including a number of boats being repaired for turnover to the Vietnamese Navy. With only a month left in-country, this news could have been a gift. "Let me know when you can work on my boat," I could have said. "I'll be at the Officer's Club."

But it didn't work that way. My boat was operating from a small base with only two others. Without me, my two partners would be at greater risk or would simply not be able to perform all the missions assigned to them. And what happened when somebody called us to provide close fire support in the middle of the night? We'd already saved one outpost from being overrun. There was no such thing as being "too short" in a situation like that.

So I hitched a boat ride to the U.S. land base at Binh Thuy and visited the Naval Operations Center. I got on the radio and called COMNAVSUPPACT (Commander, Naval Support Activities in Vietnam) in Saigon. This was—and I'm certain, still is—a gross violation of the chain of command. It was a bad thing to do—"Number Ten," as the saying went. But I was too short to worry about it.

PCF 48, with skipper Mike Peters standing in the port side pilothouse doorway, exits the Dung Island main canal having been ambushed three times in one day. About twenty Vietnamese Regional Provincial troops are on board.
COURTESY OF LOU MARUCHEAU

I explained my difficulty to the COMNAVSUPPACT duty officer. My Swift Boat was inoperable and *Krishna* was making us wait for repairs, even though my colleagues needed me for combat operations. I was marking time behind a slew of other boats that were destined for nothing more urgent than a turnover ceremony. The duty officer said he'd see what he could do, which turned out to be plenty. I learned later that COMNAVSUPPACT summoned *Krishna*'s captain to the Binh Thuy Naval Operations Center and directed him to repair my boat.

While all this was going on, my crew on its own had replaced all the injectors and changed the fuel pump on the starboard engine. We were able to get underway the next day and reached the pier at Binh Thuy, where we used the rest of the day to prepare the port engine for replacement. The next morning we returned to *Krishna*, where the port engine was pulled and replaced, although the repair crew broke the oil pan in the process. The next day they fixed that, but then they had problems with electrical wiring.

Finally, four days after we got to Binh Thuy, we left. God knows how much time they would have wasted if they hadn't been ordered to do the work. And God knows how long it would have taken if my engineman and the rest of our scruffy-looking crew hadn't done most of the job. *Krishna* did not accept my pre-repair intervention or my crew's yeoman performance with particularly good grace. They sent an officer from the ship's repair office to conduct a "surprise inspection," a textbook example of naval bureaucratic bullshit—if you can't bust them for the thing that really pisses you off, find something else. We were not impressed. The inspector abandoned the boat in a huff when the whiskey bottle he found in our refrigerator—his would-be "smoking gun"—contained only water.

Once repaired, we returned to Long Phu, conducted a couple more three-boat ops, managed to avoid getting shot at, and finally went to Cat Lo to get processed for leaving Vietnam. I never heard from *Krishna* again, nor did I get my knuckles rapped for calling up COMNAVSUPPACT to complain. I wouldn't have been surprised if I had, but it wouldn't have done any good. What were they going to do, send me to Vietnam?

Endgame

Robert O. Lincoln

Radarman Third Class Robert O. Lincoln left the Navy in 1972. After a career working in the furniture industry and eventually owning his own business, Lincoln retired in northern Michigan and passed away in December 2016.

SUPPOSEDLY, THE SHIPMATES YOU BONDED WITH DURING SWIFT BOAT training were to be the same men you spent the year with in Vietnam. Your crew, the instructors told us, was for keeps.

Maybe that was true at the beginning, but by the time we got to Cat Lo in mid-1970, things had changed. The Navy was turning over all the American Swift Boats to the Vietnamese, a process that was supposed to finish December 1. Guys were going on R&R, finishing their tours, or getting early outs and going home. New crews were not crews, it turned out. I went upriver to a place called Sa Dec, and the rest of my training mates filled in other blanks wherever—placeholders until turnover.

Soon I found myself twenty miles deep inside Cambodia aboard PCF 54, serving with a bunch of strangers. I had replaced a veteran who was probably going home. I had 360-some days and a wakeup to go. Man, would I ever get out of here?

Turnover began with a trip 200 miles up the coast to Cam Ranh Bay for overhaul. PCF 54 was dented, beat up, and leaking from countless encounters with everything from stone piers to B-40s. We were supposed to swap it for a reconditioned, turnover-ready rehab. This event was a welcome interlude. We washed away the river mud with the gorgeous

PCF 692 stands off as UDT detonate charges to remove canal barracades in 1970.
COURTESY OF JOHN W. YEOMAN

swells of the South China Sea, and the harbor at Cam Ranh was like something out of a movie—surrounded by mountains and with water so clear you could follow the fall of a dropped quarter for thirty feet.

PCF 54 looked like an abandoned orphan next to our spanking-new PCF 87, and we were happy to have it. I still didn't know much about the rest of our crew. Our Vietnamese crewman would disappear for weeks whenever he wanted to go home, then he would get arrested and reappear without explanation. Then there was "Ski," a loudmouthed New Yorker who threw a tantrum when they tried to make him an advisor to the Vietnamese Navy. He stayed with us while they set up his court-martial in Saigon. Back at Cat Lo there wasn't much left for us to do. Vietnamese boats handled all the coastal patrols and most of the routine river work. That left "make-work" for us. Really nasty make-work.

PCF 87's last American-crewed mission began November 10, 1970. Together with PCFs 45, 97, and 692, our assignment was to raid Dung Island, on Rach Eo Lon, a VC stronghold southwest of Vung Tau. We were told to find a large arms cache there and destroy it. To do the job, we were using Kit Carson Scouts—former VC who had come over to our side. As we approached the island I noticed a ten-foot-square billboard with an English inscription that read: "Americans who enter will be killed." Can't say they didn't warn us.

I was the bow gunner on the lead boat, but without a gun mount. I had to shoot my M-60 from the hip. This was called "John Wayneing" it. When you weren't shooting you cradled the M-60 like a baby. When you were on full automatic, you hung on for dear life to keep the gun from jumping out of your hands.

We turned into a canal so narrow that tree branches on either side made me sit down. I couldn't see anything. We stopped, and the Scouts got off the boat. They found the ammo dump, but instead of blowing it up, they returned to the boats carrying armloads of rockets.

What the hell? I thought. Talk about stupid. Why in God's name are we doing this?

We made it back to the relative safety of the big river just before dark. Sometime around then, while listening to the boat officer in the pilothouse behind me, I learned that the big shots back at the base wanted to show off the size of Charlie's ammo cache. We couldn't blow the stuff up. We had to bring it home. Even during the last days of American Swift Boats, by God, we could prove we weren't doing make-work.

So instead of an "attaboy," the big shots told us to go back the next day and pick up more ammo. Are you kidding?

We did it again, this time with a feeling that our luck could run out at any moment. The Scouts made trip after trip to the cache. They stacked the ammo high on the boats so the big shots could eyeball it and take pictures.

Even with this return trip, there was still no "attaboy." We needed to go back one more time, they told us, and blow up what was left of the cache. I wondered: Wouldn't it be easier—and safer—to use Black Ponies, Cobras, or mortars? We have the exact coordinates. Did the big shots really think Charlie would let us humiliate him three days in a row?

It was November 12, 1970. We got in again without trouble. The Scouts went ashore, blew the ammo dump, and came back to the boats. Now, I thought, all we have to do is get out of here and make it to the big river. But in the meantime, if Charlie wanted to find us, all he had to do was reach out his hand. We were that close to the riverbank.

As we turned into a fork in the canal I heard a blast behind me. Charlie had finally fired a rocket, but it had detonated between two boats and inflicted no damage. Even better, someone saw the smoke trail as the rocket left the jungle. We drove straight at the spot. Seconds later I was fifteen feet deep in the forest, carpeting the ground with bursts from my M-60. Then the firefight ended, and Scouts jumped from the boat to do a quick body count—the big shots had to have their body count. I never learned whether there were any bodies to count. It was still a long way to the big river, and we needed to focus on getting there alive.

We got back underway, with PCF 87 second in line now. Just ahead to starboard was a barren mud field denuded by Agent Orange. To port was dense jungle. Then I heard another explosion. The boat jumped ahead, throttles to the floor. This was standard procedure—get the hell outta there and clear the kill zone. Except the helmsman suddenly turned sharply to starboard and beached the boat in the empty mud field at full speed. I had a split second to drop the M-60 and grab a support bar to keep from being thrown overboard.

And then silence. I looked around at the helmsman sitting in the pilothouse behind me and started screaming at him for almost killing me. He interrupted. We've been hit, he said. The throttle was jammed. I jumped up and ran the six or seven steps down the port side to the fantail. Then I froze for five seconds, or maybe it was five minutes. I don't know.

"Linc!" the boat officer hollered at me as he climbed out the door of the main cabin. "Get blankets over these men!"

I started to move, except there was no place to put my foot. I couldn't see the metal surface of the boat. A rocket had hit a Scout in the chest and detonated, spraying blood and innards everywhere.

Black Ponies arrived then, and miniguns poured fire into the jungle all around us. Other boats came alongside to take some of the wounded.

PCF 45 tied up in Sa Dec after ambush in Rach Eo Lon south of Ben Tre in the mid-Mekong Delta.
COURTESY OF JOHN W. YEOMAN

I knelt beside a young Scout whose dark eyes looked into mine. His body was ripped open from throat to crotch by a gash that looked like it was eight inches deep. I couldn't believe he was still breathing, and I was terrified that I would drop him as I helped transfer his stretcher to another boat. But I didn't.

As we were being towed back to a support base, the Scouts' American advisor screamed at us, challenging our manhood because we weren't cleaning the body parts off the deck with our bare hands. Sorry big shot, I thought. I was using individual body armor plates from blown-apart flak jackets to push remains off the boat, but the advisor had a point: The sun was baking the gore onto the deck, and we had to go faster. I used my hands.

Back at the base our boat officer joined the other officers for cocktails and went to sleep in a clean bed. My two unharmed crewmates and I scrubbed the boat for most of the night and tried to sleep in the filthy main cabin. They told us only two people died in that firefight. Nobody asked me, but part of my soul died as well. I'll never forget the sight and the stench of the dead and dying on the fantail of PCF 87.

I couldn't figure out why we were sent to Dung Island three days in a row for a job that could have been done another way in a couple of hours. Was it stupidity or arrogance? This type of leadership, I figured, could cost you a war.

As for the men I served with, I couldn't tell you much about them. There was the tall skinny guy and the guy with the spiderweb tattoo covering his back. I never saw them again. I think the guy in the gun tub was named Brown. The quartermaster was blond and the boat officer was Irish. I'm the guy who threw the hearts, lungs, and shinbones into the river.

PCF 87 was the last U.S.–crewed Swift Boat to be hit and take casualties. Three weeks later we handed it over to the Vietnamese.

Not with a Bang . . . or a Whimper

John Dooley

Lt. Cdr. John Dooley left the Navy as a commander in 1980. After a second career designing stealth modifications to destroyer and cruiser hulls, he retired to his "Golf Camp" in Cape Coral, Florida.

I WAS UNDER NO ILLUSIONS WHEN I ARRIVED IN VIETNAM IN JUNE 1970. I was a lieutenant commander with ten years in the destroyer Navy, coming off a tour as an oceanographer in the Pacific. I was expecting a destroyer XO job, but my orders were to take command of the Swift Boats at Coastal Division 12 in Da Nang.

Plum job? Maybe. It was a combat assignment—definitely challenging, and at least on the face of it, a big deal. And as "sea duty," it had the same cachet as a destroyer XO slot. On the other hand, river fighting was a skill that I would have to learn on the fly. I would become part of a seriously mishandled war that looked unwinnable and was winding down. I could see the inevitable "bug out" clearly visible on the horizon and knew I would be part of the cleanup crew. This was not a big deal to the Navy, and I doubted the assignment's usefulness to my career. But so be it. Experience had taught me that whatever job the Navy gave you, you didn't piss and moan or call your mom, you just did it and reported back when it was finished.

The first thing I found when I arrived at squadron headquarters in Cat Lo was that Coastal Division 12 no longer existed. The Da Nang Swifts had been turned over to the Vietnamese Navy as part of the

The remaining U.S. Swift Boats are turned over to the Vietnamese Navy at a ceremony at Cat Lo in December 1970.
COURTESY OF JOHN DOOLEY

"Vietnamization" of the war, and my job had disappeared along with the boats. I was somewhat disappointed, but not surprised. And within a couple of days the squadron commander made me his Chief Staff Officer—his number two.

I had a staff job, but I was not just a bureaucrat. I had some clout. The squadron commander expected me to get out on the rivers and provide on-scene guidance for boats on patrol. The first thing I did was commandeer Lt. (j.g.) Andy Horne as a Mekong River tour guide. His boat had been recently Vietnamized, leaving him to serve out his last few weeks in-country in a make-work job as a "Swift Boat Training Officer" when there were no more U.S. crews to train. But Andy had patrolled large swatches of the Delta, where most of the remaining U.S. boats were operating, so I had him take me around to visit the fifty or so boats we had left.

Our destination was Sa Dec, on the Mekong River where it crosses into Cambodia. Coastal Division 13 had moved there from Cat Lo to be closer to the Cambodian incursion, which was just winding down. To get there, Andy and I scrounged "Space A" chopper flights heading more or less in the right direction; we had to make out-of-the way changeovers at Binh Thuy, My Tho, Can Tho, Chau Doc, and a number of lesser and soon-forgotten fire bases and rice paddies. This was my first taste of the Vietnam ground war. Some war.

The Delta people were clearly focused on survival rather than combat. Rice production was the main interest, both in the fields and in the markets. Despite lots of M-16 rifles in evidence at lazily guarded bridges and checkpoints, there was an overwhelming sense that the war had passed by, or at least had been postponed until the Americans left. The few U.S. Army soldiers we met were clearly garrison troops who spent their time in sandbagged barracks guarded by Vietnamese soldiers and fronted with barbed wire. At Binh Thuy I met with pilots of the Navy Black Pony A-10 detachment and was happy to hear that they would not be standing down until the end of the year along with us. Good. Overhead Navy air cover made for happier Swifties.

After two days of puddle-jumping, we reached a remote Vietnamese militia outpost only ten klicks from Sa Dec. The militiamen, known technically as Regional Forces/Provincial Forces, and colloquially by us as "Ruff-Puffs," greeted us cordially but warned us that they suspected Charlie would attack at dark. And since we were armed with only .45-caliber pistols, we weren't going to tip the odds. The Ruff-Puffs were pulling out for the night and advised us to do the same. Dusk approached, and Andy and I didn't like our options. As the friendlies moved off to the east toward town, we could feel the threat from the nearby tree line to the west. Great. Middle of nowhere, no radio, and no cavalry to ride to the rescue. It looked like my first taste of combat was going to very brief. Andy and I were digging through our packs searching for extra ammo clips when a beat-up VN Army 2.5-ton truck rattled by, hurrying to reach Sa Dec before dark. We hitched a ride.

Over beers that night, I met the Coastal Division 13 commander and a number of his boat officers and crew. I stuck around for a few days to get a feel for what the ops were like on the upper Mekong. Most boats were doing static defense—blocking crossings along the 1,000 yard-wide, fast-flowing Mekong River and a bunch of secondary waterways, to keep contraband from Cambodia from entering Vietnam. At the same time, the Swifts were supposed to keep U.S. and Vietnamese forces from inadvertently crossing the border from Vietnam into Cambodia. Keeping the combatants apart was boring—hot and tedious work during the day, nerve-racking and potentially volatile work at night.

Apart from patrols, it was obvious to me that the Navy's chief preoccupation was to keep Vietnamizing U.S. Swift Boats as fast as the Vietnamese Navy could train crews to operate them. Boats were being steadily pulled off the line at Sa Dec and sent downriver to Cat Lo. This turned out to be convenient for Andy and me after my look-see—our own return trip to Cat Lo took twelve hours, not two days. If you wanted to travel in Vietnam, I learned, you used boats. That's what Charlie did. Which, of course, was the whole point of us being there.

Sometime in September 1970, Navy commanders in Saigon devised "Blue Shark," a plan to get the most out of a fast-dwindling supply of U.S.–crewed Swift Boats. Navy SEAL teams were trying to locate and raid several VC camps thought to be holding U.S. prisoners. SEALs had operated in the Delta for some time, frequently in cooperation with Swifts, and this was to be a final effort to find the clandestine prisons while the Navy still had assets available to help out. The SEALs were perfectly capable of carrying out the raids on their own, but if things went sour, they might need backup. Now that the Cambodian adventure was winding down, the Sa Dec boats were available to provide a rapid response to SEAL ops while putting pressure on known VC strongholds. Once a Blue Shark operation was complete, the Swifts involved went back to Cat Lo to turn their boats over to the Vietnamese.

For convenience during Blue Shark, we established a command post at Long Phu, a Vietnamese Navy base at the mouth of the Mekong. There were other U.S. tenants—the Seabees who set up the base, a SEAL team, and an intelligence officer. I moved in as the Blue Shark

Swift Boat crews stand inspection for the turnover of the last of the U.S. Swift Boats to the Vietnamese Navy at Cat Lo in December 1970.
COURTESY OF JOHN DOOLEY

commander and tried to ride aboard every boat on a patrol at least once. Unlike the tedium of Sa Dec, there was still plenty of VC activity in the lower Delta, especially at night. Aided by the Navy intelligence officer at Long Phu, we identified Charlie's watery paths and procedures and had a pretty good idea of the numbers and weaponry of the fighters in the area. In the swampy, canal-laced lower Delta, feeding and arming the troops was just as important as Charlie's other mission—intimidating and taxing the farmers.

We began to annoy the VC near Long Phu and especially at Dung Island, a longtime VC hideout separated from the mainland and stuck

PCF 691 beached in a canal near Ben Tre and inserting South Vietnamese troops for a sweep during October 1970.
COURTESY OF JOHN DOOLEY

like a cork in the lower Mekong. Since the island was accessible only by boat, the intelligence folks were fairly certain that there was more than one VC prison there. We ran daytime patrols to let the locals know there was a new sheriff in town, sending two or sometimes three boats into Dung Island's canals and creeks to check ID, search sampans, and occasionally draw hostile fire.

Our forces varied from day to day. With five or six boats, we could patrol a wide area of the Mekong and aggressively probe the canals in pairs. The Swift Boat crews (with their Vietnamese Navy liaisons) were experienced in the stop-and-frisk procedures designed to separate civilians from combatants, and the precision of our intelligence improved once we detained a number of suspicious characters. Local Vietnamese Army units were eager to take advantage of our mobility, and frequently rode the boats when they raided the island.

VC snipers had always taken potshots at us when we were raiding, but once we began inserting and extracting troops and our location became more obvious, Charlie started ambushing us along our escape routes. We were challenged by rifle and RPG fire.

It was difficult to assess our effectiveness. I reported details of our daily operations to headquarters each evening via a laboriously encrypted SITREP, a format designed by the Army to tout the body count. Because we were not authorized to go ashore after a firefight, there was no way to tell whether anyone was dead. I would innocently skew the Army's statistics downward by writing "Enemy Bodies and Weapons Recovered—Zero." But I would always report a large amount of .50-caliber and 81mm mortar ammunition expended to satisfy their need for numbers. Although we captured a number of VC on the Dung Island waterways and turned them over to the VN Coastal Group at Long Phu, it was difficult to assess their importance. The intel folks labeled nearly every captive as "Village Party official" or "VC Tax Collector."

We stayed at arm's length from the SEALs, as there seemed to be no reason to call attention to our unacknowledged mutual goals. We discussed planned operations to avoid getting in each other's way and to let each other know how we could provide support if needed. The SEAL officer was always careful to tell me where he planned to end up when his op was over, but he would never tell me where he planned to go in the first place.

Seabees and Swifties got along famously. The Seabees had the tools and expertise to keep our boat engineers well supported and the boat engines in top shape. One night on Dung Island a Swift was rocked by the explosion of a command-detonated mine—probably a 55-gallon drum filled with shrapnel and C-4—buried in the mud wall of a canal. The blast caught the boat on the starboard side, spraying it with shrapnel and wounding three crewmen, one of whom was subsequently MEDEVACed. The next day, we counted over fifty hull punctures between a half inch and 1 inch in size. We careened the boat on the narrow beach along the Mekong, and the Seabees and the boat crews filled the holes with cut-to-fit wooden plugs. By next day the Seabee chief pronounced repairs complete and the boat was refloated, tested, and sent back to Cat Lo for turnover. I never should have let it leave without an escort. The plugs leaked in heavy seas and it was only the OinC's expertise that kept it afloat. This was a serious judgment error on my part. Nothing bad happened to me, to my great and undeserved good fortune.

It turned out that the SEALs never needed direct Blue Shark assistance, except for a bunch of canal incursions and feints that were supposed to cover their operations. The Navy High Command had specific rules about who was to know about the raids—and the list did not include Swift OinCs. When I briefed them about an upcoming op, I frequently set them up with "raids" that came to nothing. They must have thought the whole exercise was pretty useless.

And maybe it was. Blue Shark was not exactly a rearguard action, but it certainly felt that way. In some ways it was about as successful as the war in general—not exactly the result we were looking for. The SEALs overran some stockades and took casualties doing it, but they never found any U.S. prisoners alive.

There were other difficult moments as the U.S. Swifts approached eclipse. In October 1970 we sailed three boats upriver about twenty klicks to Ben Tre to help insert Vietnamese troops along nearby canals. The plan was either to withdraw quietly or, if necessary, hang around to provide gunfire support if the troops ran into resistance they couldn't handle. We would maneuver to block Charlie's escape route, and if that didn't work out, we would pick up the Vietnamese and return to Ben Tre. This type of mission was quite familiar to the Swift Boat crews, and though it was routine, there was nothing easy about working near Ben Tre, Ho Chi Minh's birthplace and a longtime VC hotbed.

The op started as a daylight reconnaissance but was interrupted by a number of firefights, and the Vietnamese troops got lost. It was well past midnight before we were able to get them all back aboard and return to Ben Tre. The final approach should have been easy, but the soldiers manning the mud fort at the base's north entrance opened fire on us with heavy machine guns at a range of about 750 yards. This lasted several seconds before the gunners recognized the flare that one of the boats sent up and stopped shooting. The base command knew we were coming back, but apparently the word never reached the trigger fingers. As they say: Friendly Fire Isn't.

By mid-November 1970, the last twenty or so Swifts converged on the support base at Cat Lo for repairs, overhaul, and a paint job before being turned over to the Vietnamese Navy in a formal ceremony on December 1, 1970. As a general rule, the U.S. sailors who had completed almost all of their twelve-month tours went home, and the rest of us became advisors to the Vietnamese Swifts. Cat Lo, my home for the next five months, was turned over to the Vietnamese with about twenty U.S. advisors assigned to the ship repair and engine shops.

I became the advisor to Dai Ta (Commander) Minh, in charge of Coastal Flotilla 3. He was a man my own age who, as a Catholic, had been forcibly emigrated from Hanoi in the late 1950s. Formerly a staff officer in Saigon, he was a good man, an indifferent leader, and terrified of his superiors.

My "command" as senior advisor consisted of myself, engineering and ops officers, a radioman, a yeoman, and a dozen enlisted advisors. We never had enough people to staff each boat so the advisors rotated. Many found the duty gastronomically challenging; they saw enough fish eyes to last a lifetime. Others enjoyed it. The Vietnamese appreciated them, and the coastal patrols were not nearly as arduous (or dangerous) as the rivers. Flotilla 3 had responsibility for the same vast stretches of coastline that the Swifts had patrolled during the war's early years. The Vietnamese leadership, however, was very wary of conducting sustained riverine patrols, and the boats were quick to seek a sheltered cove during the monsoon. I remember accompanying Commander Minh on one operation in the Rung Sat Special Zone where, after an unsuccessful "surprise" amphibious raid (operational security was unknown in the VN navy), we were returning to base. Since we still had plenty of ammo, I suggested a standard Swift Boat tactic to him.

"Dai Ta Minh, turn into that next big canal. It's only a klick or two long before you'll exit into deep water on the other side. Let the boats astern cover one another, and slowly sail through to see who you can surprise."

"Ah, Thieu Ta Dooley," Minh replied, lips pursed and a seriously worried look on his face. "Many VC. Not good." We continued safely back to Cat Lo.

My tour ended in the summer of 1971, and I left Vietnam. After a tour at the Naval War College, I was reintegrated into the blue-water Navy as XO of a guided missile destroyer.

From a career point of view, Swifts were neither a plus nor a minus. I never felt I had contributed to a praiseworthy, epic, patriotic endeavor. I was ten years older than most of the men who manned the Swift Boats. I was married with three children and able to regard Vietnam as just another duty station, albeit somewhat more challenging and seemingly longer lasting than others. Many Swifties told me I was crazy to accept the same risks that they did, and there were times I agreed. It may have been a pointless, ambiguous mess of a war, and I was doing a job that apparently no one else wanted, but I got the job done, didn't lose a sailor, and left Vietnam before the sorry end.

And, dammit: Long after it was all over and I was living in Florida, I would stop short whenever I heard the throaty rumble of a boat's diesel starting up like those twin 12-cylinder General Motors Swift engines. For a moment I was somewhere else.

Chapter Eight

Aftermath

"Swiftboat" Is Not a Verb

On Thursday evening July 29, 2004, Sen. John Kerry of Massachusetts stepped to the podium at Boston's FleetCenter to accept the Democratic Party nomination for president: "I'm John Kerry," he said in a loud voice, raising his right hand in a salute. "And I'm reporting for duty!"

This was Kerry's awkward but defiant response to an equally awkward but defiant smear campaign. A group of Swift Boat veterans mounted the campaign to oppose his candidacy by casting doubt on his performance as a Swift OinC during SEALORDS, and by denouncing his later leadership in the protest organization Vietnam Veterans Against the War.

Kerry had always been a polarizing figure among Swift Boat veterans—at once the most famous of their number and a focus of animosity because of his career as an antiwar activist. Kerry lost the 2004 election, in part, perhaps, because of the Swift Boat veterans' opposition.

Regardless of their individual political views, it was hard for any former Swift Boat sailor to view the long-term consequences of the anti-Kerry movement with anything but dismay. The 2004 campaign had coined the verb "to swiftboat"—a pejorative denoting any particularly heavy-handed political smear. Nearly thirty-five years after Swift Boats disappeared from the active-service Navy, was "swiftboating" to be the only thing that people remembered about them?

There was more to say. In 1970, when the last Swift Boats were turned over to the Vietnamese, the Brown Water Navy's war—apart from the advisors who lingered on—was over. Swift sailors, like other servicemen returning to civilian life, found a nation divided because of the Vietnam War. In many cases, former friends and even family members harshly judged them simply for having been in the armed forces. Some veterans retreated from everyday American life and the unforeseen burdens that it imposed. Others became activists, both denouncing and defending the war.

Eventually the Swift veterans, like their colleagues from other services, had to confront the future. Many knew they would never do anything that could match riding a thirty-knot Swift Boat at full bore in the Mekong Delta with guns blazing. They needed something else to do. Some made the transition easily. Others needed more time. Some found that the horrible images they carried in their heads would not go away. There was not yet a name for post-traumatic stress disorder, but as the years passed many veterans understood that there was something wrong with them that needed to be fixed. And some never fixed it.

As for the boats themselves, their day had ended, and the Navy largely forgot them. There were holdovers. PCFs 1 and 2, the first two Mark Is that went to Coronado as training boats in 1965, showed up at the U.S. Southern Command in Panama in the late 1980s. Used to train the navies of our Latin American allies in small-boat handling and maintenance, SouthCom pressed them back into service to escort ships through the Panama Canal during the Panama invasion in late 1989 and early 1990. In 1995, PCF 1 was transferred to the National Navy Museum at the Washington (D.C.) Navy Yard and put on permanent display. PCF 2 began a new career as an oceanographic research vessel at Tidewater Community College in Norfolk, Virginia.

PCF 104, another training boat, was rescued from a junkyard in Bangor, Washington, and then restored and put on display at the Coronado Amphibious Base memorial to the Brown Water Navy.

PCF 816, a Mark II and apparently the last boat ever to find a new home, had been donated by the Navy in 1971 to the government of Malta, where it served for nearly forty years as a coastal defense vessel. In 2012 Malta retired PCF 816 and donated it to the Maritime Museum of San Diego for exhibition and conservation. The Swift Boat Sailors Association, the Swift veterans' organization, arranged the acquisition of the boat and its transport from Malta to San Diego; the veterans then worked in conjunction with the Maritime Museum to restore it. PCF 816 became a permanent exhibit at the museum and was put to work giving regular tours of San Diego harbor.[1]

When Swift Boat sailors gathered at regular reunions to tell sea stories, they had a different definition of *swiftboating*—a noun, not a verb.

Swiftboating was an unforgettable experience for 3,600 young men, most under twenty-five years old, who held positions of leadership and responsibility in a dangerous, high-pressure environment. In part they took the job because nobody else wanted it. In some cases, they had no choice.

Swiftboating meant fighting in the closest confines imaginable—six men on a fifty-foot boat with an aluminum hull unable to withstand the impact of even the smallest homemade grenades. Swift Boat crews understood that if one man was wounded in a firefight, chances were that others would also be wounded—or killed. There was no ducking out on a Swift Boat. Everybody took the same risks.

Swiftboating endured long after the boats themselves were gone. Some Swift veterans were successful and some were not. Some lived happily ever after while others struggled to cope. Some stayed many years in the Navy, while others left as soon as they got home. But whenever they saw each other, it did not matter how much money their former shipmates had earned or how bad their personal problems were. Even decades later, they knew they could trust one another with their lives.

Slaying Goliath

Duane Holman and Jenny Barr

Quartermaster Second Class Duane Holman left the Navy in December 1970. He lived in Eau Claire, Wisconsin, and worked as a surveyor with private engineering firms for more than forty years.

Jenny Barr graduated from the University of Wisconsin-Stout and worked for Nestle Nutrition, in Eau Claire, Wisconsin, as a formulation specialist.

DUANE

GROWING UP IN THE MID-1960S, I KNEW ABOUT VIETNAM. EVERYONE knew or had heard of someone who died in Vietnam. I tried not to think about it, but of course I thought about it all the time. It was Goliath, the one you couldn't avoid, and I wondered if I would be David enough to survive.

I graduated from high school and had just completed an associate's degree in mechanical design, hoping to become a draftsman. I was ready to go to work, and I was more than qualified. But in 1967 that didn't matter. One of the first questions on every application form was about my draft status. I was 1-A, which made me instantly eligible for military service. No sane employer would consider hiring me only to lose me in a few months. A convicted felon had a better chance of getting a job.

So, Goliath. You could call me a draft dodger, but I didn't want to go to Vietnam. So I enlisted in the Navy. My plan worked well at first, landing me a cushy staff job in Okinawa. But as I was getting ready to

Quartermaster Duane Holman.
COURTESY OF DUANE HOLMAN

return home and get married in October 1969, I received orders to—it couldn't be true—Swift Boats in Vietnam.

Time stopped for me. I thought only volunteers went to Swift Boats. I guess not. Had I made a mistake? Was this punishment for the time I broke my superior's personalized squadron coffee cup and tossed it in the trash?

"Where's my coffee cup?" he asked.

"I don't know," I replied. I wasn't stupid.

But maybe he wasn't, either, and maybe he volunteered me for Vietnam. Vindictive.

My emotions were all over the place because of the horrific stories we were hearing. This was the year we learned about the 1968 My Lai massacre. My fiancée, Rosemary, and I were reluctant to go through with the wedding. I remembered the Navy's boot camp message: if you needed a wife, we would have issued you one. The hell with it. Against all the advice we were hearing, and our own common sense, we got married anyway. Of the decisions I made in life, this one was one of the best.

The journey to Vietnam was awful—twenty hours in flight, a dozen time zones, no sleep, airplane food, and nerves. That was just to get to

Quartermaster Duane Holman.
COURTESY OF DUANE HOLMAN

Saigon. Then the hydraulics failed on the feeder that was taking me to the Delta, and we almost slid off the runway returning to Tan Son Nhut.

By the time I reached the Swift base at An Thoi and saw my boat, I was totally frazzled and homesick. A big Lone Star flag flew below the boat's American flag. With my imagination running wild, I was thinking it would be a miracle for a Yankee from Wisconsin to fit in with this group.

The crew was standoffish at our first meeting. I felt like the weakest dog joining the wolf pack, and immediately I sank into deep despair. Then the boat's Leading Petty Officer appeared. This was Charlie, who was from Texas and had brought the flag. Forty years later my daughter Jenny met him for the first time and described him perfectly: "Someone who seems to have everything totally under control yet instantly puts everyone at ease." Which is exactly what he did for me. He became a friend for life.

Charlie may have made me feel like I belonged, but I knew better. I was a Quartermaster Second Class who had never even been to sea, and I was surrounded by shipmates handpicked for their bravery, integrity, and skills. How did I come to be part of this elite group?

We patrolled the rivers of the lower Mekong Delta, and every mission was stressful. About a month into my tour, we were patrolling the Cambodian border and had just beached our boat on the Cambodian side when a water mine exploded beneath us. I was driving, and my mind blanked. I thought we were sinking. Luckily the OinC grabbed the throttles to get us out of there. We lost a skeg, but were otherwise undamaged. The enemy, I soon learned, used mines to create confusion, then opened fire on you before you figured out what was going on. The rest of the crew already knew this and had reacted instantly. Swift Boats were not a John Wayne movie—this was the real thing, and the bad guys wanted to kill you. I was scared to death.

I was also green. But I got better. I could drive at night up canals that were narrower than our boat was long just by using the radar. I ran aground a lot (everyone did), but I was also good at getting loose. I could drive through firefights without losing control. I had the helm most of the time, but sometimes I was a gunner, which was easier. As a gunner you could put your finger on the trigger and hold it there. On the helm, your job was defensive—you were always thinking about how to get away.

Maybe it was a defense mechanism, but I later found myself focusing on lighter moments. I remember laughing with admiration at the ingenuity of the Vietnamese country people who could enclose two full-grown pigs in a wicker pen in the center of a sampan, a vessel smaller than a canoe, and have the pigs lie comatose while they were carried to market.

We spent as much ammo on varmints as we did on the Viet Cong. If we saw a sea snake swimming nearby we would use everything except the 81mm mortar to take him out. We never succeeded. Concussion grenades, machine gun fire—nothing worked. I once estimated that we spent thousands of dollars' worth of ammunition on just one of these events. On another occasion we left the river to swim in the Gulf of Thailand and were interrupted by someone hollering "Shark!" We scrambled aboard and tore up the ocean with machine guns. We spent thousands that day too—with, of course, nothing to show for it except our amusement.

A sampan comes alongside to be inspected for contraband.
COURTESY OF DUANE HOLMAN

I arrived home for good in December 1970, just before Christmas, and the holidays were great. Then came January 2. Rosemary went back to work. My friends went to work. I stayed home. I was the only one without a life. The one thing I had so dreaded—going into the military—I began to miss. The three-plus years I had spent on active duty seemed almost like a lost friend. Back then I was somebody. I had a purpose. Now everyone had jobs but me. One thing I had never understood was why so many sailors left the Navy only to reenlist months later. I knew now. The world was closing in on me. On December 31, I was home and on top of the world; on January 2, I was at the lowest point of my life.

Nothing I learned in Vietnam was going to do me any good in a small town in Wisconsin, or so I thought. I could drive boats at high speed. I was qualified in a dozen different sidearms and heavy weapons. So what? I was depressed. Everybody at home had at least a four-year head start on me, and when I needed hope the most, an intense job search turned up nothing at all. After my last check came from the Navy, and I officially became a civilian, I was forced to apply for unemployment. You would have thought I had robbed a liquor store. First came the guilt this guy put on me for not working. He nearly had me convinced I wasn't even qualified for the help.

I also had to listen to my brother-in-law talk about how disgraceful it was for me to collect unemployment, and when I told him I was thinking of going back to school on the GI Bill, he was even worse. For some reason he was very critical of the military, and I never knew why. Folks like that were what I called "scab pickers." They were always after me; I guess when you are down you are vulnerable. Bad-mouthing me made them feel better themselves. I spent a lot of time thinking about clever replies I could have used.

So veterans weren't catching any breaks. But I didn't really expect any. I had never been a jock or a great achiever. I'd never received special treatment. Admiration would have been nice, but I was used to being ignored, so that was actually an advantage at this time. No big deal.

So I sucked it up. The very next spring I went to Madison to visit the Madison Area Technical College in search of a career. There were anti-Vietnam demonstrations going on, and I saw boarded-up and broken windows damaged by the protesters. The school counselor showed me a list of courses. I thought commercial art looked interesting, so we visited a class. I walked in with my military-issue short haircut, and every student had long hair and appeared to be rebelling against everything. The counselor took a look at my reaction, gently turned me around, and walked me out. Maybe with my math background I would consider surveying and engineering, he suggested. I registered for the fall semester and breathed a small sigh of relief.

In the spring my uncle gave me a job at the local farm supply store to tide me over until the fall. This brought purpose back in my life, along with some money. And then I graduated with straight A's, went to work immediately, and became a licensed land surveyor. I never looked back.

Being on Swift Boats gave me an education, but more than that, it enabled me to face any challenge, a reward beyond price. You see, my Goliath was dead. He was slain in the Mekong Delta.

JENNY

When I was really young, he was just "Dad"—the man who gave me whisker rubs with his beard and acted goofy to make us laugh. We lived in a nice, new middle-class house in Eau Claire, Wisconsin, with nice things, and I assumed life had always been that way. Dad, Mom, my brother, the family, the house. A good way to be.

One day, when I was maybe nine or ten, I was exploring in the basement, the way kids do, and I came across a big black trunk sitting on the cement floor. It had shiny buckles and smelled old and musty when I opened it, like it had been closed for a long time. Inside I found folded-up maps with what looked like Japanese writing on them. I found a plastic bag full of patches and medals. One of the patches had Snoopy on it, and another had a black cat. What were they for? And there was a white sailor suit. Maybe I could wear it for Halloween.

I shuffled through moldy papers and documents that didn't interest me very much. Then I found the pictures: Asian children with tropical foliage in the background and my Dad kneeling next to them; Dad with guys I had never met; Dad on a boat in his swim trunks. He looked much younger and almost starved. I could see his ribs and hip bones. Other photos showed a younger version of my Mom with a funny hairdo. She had written notes to my Dad on the backs of some of the pictures. What was this all about? All of a sudden Dad was mysterious.

So I asked him and learned he had been in the Navy, fighting a war in Vietnam. Huh . . . really, a war? My nice Dad was in a war? This was news to my brother and me. Next question, of course: Did you ever shoot anyone? I couldn't imagine my Dad hurting anybody. He said he had to shoot sometimes because people were shooting at him, but he told us he hoped he had never killed anyone. "Bad guys," he said, "had kids at home, too." He didn't want them to be without their dads.

That was strange. I thought bad guys were bad guys. I wanted to know if he was scared. I didn't think my Dad was scared of anything, and I was suddenly very worried about him. I wanted to protect him.

He was scared lots of times, he said. Mostly he drove a boat around and didn't shoot the guns. And most of the time, nothing happened. He and his friends got to swim a lot, and they even had a dog on the boat

Civilian Duane Holman with Jenny, his first child, after returning home from active duty.
COURTESY OF DUANE HOLMAN

for a while. That didn't sound so bad (although he told me later that the dog went missing one day).

But I wanted to know more. I remember one Sunday when I was about twelve, Dad stood up during Communion meditation and described his S.E.R.E. training—prisoner of war simulation. He endured hunger and beatings so that he would know what to expect if he was captured. He hadn't ever told us anything about this. It sounded awful, but at the same time, inspiring. When he sat down afterward he asked my Mom quietly, "Did that sound okay?" She assured him that it was very good.

In the years that followed I discovered that I had friends whose dads were in Vietnam but they weren't supposed to talk or ask about it. Other dads hadn't gone to Vietnam. One was able to claim a medical condition (it wasn't obvious to me) and another was in college. I remember thinking that they had cheated. Then much later I found out that my Dad went into the Navy because he didn't want to get drafted into the Army or Marine Corps. At least he didn't try to cheat and not go at all.

Dad always made it sound like his own experience was unremarkable, but I didn't understand his thinking. I don't think anybody does, unless they're his age or older. Nobody my age ever got drafted. Nobody I knew ever had to serve. Nobody I ever knew was even asked to serve. For someone like me, Vietnam and war were both terrifying and fascinating. For Dad, Vietnam was the menacing centerpiece of his youthful landscape. You did what you could—enlisted in the Navy, went to college, went to Canada, went to jail, or got drafted and joined the marines.

The black trunk sat unopened, but Vietnam had a way of coming back to life. I remember Dad reacting to movies like *Good Morning, Vietnam* and *Forrest Gump*, and they sparked memories. "'Charlie' is what we called the VC," he would say, or he would point out an airplane or a truck that was familiar from those days. And even though *M*A*S*H* was based on the Korean War, we enjoyed watching it with Dad because it, like the movies, cast light on some very dark times. On family road trips, we were accustomed to stopping at Naval bases to tour ships and planes—further reminders of the Vietnam puzzle I was trying to put together.

I first learned Dad had been on Swift Boats when John Kerry ran for president in 2004. By that time I had been to college, gotten married, and had two kids of my own. For years I had had a general idea that Dad had spent his time on a big ship cruising around the ocean, nice and safe. It was a comfortable vision. Now, all of a sudden, he was mysterious again.

He referred me to a website where I could look up his PCFs and find his name and the names of his crewmates. I decided for Christmas that year to make a scrapbook from the website information and the contents of the trunk. I went through drums of old slides and printed out the ones that seemed significant. I finally learned that Snoopy was the mascot for Coastal Division 11 at An Thoi, the "Numbah One Watchdogs." The cat was from Coastal Division 13, Cat Lo.

One summer one of my Dad's former shipmates—Charlie—came up from Texas for a visit. He was possibly one of those guys whose picture I had seen in the trunk. He and Dad picked up right where they had left off, talking about experiences they had shared forty years earlier. Charlie mentioned a Swift Boat reunion in San Antonio, Texas, the next year—2011—but my mom had a degenerative condition caused by chronic Lyme disease and was failing rapidly. Dad was her caregiver, and a trip to San Antonio seemed out of the question. But maybe we could go, if I went along to help?

During his visit Charlie recommended that Dad read *War on the Rivers*, by Wey Symmes. It had a tremendous emotional impact on him, and I read it when he was finished. Finally, we were able to talk about specific experiences: traveling up dangerous waterways; anticipating a firefight on every patrol; boarding boats to search for contraband. It was the unknown and the unseen that frayed his nerves and those of his shipmates. To me, the child of a different generation, these situations and experiences seemed intolerable.

Mom passed away in March of 2011. I was worried about Dad because he was alone for the first time in forty-two years. After six weeks or so, I suggested he go to the Swift Boat reunion. He wasn't interested, but I kept prodding, and Charlie kept calling, and finally he agreed. Hearing his voice over the phone when he called from San Antonio and seeing the difference in him when he came back, I knew the trip was exactly what he needed.

He had told me so many times that no matter what happened to him, Swift Boats reminded him that "if I could get through that, I can get through anything." For me he was always indestructible. Finally, as a Swiftie kid, I knew why.

The Real World

Guy Gugliotta

Lt. (j.g.) Guy Gugliotta worked in New York, Latin America, and Washington D.C. for thirty-five years for United Press International, the Miami Herald, *and the* Washington Post *before becoming a freelance journalist and book author.*

I DON'T REALLY REMEMBER LEAVING VIETNAM, EXCEPT THAT IT HAPpened sometime in early November 1970. I was at Cat Lo, the last remaining Swift base that hadn't been Vietnamized, and my old crew—the five guys who had been shot at with me, and who had been the most important people in my life—were already gone. That left me as a pickup Officer-in-Charge working with pickup crews. They were nice folks, but I couldn't tell you their names.

That's probably because I had started to check out. Like everybody else, I had spent a lot of time thinking and talking about the Real World, as in, when I get back to the Real World, I can get ice cream anytime I want, or, when I get back to the Real World, I won't ever drink warm beer again; or sleep on a plastic mat with mosquito netting wrapped around my face; or wear clean clothes that feel like they've been treated with fire retardant; or smell charcoal cooking fires everywhere I go. I had counted down my year day by day, and I was short—"so short I can sit upside a dime and not see over the edge."

And then it finally happened. I'd like to tell you that going back to the Real World was ecstasy—deliverance from evil, dawn of a sunny day, a heavy sigh of relief. Or even that it was a horror—night sweats, problems coping with everyday tasks, inability to carry on a coherent conversation. But reality, for me, was difficult to describe. It still is, truth be told.

It still surprises me that my departure remains a mystery to me. I know I went to Saigon, because it was the only place you could get out, but even though I had hardly ever seen the place, I couldn't tell you what I did there or even if I spent the night. I know I flew home on a charter jet filled with servicemen, but apparently I didn't have profound thoughts before takeoff, or I would be able to tell you what they were.

I remember only two things. The first was the one-hour stopover in Anchorage, Alaska, and the walk down the long, wide, bleak, badly lit corridor leading to our U.S.–bound flight. Halfway along, we passed the passengers coming in the other direction on their way to Vietnam. I had made that walk nearly a year earlier—depressed, scared, and wondering why the returning guys weren't joking and laughing, teasing us and giving us the finger.

Now I was a returning guy, and I wasn't joking and laughing, either. Instead, I felt separated from myself, an unpleasant feeling that I would come to know well in the coming months. This wasn't me walking down the polished corridor, I thought. I didn't belong here. I belonged . . . no, not there. I don't know where, but not here.

The second thing I remember was landing at McGuire Air Force Base in central New Jersey. I don't know what I expected as a Real World introduction, but zero is what I got. It was four in the morning and there was nothing at all except an empty parking lot and a van to take some of us to Kennedy Airport. The driver lived in Trenton, and one of my fellow passengers grew up there. They talked nonstop the whole trip, treating this like it was an early-morning commute. I felt like we were on Mars.

When your tour ended, the Navy would fly you anywhere you wanted to go in the United States. I picked Boston, where I had spent a lot of time as a Navy ensign raising hell at local saloons. Where better to acclimatize myself to the Real World? I had no history in Boston, I knew almost no one, and if I screwed up, no one would see me. Much later, I realized that I must have suspected that the Real World might not be the hoped-for cakewalk.

I got to JFK at dawn, bought a standby ticket, and went to the gate. The stewardess (we called them stewardesses then) saw my uniform and put me in first class. Working people always cut us a break. In those days everybody had either served or had family who had served.

I reached Boston around 0800. I had called an old Navy friend who agreed to put me up for a few days. My plan was to get out of the Navy and spend some time and money (I was loaded after spending most of the year on Uncle Sam's nickel) while I figured out how to be a civilian. Only then would I fly home to San Francisco, see my folks, and try to resume my romance with the girlfriend I suspected had abandoned me during my long absence.

I checked into the airport hotel at Boston intending to take a nap, and I instead slept for nine hours. My buddy picked me up, took me to his fiancée's apartment, and left me there. He was in business school, which made him somewhat frantic almost all the time. The fiancée was nice. I drank scotch with her and watched Monday Night Football for the first time ever.

My buddy said I was taciturn and reserved. I shrugged. He had to study; I wanted to party, but when we tried that out, I was bored. I called my girlfriend. I tried to make a joke. It felt wrong. I was nervous. She was nervous. This isn't me, I thought—the Anchorage feeling again.

I didn't, however, entirely take leave of my senses. I visited the First Naval District office the morning of November 9, 1970, and was separated from active duty after enduring a pep talk from a lieutenant commander about why I should stay in, go to destroyer school, and become CO of a tin can when I was thirty-seven. I was barely twenty-four. Destroyer school? Are you shitting me?

My Boston stay did not improve. I felt like a foreigner, and my buddy and I no longer seemed to speak the same language. Maybe it would be better if I went home, I thought, so I left early and flew to San Francisco. My girlfriend apparently hadn't found anyone else, or maybe she just hid it well, but we were indeed finished. I didn't accept this right away, and I was devastated.

I realized much later that this experience, dreadful though it was, offered a useful insight that I had missed completely. Vietnam was supposed to be dangerous, terrifying, and traumatic, and it was. But war is also very simple. They feed you, clothe you, sell you cheap drinks, plan your schedule, define your goals, and show you a movie every night at 1930 hours. There was nothing you could do about your girlfriend, so give it a rest. You'd think about it later.

Well, later was now. In the Real World you had a love life—or not. You had to talk to children, women, and old people. You had to buy presents for people, call people on the telephone, pick up orange juice on your way home, make an appointment for your little brother at the orthodontist. The Real World was complicated and emotional. You could hurt someone's feelings. Someone could hurt your feelings. The Real World was dangerous, terrifying, and traumatic.

So, okay. I opened a bank account, got a driver's license, did my own laundry (with detergent), read Western novels by Louis L'Amour, and began to think about what to do next. Maybe it wasn't anybody's fault that my girlfriend and I couldn't get back together. Maybe I had changed, and my relationship with the Real World needed to change. I had to figure it out.

How different was I? Once a notorious big mouth, I now had little to say, and everybody noticed that. But there were other things. I no longer cared what people thought about me. And, except for my parents, who, bless their hearts, didn't bother me or ask me any questions, I didn't trust anyone.

This was bad because I could be a very cold bastard. But it was good, because it was hard to hurt me, and I no longer paid attention to minutiae. I took the Graduate Record Exams and scored 250 points higher than I had scored on the College Boards. I was a great interview, able to communicate with potential employers with utter clarity. Being in Swift Boats—a discipline that taught no obvious marketable skills—had apparently given me a boundless capacity to focus. I had needed that in the Delta. Apparently, it was also useful in the Real World.

I decided that I wanted a career where I would go to exotic places, and that Latin America would be best. I don't know why I got this idea, but it, too, probably came from Vietnam, an atavistic urge to seek out uncertainty and adventure. And I had a little Spanish. So I spent some time in Monterey, California, at a small school that accepted graduate students in Latin American Studies, and then went to New York to study international affairs at Columbia University. I figured I would join a nonprofit or become a diplomat.

I had no closure with my old girlfriend, no interaction with my old friend in Boston, and no correspondence with my crew in Vietnam. But now, although I still had the Anchorage feeling, I also understood that I was separating from my old life. The new me, not a person I really knew or liked yet, was now my Real World. I had to get used to it.

One thing that hadn't changed was my attitude toward school. I had no patience for it. The novelty of the experience had gotten me through Monterey, but at Columbia my resolve was fraying badly. I signed up for a heavy course load so I could finish a semester early. I took the Foreign Service exam and passed it. I needed to hang on for six more months. The course book offered three graduate credits for an internship at the New York desk of the news service United Press International. No final, no paper—just spend Wednesdays doing "rewrite," whatever that was. I showed up at UPI and was put to work at one of a dozen huge Smith Corona manual typewriters. "Take in City Hall on line four," the editor said by way of introduction, and walked away.

I picked up the receiver: "Gugliotta," I said.

"Yeah?" said a voice, and began dictating a story. I looked around. My woman colleagues could all type, but the guys used only two fingers or four—they looked at the keys, hit them way too hard, jammed the carriage, and made a lot of mistakes, which they fixed with a pencil. I can do this, I thought.

The next week was more of the same, except I came in later and was supposed to stay later. By 6 p.m. I was the only person left in rewrite. Around then the cops called. A teenage mugger had killed a Columbia professor on Amsterdam Avenue as he walked to the Harlem train station.

"You're at Columbia, right?" said the deputy night editor, a woman my own age with an extremely loud voice. "Find out about this guy."

A reference librarian at Columbia filled me in on the man's entire life with effortless dispatch. I shouted some of the details to the deputy editor.

"Gimme three graphs," she said, and turned back to the phone. I pounded out three paragraphs and handed them to her.

"That's good," she said. "Gimme the rest." I kept typing.

She wrote the story again and I gave her three more paragraphs. Then she did a "write-thru" using feeds from our on-scene reporter, information from the cops, and about 250 words of background from me.

"That's great," beamed the night editor. He turned the dial on the radio, running through the drive-time stations. "Everybody's using our stuff."

Teletype machines were clanging "Bulletins" and "Urgents" that I had helped write. Telephones rang off the hook. People were shouting across the room to make sure the story got on the national wire. I stood up.

Maybe I was still feeling my way into the rest of my life, but for the first time in a while I had the answer to something: They pay you to do this in the Real World?

Wow, I thought. Sign me up.

Encore

John R. Juarez

Hull Maintenance Technician First Class John R. Juarez retired from the Navy in 1999 and became a field service technician specializing in industrial water purification. Based in Pensacola, Florida, he traveled the world as a consultant to paper mills, pharmaceutical companies, power plants, and microchip factories.

I ARRIVED IN PANAMA IN SEPTEMBER 1988 WITH ORDERS TO THE U.S. Naval Small Craft Instruction and Technical Training School, where I would help teach navy and national police personnel from Central America, South America, and the Caribbean Basin how to maintain and operate small patrol boats. Our group worked with a 100-foot command boat, two Boston Whalers, several Vietnam-vintage landing craft—and two Swift Boats, PCF 1 and PCF 2. The only thing I knew about Swift Boats was that the Navy had used them during the Vietnam War. I didn't know where our two had come from or how they had gotten to Panama, but they were in good shape given their age—at least as far as I could tell.

I was a First Class Hull Maintenance Technician, a welder with no experience in Swift Boat engines, electronic equipment, or weapons. But I knew a lot about aluminum hulls and how to repair ships and small boats. And I spoke Spanish as a second language. My paternal grandparents emigrated from Mexico and settled in Kansas. I had learned Spanish while living in Chile and Venezuela when my father, also a Navy veteran, was stationed there. Panama had the only U.S. Navy school worldwide that taught in any language other than English.

It was a good life. I was only twenty-seven, on my third duty station with the Navy, and now here I was with my wife and two small boys living in this beautiful neighborhood of whitewashed houses at Fort Amador, one of the many U.S. military bases guarding the Panama Canal. We had all the comforts of stateside living available to us on the various U.S. bases. The cost of living was very low, and there was plenty of green space for the kids and lots to do. The Canal—forty-eight miles long—ran from Colon on the Atlantic side to Balboa on the Pacific. We were on the Pacific side, right across the Bay of Panama from Panama City.

We had no worries where we were, but outside our gates the political situation had been deteriorating for some time. In 1988, U.S. courts had indicted Panama's strongman, General Manuel Antonio Noriega, for drug trafficking. The United States suggested that he step down, but Noriega paid no attention.

In May 1989, eight months after we arrived, Noriega's handpicked presidential candidate lost the elections, but Noriega nullified the result and personally took over the government. Frequent street demonstrations and civil disturbances in the city and around the U.S. bases heightened tensions, and U.S. dissatisfaction with Noriega hadn't changed with the arrival of new U.S. president George H. W. Bush earlier that year. We held frequent military exercises and developed—and practiced—several plans designed to ensure the safety of dependent families, including evacuation if it became necessary.

In October 1989, a faction of the Panamanian Defense Forces tried to overthrow Noriega but failed, and on December 15, the Panama General Assembly, controlled by Noriega, passed a resolution declaring that a state of war existed between Panama and the United States. The following evening a contingent of Defense Forces opened fire on four American military officers in a civilian vehicle, killing Marine lieutenant Roberto Paz. President Bush gave the order to invade.

On the afternoon of December 19, 1989 our Commanding Officer held an emergency meeting, summoning all of us to our admin and student barracks buildings. As I arrived, I noticed that some of the indoor passageways were blocked off, and a bunch of guys with long hair and beards were sitting around, checking out web gear and weapons. The CO told us that we might notice folks "who didn't appear military," but "rest assured, many of them are higher rank than most of you."

"Don't talk to them," he said, but if they asked us for anything, we had permission to beg, borrow, or literally steal it for them.

I went home full of apprehension and excitement. My wife wanted to know what was happening. One of our neighbors had just called his wife and told her to pack up and go to nearby Rodman Naval Station. I told her there was nothing going on—at least so far—but that I had seen mean-looking guys with fancy equipment. I said I thought they were either Delta Force or CIA and suggested they would try to "snatch" Noriega that night. The kids went to bed around 2000. We sat down to watch some sort of Christmas event that Bush was attending. I said to my wife that he wouldn't be at the gala if he was planning anything here.

Wrong. About 2345 I heard a short burst of machine gun fire in the distance. My wife sat up in bed and asked what was happening. "Must be the dumb Panamanians having an accidental discharge during the turnover of the watch," I replied. A minute or two later I heard a longer burst. It was no accident.

Now I was worried. I asked my wife to go to the boys' room and stay there so I would know where they were. I retrieved my .45-caliber pistol from my room and went to the front window to watch the street. My biggest fear was that Defense Force troops would infiltrate our housing to kidnap dependents, as Noriega had threatened.

Suddenly the whole sky lit up like the Fourth of July. Explosions echoed from the Panamanian Defense Force barracks just blocks away. Tracers flew in all directions, and streams of red tracer rained down from what I later learned were U.S. Air Force C-130 Specter gunships. It was then that I noticed men coming toward us, flitting from shadow to shadow as they moved closer to our neighborhood. "Oh, hell," I thought. "Here we go." I had learned the basics of weapons handling in boot camp, and I had quite a bit of training in Panama in small arms and in patrolling techniques as a member of the base's auxiliary security force. I thought about all the years growing up playing "army," and how cool I thought it would be to go to war. Well, here it was. I cocked my .45 and waited.

I watched one of the shadows move down the street until it stepped into the light. It was an American soldier. I exhaled. He ran up to our door. We had five minutes to get ready to leave, he said. Did we know which of our neighbors were home? We told him. He left and returned exactly five minutes later, almost to the second. We joined him, and together with a half-dozen other soldiers we ran from our enlisted housing compound to the adjacent neighborhood where the officers lived. We scrambled up a small hill beneath mango trees whose leaves were being shredded by Panamanian machine gun fire. Powerless to protect my wife and the boys, I was more scared than I had ever been in my life. We spent the night below one of the officers' houses, whose bottom floor was a screened patio.

We stayed there the next day until about 1600, when the soldiers allowed us to return home. That evening the training school called me up. The next morning an armed bus would come by to pick me up, the caller said. I should bring my field gear and be ready to spend at least a week away from home.

We gathered at the school that morning. The CO told us that Special Boat Unit 26, the local Navy experts in small boat warfare, had been sent to help the Special Ops types. That meant that we would be providing escort for High Value Transits—big ships—traveling through the canal.

And so I became the aft gunner on PCF 1, in charge of the over-under .50-caliber machine gun mounted on top of the 81mm mortar. The Command and Control Boat went to Gatun Lake, right in the middle of the canal, to provide food, fuel, and support for the rest of us. The Boston Whalers patrolled the multitude of islands in the lake; the PCFs escorted ships from the gates of the Pedro Miguel Locks on the Pacific side, through the Culebra Cut and Gatun Lake to the Gatun Locks on the Atlantic side. Then we picked up another ship and made the transit in the opposite direction. We always traveled together, one at the front of the ship and the other bringing up the rear. We didn't "lock through" with the ships, but we made up to four trips a day back and forth.

I had always thought that in order to "prove myself" I would like to fight for our country, but doing it is a lot different from watching it at the movies. It can be really exciting, but it can also be downright boring. And it's always complicated.

We spent our first night out snugged up close to the wall in the Pedro Miguel Locks, the first step down from Gatun Lake on the way to the Pacific. At one point a Panama Canal Commission employee visited us and told us that the Panamanian Defense Force police had taken over a house a few blocks away. We were moored in the lock and couldn't take the boats anywhere, but our captain radioed this info along, and we thought we'd be sent to investigate. I got picked to go. Scared as I was, I was getting up for it, but then the powers that be changed course and decided to send someone else. Shortly after midnight a couple of rounds of rifle fire hit close by. We couldn't tell if it was sniper fire from a nearby hill or just stray bullets, but we stayed under cover inside the boats and below the cement lock walls if we had to go outside the rest of the night. That was the last night we spent closed up in the locks. The rest of the time we were in Gatun Lake, either at the Canal Commission piers or anchored out, and were free to pick up and move whenever we wanted.

For the ten days—including Christmas—we were out on the water, our command boat was either moored in Gatun Lake or tied up at the piers to avoid setting a pattern. Each night the Swifts and the Whalers linked up with the command boat to refuel and make any needed repairs. This quickly led to a routine that got more tedious as time passed.

The invasion's High Command had decreed there would be no alcohol sales for the time being, but we were not impressed. After all, we lived in Panama. So several times, while waiting on a High Value Transit to "lock through," we would pull into one of the many small towns along the shores of Gatun Lake, stop at a local kiosk, and pick up a hot plate lunch and a case of beer. In the evenings, after refueling, eating, and cleaning up the boat, our grizzled Vietnam veteran warrant officer would call the crew to the forecastle for "training," which consisted of drinking enough beer to catch a decent buzz, but not enough to get drunk. Everybody could still function. Beer, real training, and joke-telling helped calm us down. We spent our nights on watch, wearing night-vision goggles to keep an eye on the boats and check for bad guys.

One day after escorting a ship to the Atlantic side we came around an island in the lake and saw something suspicious floating in the water. We reported it to our CO, who was on the command boat, and he decided to investigate personally. He took a look and decided the object was a floating water mine, and reported it. His boss told us to destroy it with .50-caliber machine gun fire. Both PCFs opened up with all six .50-caliber machine guns. Plastic and foam flew sky-high from an Igloo cooler that a fisherman had lost.

A few days after that we received a report of unidentified watercraft five miles up the canal from us. The Boston Whalers started off in pursuit but couldn't travel fast enough, so both PCFs broke away from escorts and took off. We were pretty keyed up, but after a short run we could see that our two targets were high-speed SEAL insertion boats. As we came up on them—about 1,000 yards away—an Apache attack helicopter popped up from behind a small island, ready to blow us away with a rocket or with the 30mm Gatling gun that kept tracking back and forth between us and our sister PCF. It didn't take long before he saw the U.S. flags and realized we were "friendlies." And in the blink of an eye he was gone. Thank God.

Next came the day when we ferried a dozen or so journalists around the canal. They had no particular interest in what we had been doing or in the boats. Instead, they kept asking when the canal was built, how wide it was, how many ships used it? It was ridiculous. I told them I was a Navy welder. What the hell did I know about the canal? I didn't build the damn thing. Still, it wasn't a total lost cause. I posed for a picture that made the AP wire, appeared in over thirty stateside papers, and ended up as the centerfold of an enormous coffee table book about the invasion.

And then it was over. After escorting ships from multiple countries for about three weeks, we packed it in around mid-January 1990. It was a relief to finally go home and see the family. By that time the war, such as it was, had ended and U.S. forces were pulling out. Panama had a civilian president and Noriega was in federal prison in the United States awaiting trial for drug trafficking. Twenty-three Americans died in the fighting, as had about 500 Panamanians. Fewer than half of the Panamanians killed were soldiers. It was a hell of a way to spend the holiday season.

Legacy

Suzanne Edwards

Suzanne Edwards of Thornton, Pennsylvania, founded the website "Legacies of Swift Boat Sailors" in 2013 to preserve and promote the history of Swift Boat sailors and to serve as a repository for documents, photos, film, and video for Swift families, friends, and supporters.

My father, James C. Edwards, to hear him tell it, was something of a rabble-rouser as a teenager in Wheeling, West Virginia, so it came as no surprise to anyone when he hit former President Herbert Hoover with an egg during a spring parade in 1956. It was all in fun, but the cops were not amused, and they hauled him off to the judge. His predicament was described to him this way:

"Young man, it is your choice," the judge said. "Go directly to juvenile detention, or march yourself down to the recruiting center and sign up for the Army." My father—again, no surprise—enlisted a few weeks later on June 17, 1956. He was sixteen. I don't know whether he had to lie about his age.

Funny story? It was practically the only thing my siblings and I, and even my mother, knew about my dad's thirteen-year service career in both the Army and the Navy. He retired as an E-5 Gunner's Mate after his last assignment aboard a Swift Boat in Qui Nhon. He never talked about that, nor did he talk about why he would not talk about it. He would become evasive and withdrawn if you pushed him. He never hurt us, but we learned not to ask. But I always wanted to know, and

Sue Edwards circa early 1970s.
COURTESY OF SUE EDWARDS

sometime around 2003, I decided to find out. This is his story—and, in many ways, my own.

My dad served in the Army First Division, the "Big Red One," for four years, then re-upped in the Navy as a gunner's mate. He became a tin can sailor, serving on three different destroyers and then made his way to Qui Nhon and the Swifts in 1968.

"Things happened there," he said once, but only once.

I guess I always knew this. I remember being around four years old, sneaking into my parents' bedroom one morning to "surprise" my father. Before I jumped on him, my mom stopped me. "Never try that again," she said. Long afterward, I found out that dad always slept on the floor during those first years home from Vietnam, so he wouldn't hurt my mom after having night terrors.

Don't get me wrong. I loved my father desperately, and as a young girl I felt loved and protected by him, even if he was not wholly accessible.

He could laugh heartily, debate politics, and sing (he would sing "A You're Adorable" to my mom at large family parties). He would call me Maran when he lifted me up and shook me into my tights for Sunday school. (My middle name is Katherine, which became catamaran, which became Maran . . . you get the picture.)

But there was always the line I could not cross. Once I thought it might be funny if I let the family dog wake him up. I let Bear jump on his bed to kiss him, anticipating that he would gently chastise me and then hug me and laugh at my devious plan. Instead, he sprang to his feet, knocking the dog to the floor. He was enraged—the kind of anger that you can feel. I ran. He never yelled at me. He never said anything at all. But I got the message: don't do it again.

We lived in Drexel Hill and Aston, Pennsylvania. Dad worked hard in security and as a warehouseman, drank his beer, watched war movies, and hummed country music songs. As a teenager I began to understand that he struggled with overt closeness, even with those dearest to him, and I began to wonder why. He never offered a real reply, but that was okay because deep down I knew I would always be daddy's girl.

I grew up, got married, and had a son. Two peas in a pod they were. This little man was this grown man's best friend; my father protected Nick as though he was his own, and palled around with him like he had never done with his own kids. Maybe he trusted him more, because my son was innocent and didn't know granddad's issues.

One afternoon in 2003, when Nick was about six, we were all together when I heard my dad call for me. He was watching yet another documentary on the Vietnam War. He wanted me to come in, because his boat was on television. I remember thinking how odd this was after so many years. The Swift Boat was smaller than I had pictured it. Actually, I guess I never really pictured it at all. At first he was excited, but then the all-too-familiar look washed over his face. It's hard to explain, but it was like the five stages of grief in one sweep, transforming a smile into a distant gaze.

Still, maybe this was an opportunity, so I took a risk. Father's Day was approaching, and I decided to see if I could find the perfect picture of the Swift Boat I saw on TV and give it to him. I worked as a paralegal, and knew how to find things. It wasn't hard. I searched "Swift Boats" on the Internet, and, of course, there it was. Not only pictures, but names—his name and the names of his shipmates. Was this Pandora's Box? If I showed him what I had found, would I lose him altogether? I loved him deeply. My intentions were good, and he would understand that. I decided to go for it.

I handed over the package like a peace offering—a means, I hoped, to soothe the conflicts within. He opened the package and said nothing. He looked at all the pages and said nothing. He put it all back in the envelope and said nothing. He turned back to the television and said nothing. Fair enough. No verdict. So I said nothing.

The next day I visited again, just to sit beside him. It was our way of being close. I was shocked when he pulled out the package. It sat on a table in the middle of the room. I waited. Finally, he spoke, asking if I had talked to anyone mentioned in the pages. "No," I said, but I had found more information. For a moment his eyes gleamed. He wanted to know what else I had. "Not much," I said. I wanted to get his service record. "Permission granted," he said with a slight smile.

Eventually it came. He began to feel safe telling me some things, and then more. He wanted me to contact his shipmates, make sure they were alive. He was letting me in—not all the way, but eventually enough so I could learn about the event that had most troubled him for so many years.

It happened on November 8, 1968. The previous day my dad had done maintenance on PCF 89 before it went on patrol. On November 8, PCF 89 went to sea and was called upon to provide 81mm mortar support for an Army unit under attack. The boat started to drift and the crew ceased firing until the boat could be anchored more securely. Orders came once again to commence firing. There was a sudden loud explosion, a flash, and then an awful stillness. Two men were dead and three severely injured.

My dad was distraught when he heard about the incident. He had just worked on PCF 89's mortar. Had it jammed? Five days later word came down: the explosion was caused by the accidental double-loading of the mortar when firing resumed. My dad hadn't caused it, but this, I had long ago learned, was cold comfort. Intellectually he might have known he was not to blame, but he carried the guilt with him for the rest of his life.

On May 8, 2010, I went to sit with my dad again, but this time at the hospital. Dad had long suffered from COPD and was battling cancer. I brought him a strawberry milkshake. He asked me to sit down and told me he had made a decision. It was his time, he said. He didn't want to struggle to stay alive anymore. I was heartbroken and said so. "Don't be afraid for me, I am not afraid," he said. "Don't feel pity for me. I have chosen my own destiny. Don't try to fight me on this. I have lived with integrity and should be allowed to die with dignity. What you can do for me is to sit here and hold my hand, talk to me even when I don't respond, and live with no regrets." He died the next day. It was Mother's Day.

You would think the story would end there, but it doesn't. One day in 2008 I was looking at Facebook when a page entitled "Swift Boat is a Noun . . . (not a verb)" was offered as a suggested group. At the time, I was deep into my search for people who may have known my dad, so I joined up. I soon met "Kat," whose father, like mine, served on Swift Boats in Qui Nhon. But my father had come home, while hers had died on patrol.

Nearly three years passed. We talked often about our fathers, our kids, our life experiences. We leaned on each other during bad moments, and shared secrets. Kat got divorced and took her maiden name—Katherine Wallace—again. The surname seemed oddly familiar, but I brushed it off—of course it was familiar, she was my friend.

Then suddenly I knew. Her father, Lt. (j.g.) Richard Wallace, was one of the men who died in the mortar explosion on the fantail of PCF 89. Kat and I had been friends for three years. My dad had died. It was time to ask for the forgiveness he had sought all those years. I let Kat know what I had figured out, and told her that my dad always believed he was partially responsible for her father's death, even if he was not the direct cause.

Kat brought closure. She and her family had learned long ago what had happened on that day, she said. They knew it was an accident. My father had nothing to do with it. He could finally rest in peace. Two daughters, both of us burdened with what I call "Second Generation Legacies," had found each other by chance at the right time, in the right place, for the right reasons, and we had been able to finish the story. Perhaps this is now our legacy of the Vietnam War.

Afterword

This project had its beginning in 2008, when a group of Swift Boat veterans joined forces with the Maritime Museum of San Diego to bring home PCF 816 from the Republic of Malta, where it had finally retired after a successful career conducting coastal patrols and search and rescue missions for the Maltese Navy since 1971.

To help raise funds for this venture, former Swift Boat officer John Yeoman, living in Hawaii, wrote a short blue informational pamphlet detailing the history of Swift Boats, provided a schematic drawing, and described how the Maritime Museum, with the blessing of the Maltese government and the hard work of Swift veterans, intended to restore the boat as a permanent Museum exhibit. San Diego's Naval Base Coronado had served as the U.S. Navy's first Swift Boat training center.

It took four years of fundraising and diplomacy, but the boat was lifted aboard a cargo ship and reached San Diego on August 29, 2012. There, dozens of Swift veteran volunteers got it in shape in time to open the exhibit and conduct tours of San Diego harbor during the Swift Boat Sailors Association reunion in May 2013.

It was at the reunion that Museum publications editor Neva Sullaway met John Yeoman, and the idea of expanding the blue pamphlet into a commemorative journal under the Museum's flagship publication, *Mains'l Haul—A Journal of Pacific Maritime History,* began to gel. Together they planned the layout of the publication and asked Swift Boat veterans to contribute stories about their experiences in Vietnam.

John prevailed on fellow Swift officer Guy Gugliotta, a New York–based freelance writer and newspaperman, to edit the contributions with help from Ted Kenny, another former Swift officer who had retired in Denver and embarked on a new career as a blogger.

The response was astounding. Swift veterans and some of their family members, many of whom had never before attempted any serious creative writing, submitted outstanding stories. Some were humorous, some were sad, some were bitter, and some were sardonic, but all of them were remarkable for their ambition, creativity, and honesty.

Even as the *Journal* was nearing completion Guy began thinking about expanding this first memoir into a full-length book—doubling the number of stories and framing them with accompanying historical background to make them accessible to a broader audience.

In October 2014, John, Neva, and Guy met with Dr. Ray Ashley, the President and CEO of the Maritime Museum of San Diego, to ask for and receive his blessing and cooperation for the new project. John and Neva reached out to Swift veterans for new stories and photos, and Guy began a new round of editing. We owe a debt of gratitude to Dr. Ashley for his and the Museum's unflagging support and enthusiasm, and to Deborah Grosvenor, of the Grosvenor Literary Agency, for her encouragement and advice. The result is this book.

—*Neva Sullaway and John Yeoman*, August 2016

Glossary

Ammi pontoons: Barges measuring 30 feet by 90 feet. Ammi pontoons were lashed together in groups and anchored in rivers to form advanced tactical support bases (ATSBs) that would support local operations of PBRs, riverine assault craft, and Swift Boats.

ASAP: As soon as possible

Beach Jumpers: U.S. Navy special warfare units organized during World War II by Lt. Douglas Fairbanks Jr. They specialized in deception and psychological warfare. Their deception equipment included the multi-component "heater," consisting of a wire recorder, a 5-phase amplifier, and a 1,000-watt, 12-horn speaker. By using the heater and other specialized equipment, a few dozen Beach Jumpers could make the enemy think that they were a 70,000-man amphibious landing force.

BuShips: Bureau of Ships, a department of the U.S. Navy involved in design, shipbuilding, maintenance, and administration. It was abolished in March 1966 and succeeded by Naval Ship Systems Command (NAVSHIPS).

"Charlie": Viet Cong insurgent

CO: Commanding Officer

CosDiv: Coastal Division

DMZ: Demilitarized Zone. An example is the 17th parallel, which formed the border between North and South Vietnam in the South China Sea.

EOD: Explosive Ordinance Disposal personnel

GTMO: U.S. Navy base at Guantanamo Bay, Cuba

Kit Carson Scouts (KCS): Also known as "Hoi Chan," a term loosely translated as "members who have returned to the righteous side." It referred to a program that used former Viet Cong combatants as intelligence scouts.

Klick (or Click): A measure of 1,000 meters. Derived from "kilometer."

Knot: A measure of speed. "Three knots" indicates three nautical miles per hour. A nautical mile is 2,000 yards, compared to a land mile of 1,780 yards. Hence, 3 knots would be about 1.1 times faster than 3 miles per hour. Thirty knots would be equivalent to 33 miles per hour.

Lt. (j.g.): Lieutenant Junior Grade. An officer rank between ensign and lieutenant.

LSD: Landing Ship Dock, a U.S. Navy vessel, approximately 600 feet long and 85 feet wide with a well dock for transporting and launching landing craft and amphibious vehicles. Swift Boats were transported from the United States to Vietnam in the well docks of these craft, as were the ammi pontoon barges that were taken from Saigon to Ca Mau as part of Seafloat.

LST: Landing Ship Tank, a U.S. Navy vessel. Created during World War II to support amphibious operations by carrying vehicles, cargo, and landing troops directly onto unimproved shore. Used in Vietnam as "mother ships" for Swift Boats, PBRs and riverine assault craft. About 380 feet long and 65 feet wide.

LZ: Landing Zone

MEDEVAC: A helicopter used to medically evacuate personnel from combat areas

NROTC: Naval Reserve Officer Training Corps

NVA: North Vietnamese Army

OCS: Officer Candidate School

OinC: Officer-in-Charge. Designation given to those in command of a Swift Boat. Equivalent to the captain of a ship.

OOD-Underway: Officer of the Deck. The person on a ship's bridge who directs the movements of a ship.

Operation Game Warden: The U.S. Navy operation undertaken in December 1965 to deny enemy movement and resupply on the major rivers of the Mekong Delta and Rung Sat Special Zone in South Vietnam. Task Force 116 or TF 116.

Operation Giant Slingshot: U.S. Navy operation centered on the strategically significant Parrot's Beak region of Vietnam, which approached within 25 miles of Saigon. The two rivers that formed either side of the Parrot's Beak were almost entirely under enemy control at the beginning of the operation.

Operation Jackstay: Operation conducted in March 1966 in the Rung Sat Special Zone, 35 miles south of Saigon. It was the first full-scale U.S. amphibious operation to be carried out in the Mekong Delta.

Operation Market Time: U.S. Navy mission to conduct surveillance, gunfire support, visit-and-search, and other operations along the 1,200-mile coast of South Vietnam in order to detect and prevent Communist infiltration from sea. Task Force 115 or TF 115.

PBR: Patrol Boat River

PCF: Patrol Craft Fast; official designation for a Swift Boat.

PSYOPS: Psychological Operations

P-3 Orion: A four-engine turboprop aircraft based on the Lockheed L-188 Electra commercial aircraft. Used for antisubmarine operations and maritime surveillance.

R&R: Rest and Recreation

RAG: Riverine Assault Group or River Assault Force. U.S. Navy vessels that transported U.S. Army troops and provided gunfire support. They conducted riverine assault operations in the Mekong Delta to destroy Viet Cong main and local force units and their resources and to extend control of waterway systems and contiguous areas. Task Force 117 or TF 117.

RF-PF (Ruff-Puff): Regional Force (at the provincial level)/Popular Force (at the district government level) troops.

Seafloat: A mobile advanced tactical support base (MATSB) comprised thirteen ammi pontoon barges lashed together and anchored in the Cua Lon River in the lower Ca Mau Peninsula of the Mekong Delta. A land base could not be approved by the Vietnamese government, and such a base in the middle of a vast enemy-controlled area would have been very difficult to defend.

SEAL: Sea Air Land, the U.S. Navy special operations group.

SEALORDS: Southeast Asia Lake, Ocean, River and Delta Strategy. A U.S. Navy operation begun on 5 November 1968 comprising the combined assets of the Market Time units TF 115, Game Warden units TF 116, and River Assault Group units TF 117. Its objective was harassment of Viet Cong strongholds in the Mekong Delta and interdiction of supplies infiltrated from Cambodia.

Seawolf, Seawolves: A U.S. Navy helicopter gunship capable of carrying either 10 troops or 4 litters or 2,000 pounds of cargo in addition to its weaponry.

S.E.R.E.: Survival Evasion Resistance Escape. Survival training. (Some joked that this was training for marriage.)

Short: Very few days left before going home.

Skimmer: A 12- to 18-foot fiberglass skiff powered by outboard engines.

Solid Anchor: A land base built on the north side of the Cua Lon River opposite the MATSB floating base of Seafloat.

Tango Boat: Also known as Armored Troop Carriers (ATC). World War II LCM-6 landing craft modified for troop carrying riverine patrol missions.

UDT: Underwater Demolition Team: U.S. Navy frogmen.

Viet Cong or VC: Communist insurgents fighting the government forces of South Vietnam

WHEC: Water High Endurance Cutter, a U.S. Coast Guard vessel

WPB: Water Patrol Boat, an 81-foot U.S. Coast Guard vessel

ENLISTED SAILOR RATINGS AND RANKINGS

BM: Boatswain's Mate. Cares for the vessel's exterior.

EN: Engineman

QM: Quartermaster

RD: Radarman

E-4: 3rd class petty officer

E-5: 2nd class petty officer

E-6: 1st class petty officer

Chief: Rank one level above a 1st class petty officer. A senior and experienced petty officer with many years of service. Adept at demonstrating how things are done in the Navy to young enlisted men, ensigns, and lieutenants junior grade

Notes

Introduction

1. www.shipbuildinghistory.com/history/shipyards/small/active/swiftships.htm.
2. Frank Uhlig, Jr., ed. *Vietnam: The Naval Story* (Annapolis, MD: Naval Institute Press, 1986), 278.
3. Ibid., 278–79.
4. Game Warden, Center for Naval Analyses (Arlington, VA: Operations Evaluation Group, January 1976), Annex A.
5. Uhlig, 280.
6. CDR R. L. Schreadley, USN (Ret.), *From the Rivers to the Sea: The U.S. Navy in Vietnam* (Annapolis, MD: Naval Institute Press, 1992), 56–73.
7. Uhlig, 281.
8. Uhlig, 283–84.
9. Uhlig, 281–82.
10. Gordon L. Rottman and Hugh Johnson, *Vietnam Riverine Craft 1962–75* (Oxford UK: Osprey Publishing, 2006), 15–16.

Chapter 1

1. COMNAVFORV Monthly Operational Summary, October 1965.
2. Ibid.
3. Ibid., January 1967.
4. Ibid., February 1966.
5. Ibid., March 1966.
6. Ibid., May 1966.
7. Ibid., October 1966.
8. Ibid., November 1966.

Chapter 2

1. COMNAVFORV Monthly Operational Summary, July 1966.
2. Ibid., March 1968.
3. Rottman and Johnson, 12–14.
4. COMNAVFORV Monthly Operational Summary, December 1967.

5. Ibid., September 1967.
6. Ibid., December 1967.
7. Ibid., November 1967.

Chapter 3

1. COMNAVFORV Monthly Operational Summary, February and March 1967.
2. Naval History Department. *Riverine Warfare: The US Navy's Operations on Inland Waters* (Navy Department, Revised 1969), 46.
3. COMNAVFORV Monthly Operational Summary, July 1968; James Steffes, *Swift Boat Down: The Real Story of the Sinking of PCF 19* (Bloomington, IN: Xlibris, 2005).
4. COMNAVFORV Monthly Operational Summary, July 1968.

Chapter 4

1. COMNAVFORV Monthly Operational Summary, November 1968.
2. Ibid., December 1968.
3. Ibid., January 1969.
4. Ibid., February 1969.
5. Ibid., March 1969.
6. Ibid., February 1969.
7. Ibid.
8. Ibid., April 1969.
9. Ibid., May 1969.

Chapter 5

1. Schreadley, 215–50; Operation SEALORDS, 37–40.
2. COMNAVFORV Monthly Operational Summary, October 1969.

Chapter 6

1. COMNAVFORV Monthly Operational Summary, May 1969.
2. Ibid., January 1970.
3. Ibid., April 1970.
4. Ibid., May 1970.
5. Ibid..
6. Ibid., June 1970.

Chapter 7

1. COMNAVFORV Monthly Operational Summary, March 1970.
2. Ibid., May 1970.
3. Ibid., June 1970
4. Ibid.
5. Ibid.

6. Ibid.
7. Ibid., August 1970.
8. Ibid., July 1970.
9. Ibid., August 1970.
10. Ibid., September 1970.
11. Ibid., October 1970.
12. Ibid., September and October 1970.
13. Ibid., November 1970.
14. Ibid., December 1970.

Chapter 8

1. Neva Sullaway and Guy Gugliotta, eds. *Restoration of a Legacy: Swift Boats and Their Sailors* (San Diego: Maritime Museum of San Diego, 2014).

Selected Bibliography

Commander U.S. Naval Forces Vietnam. *Monthly Operational Summaries*. Washington, DC, January 1963–1971.

Daniels, Victor, and Judith C. Erdheim. *Game Warden*. Arlington, VA: Center for Naval Analyses, 1976.

Marolda, Edward J., and R. Blake Dunnavent. *Combat at Close Quarters*. Washington, DC: Naval History & Heritage Command, 2015.

Marolda, Edward J. *Riverine Warfare: The US Navy's Operations on Inland Waters*. Washington, DC: U.S. Navy Naval History Division, 2006

McQuilkin, William C. "Operation SEALORDS: A Front in a Frontless War: An Analysis of the Brown-Water Navy in Vietnam." Thesis, U.S. Army Command and General Staff College, 1997.

Moise, Edwin E. "Vietnam War Bibliography." http://www.clemson.edu/caah/history/FacultyPages/EdMoise/bibliography.html.

Scheffer, Jason B. *The Rise and Fall of the Brown Water Navy: Changes in the United States Navy Riverine Warfare Capabilities from the Vietnam War to Operation Iraqi Freedom*. Fort Leavenworth, KS: U.S. Army Command and General Staff College, 2005.

Schreadly, Richard L. *From the Rivers to the Sea: The U.S. Navy in Vietnam*. Annapolis, MD: Naval Institute Press, 1992.

Uhlig, Frank, Jr., ed. *Vietnam: The Navy Story*. Annapolis, MD. Naval Institute Press, 1986.

Upton, Peter N., and Steve Waterman. "Underwater Demolition Team 13." San Diego: Cruise book submitted to the Western Pacific Fleet, 1969.

Additional Reading

Books and Articles

Erwin, Virgil. *Cat Lo: A Memoir of Invincible Youth*. Indianapolis: Dog Ear Publishing, 2009.

Forbes, John, and Robert Williams. *Riverine Force*. New York: Bantam Books, 1987.

Irwin, Larry. "Memories of Life Aboard a Swift Boat, 1967." http://swiftboatsailors memorial.com/files/original/348063df6726a55ad7d88c3d16f322a9.pdf

Rottman, Gordon L., and Hugh Johnson. *Vietnam Riverine Craft, 1962–1975*. Oxford: Osprey, 2006.

Shirley, Robert B. "Patrol Craft Fast 45." http://pcf45.com.
Steffes, James. *Swift Boat Down: The Real Story of the Sinking of PCF 19*. Bloomington, IN: Xlibris, 2005.
Symmes, Weymouth D. *War on the Rivers*. Missoula, MT: Pictorial Histories, 2004.

Websites

Blankenship, Don. "River Vet." (Swift Boats, PBRs, and Riverine Assault Craft). http://www.rivervet.com/swifts.htm.
Maps of South Vietnam. http://911gfx.nexus.net/SVNmap.html, http://911gfx.nexus.net/sea-ao.html
Swift Boat Sailors Memorial. http://swiftboatsailorsmemorial.com.
Vietnam Unit Memorial, San Diego. http://www.vummf.org/default.aspx.
Spratt, Jack. "PCF 48, 1970." http://www.oocities.org/swift48rvn/photos.htm.
Wasikowski, Larry. Coastal Squadron One—Swift Boat Crew Directory. http://swiftboats.net.

Index